PUBLIC COMMUNICATION

THE NEW IMPERATIVES

SAGE Communications in Society

New Communication Technologies and the Public Interest

Comparative Perspectives on
Policy and Research

edited by
Marjorie Ferguson

New Media Politics

Comparative Perspectives in
Western Europe

edited for the Euromedia Research Group by
Denis McQuail and Karen Siune

The Myth of the Information Revolution

Social and Ethical Implications of
Communication Technology

edited by
Michael Traber

PUBLIC COMMUNICATION

THE NEW IMPERATIVES

Future Directions for
Media Research

edited by
Marjorie Ferguson

⑤ SAGE Publications
London · Newbury Park · New Delhi

Foreword and editorial arrangement
© Marjorie Ferguson 1990
Chapter 1 © Graham Murdock 1990
Chapter 2 © William H. Melody 1990
Chapter 3 © James Michael 1990
Chapter 4 © Philip Schlesinger 1990
Chapter 5 © Peter Golding 1990
Chapter 6 © Jay G. Blumler 1990
Chapter 7 © James Curran 1990
Chapter 8 © Denis McQuail 1990
Chapter 9 © Marjorie Ferguson 1990
Chapter 10 © Roger Silverstone 1990

First published 1990

SAGE Publications Ltd
28 Banner Street
London EC1Y 8QE

SAGE Publications Inc
2111 West Hillcrest Drive
Newbury Park, California 91320

SAGE Publications India Pvt Ltd
32, M–Block Market
Greater Kailash – I
New Delhi 110 048

British Library Cataloguing in Publication data

Public communication: the new imperatives: future
   directions for media research. – (Sage Communications in Society)
   1. Mass communication
   I. Ferguson, Marjorie   II. Series
   302,2'34

ISBN 0–8039–8267–4
ISBN 0–8039–8268–2 pbk

Library of Congress catalog card number 89–62648

Typeset by Photoprint, Torquay, Devon
Printed in Great Britain by Billing and Son, Worcester

Contents

Notes on the Contributors   vii
Acknowledgements   viii

Foreword   ix

PART ONE   Transforming Media Structures:
           Ownership, Policy and Regulation

1 Redrawing the Map of the Communications Industries:
   Concentration and Ownership in the Era of Privatization
   Graham Murdock   1

2 Communication Policy in the Global Information
   Economy: Whither the Public Interest?
   William H. Melody   16

3 Regulating Communications Media: From the Discretion
   of Sound Chaps to the Arguments of Lawyers
   James Michael   40

PART TWO   Changing Media Processes:
           Politics and Power

4 Rethinking the Sociology of Journalism: Source Strategies
   and the Limits of Media-Centrism
   Philip Schlesinger   61

5 Political Communication and Citizenship: The Media
   and Democracy in an Inegalitarian Social Order
   Peter Golding   84

6 Elections, the Media and the Modern Publicity Process
   Jay G. Blumler   101

7 Culturalist Perspectives of News Organizations:
   A Reappraisal and a Case Study
   James Curran   114

PART THREE   Rethinking Concepts and Methods:
Traditions, Technologies and Audiences

8   Communication Research Past, Present and Future:
American Roots and European Branches
Denis McQuail   135

9   Electronic Media and the Redefining of Time and Space
Marjorie Ferguson   152

10   Television and Everyday Life: Towards an Anthropology
of the Television Audience
Roger Silverstone   173

References   190
Index   205

The Contributors

Jay G. Blumler has directed the Centre for Television Research, University of Leeds, and is Associate Director of the Centre for Research in Public Communication, College of Journalism, University of Maryland.

James Curran is Professor of Communications at Goldsmiths' College, University of London.

Marjorie Ferguson, formerly at the London School of Economics and Political Science, is Associate Professor at the University of Maryland.

Peter Golding is Senior Research Fellow at the Centre for Mass Communication Research, University of Leicester and Professor of Sociology designate at the University of Loughborough.

Denis McQuail is Professor of Mass Communication at the University of Amsterdam.

William H. Melody is Director of the Centre for International Research on Communication and Information Technologies (CIRCIT), Melbourne, and Visiting Professor at the University of Melbourne and Monash University.

James Michael is Director of the Centre in Communication and Information Law, University College London.

Graham Murdock is Research Fellow at the Centre for Mass Communication Research, University of Leicester.

Philip Schlesinger is Professor of Film and Media Studies at the University of Stirling.

Roger Silverstone is Director of the Centre for Research into Innovation, Culture and Technology and Reader in Sociology Brunel University.

Acknowledgements

This book results from a two-day workshop devoted to 'Classic Issues of Mass Communication Research'. This meeting was sponsored by the Economic and Social Research Council's Programme on Information and Communication Technologies (PICT) and held at Madingley Hall in Cambridge on 27–9 April 1988. I would like to thank the Council, PICT and its founding Director, Professor William H. Melody, for their support of this venture.

The workshop provided a distinguished group of British media scholars with a rare opportunity for substantive interchange and fruitful debate. Their extensive critique of 'classic issues' culminated in broad agreement about 'new imperatives' for future research. As this volume attests, these concerns focus on the changing structures and processes of public communication and the many conceptual, policy and methodological questions they raise.

Finally, I want to record my warmest personal thanks, first to all the participants who made this workshop such a worthwhile scholarly experience, and second, to those who assisted so ably in London and Washington with the organization of that meeting and the preparation of this book: Pam Deane, Pam Hodges, Jo James, Archana Kumar and Lois Reynolds.

Marjorie Ferguson
University of Maryland

Foreword

Evidence of belief in the power of modern media to penetrate and influence political, economic, cultural and social spheres, together with evidence of restructuring in the cultural and information industries nationally and internationally, has highlighted the centrality of media institutions to public and daily life.

Historically, the role assigned to public communication has been a functional one. In liberal democratic societies, structures of media ownership and regulation, processes of media production and consumption are seen as causally related to the openness or closedness, the richness or impoverishment of civic and cultural discourse in the public sphere. Construed in this light, public communication serves as a form of social litmus paper attesting to the health, or otherwise, of the body politic.

Public communication, then, refers to those processes of information and cultural exchange between media institutions, products and publics which are socially shared, widely available and communal in character. It consists of a complex series of interactions between the economic and political institutions that determine media structures, the technologies and techniques used to create and distribute their products, and the content choices thus laid before an array of audiences.

The transformation of media environments around the world in recent times, however, has had profound consequences for public communication at all levels from local to international. The sources of and forces for change have been primarily economic, political and technological. Their consequences, direct and indirect, have also affected social and cultural forms, norms and behaviours.

Any analysis of contemporary systems of public communication therefore requires that they be located within this context of evolution in the media environment. Three areas have been in the forefront of change: the shift from national to international markets, the convergence of telecommunications and broadcasting services and the spread of 'liberalization' policies. The intensification of market ideology applied to cultural as well as economic goods, together with innovation in fibre optic cable, digital and satellite technologies has assisted the internationalization of public communication systems and ownership.

Changes in the marketplace are matched by metamorphosis

within media production, distribution and reception processes. Unintended as well as intended consequences have followed. Advances in the portable video technology of electronic media production, for example, have led both to more candid and more pre-packaged television news. Vertical integration of production and distribution services within multi-media corporations has further concentrated ownership power – from the initial concept to the final 'spin-offs' and marketing of the product. Such developments have implications for public and social policy. Just two of the issues which give cause for concern are the increase in political, official and corporate 'information management' in print and electronic media, and the widening differentials of access and choice in the marketplace of ideas within and between nations.

Concurrent with these developments, the audiences of public communication have become more fragmented and their reception processes more privatized. The domestication of media consumption focused on household television sets, VCRs and computers continues. Paradoxically, this both enhances and subverts audience participation as an aspect of public communication, seen as integral to the democratic process. Participation is enhanced by television remote and VCR technology; content choices are subverted by commercial pressures to maximize audiences.

In many ways the wheel of scholarly enquiry has come full circle. The issues raised by the role and nature of public communication today echo concerns pursued by early pioneers of mass communication research. They, too, were interested in questions which dealt with the role of 'propaganda' in public opinion formation, or the relationship between information access, freedom of the press and the democratic process.

In exploring the changing nature and role of public communication into the 1990s, the contributors to this book consider a wide spectrum of scholarly questions, policy priorities and political issues. Their work is grouped into three sections within which each chapter provides its own imperatives for further reflection and research.

Part One examines how changes in ownership, policy and regulation are 'Transforming Media Structures'. In the opening chapter, Graham Murdock surveys important questions arising from the concentration of corporate, cross-media ownership in the print and broadcasting industries. He explores how the economic organization of the communication industry structures the range and contents of the symbolic goods circulated for public consumption; and asks whether or not a communication system organized exclusively around market dynamics and private ownership can provide the full range of information and communication resources for democracy.

William Melody pursues the question of a better informed and more participatory citizenry in relation to communications policies relevant to a global information economy. He asks 'whither the public interest?' when the locus of policy is moving from the national to the international stage and when its focus is more on private than on public interest objectives. Conceding that the new technologies have expanded opportunities for some users and producers, he argues for an overall policy framework in the public interest which will address issues of communication disparity both within and among nations.

The structure of international regulation is crucial to such ends, and James Michael discusses the qualitative differences involved in the regulation of communication and information media. Arguing that imparting information is a human right as well as an economic activity, he compares aspects of broadcasting and telecommunication regulation the United States, Britain and the rest of the European Community in an era of 'de-regulation'.

In Part Two, 'Changing Media Processes', four authors examine the relationship between politics and power, applying a variety of critical approaches to the conceptual and methodological issues raised by the political and media production processes. Philip Schlesinger enjoins us to rethink the sociology of journalism and take a closer look at the questions raised by source strategies. These will quickly reveal the limits of media-centrism as propounded by theorists of media dominance, he argues, going on to develop an analytical model for the examination of the role of sources in influencing the form and content of public communication.

Jay Blumler explores debate about media power and its relationship to the political process in relation to the electoral arena. Viewing the mass media as central to the conduct of political life, he focuses on the emergence of the 'modern publicity process' as a key element in the growing intimacy between the political and media spheres. Blumler notes how political actors are directing more resources to competitive media strategies, and how these processes appear to operate more intensively in some societies than others.

Our critical attention is directed to the political role of communications institutions in industrial democracies by Peter Golding. Pointing to the flaws in the cultural and technological determinism of much recent work in the field, he provides a methodological critique of those positions. Conceptually and empirically he urges us to address questions about the unequal access to information faced by large sections of society and suggests we incorporate a concept of social citizenship in our work to this end. The deficiencies of cultural perspectives for the investigation of news organizations are addressed by James Curran. Although different culturalist interpretations are located in differing models of society, all share a contradictory contention that control of the media is located largely outside the media. Such explanations, Curran contends, fail to account for content differences between print and electronic media and often exaggerate the extent of journalists' autonomy.

Part Three, 'Rethinking Concepts and Methods', surveys some of the research imperatives, both new and old, relevant to the changing face of public communication today. Taking a comparative perspective, Denis McQuail explores the similarities and differences between the foci of current communication research in Europe with the earlier, 'classic' period of American scholarship. Arguing that communication research reflects the pressures and influences of the surrounding culture and society, he compares the issues that engaged early American scholars with the institutional and technological changes currently reshaping the European research agenda.

Marjorie Ferguson explores the impact of electronic media on two basic categories of public communication, time and space. Arguing that a 'techno-orthodoxy' that claims new media have reduced time–space significances is misleading, Ferguson contends their importance is being magnified. She cites evidence from the telecommunication and television markets, insights from the literature and the paradox of time–space imperatives in the media production and political image processes to support her thesis.

The final chapter addresses a central dimension of public communication, the audience. Without taking into account the variety of media audiences and their social contexts there can be no full understanding of the nature of public communication in any society. Roger Silverstone makes the case that an increasingly complex mass media environment requires us to develop an increasingly sophisticated view and methodology of the audience. An anthropological approach to the study of the television audience, he argues, one that views them as active consumers and makes allowance for the place of the audience in everyday life, is a step in this direction.

As the contributors to this book make clear, there are many conceptual paths and empirical routes to the study of public communication. Nevertheless, all the authors share a broad set of normative concerns and intellectual understandings which highlight the renewed salience of communication in the public sphere.

Subsequently, the events that occurred in Tiananmen Square, Beijing in June 1989 sharply focused several of these preoccupations about communication in the public sphere. In the context of changing media environments worldwide and global trends towards a more accessible and international communication system, the limitations of live satellite television, direct dial telephone and facsimile technology for free information flow were revealed; and the imbalance of power between democratic ideas and media channels opposed by military might and authoritarian bureaucracy reaffirmed.

To speak of media power structures and public communication processes in any society is to invoke relative rather than absolute criteria. Historically, as the case of China reaffirms, public communication is Janus-faced. The media of mass communication can be used either as a vehicle for political change and mobilization or as a vehicle for repressive social and political control. Both aspects, their power and their powerlessness, provide imperatives for further research.

Marjorie Ferguson
University of Maryland

To

Professor Hilde Himmelweit

in memory of her lasting contribution
to the field
and her spirited interventions
at Madingley

PART ONE

TRANSFORMING MEDIA STRUCTURES

Ownership, Policy and Regulation

1

Redrawing the Map of the Communications Industries: Concentration and Ownership in the Era of Privatization

Graham Murdock

At the outset of the modern media age, in the first half of the nineteenth century, most commentators generally saw no contradiction between the private ownership of the press (the major medium of the time) and its public, political roles as a channel for strategic information and a forum for political debate. Freedom of the press was synonymous with the absence of government censorship and licensing and the freedom to operate unhindered in the marketplace. Newspapers were viewed as a voice on a par with individual voices, and the advocation of press freedom was seen as a logical extension of the general defence of free speech. This was plausible so long as most proprietors owned only one title and the costs of entering the market were relatively low. As the century wore on, however, and newspaper production became more sophisticated both technologically and operationally, rising costs increasingly restricted entry to major markets and drove smaller titles out of business, while the larger, wealthier concerns expanded their operations. By the beginning of this century the age of chain ownership and the press barons had arrived, prompting liberal democratic commentators to acknowledge a growing contradiction between the idealized role of the press as a key resource for citizenship and its economic base in private ownership. As the American writer, Delos Wilcox, author of one of the earlier systematic analyses of press content, observed in 1900:

> The newspaper is pre-eminently a public and not a private institution,

the principal organ of society for distributing what we might call working information . . . . The vital question is, from the social standpoint, the question of control. Who shall be responsible for the newspaper? It is rationally absurd that an intelligent, self-governing community should be the helpless victim of the caprice of newspapers managed solely for individual profit. (Wilcox, 1900: 86–9)

Wilcox's concern is more pertinent than ever as we move into an era where the combination of technological change and privatization policies are creating massive communications conglomerates with an unrivalled capacity to shape the symbolic environment which we all inhabit.

Old problems, new contexts

The last two years or so have seen a series of major acquisitions and mergers in the communications industries in Europe, North America and around the world. They include: Sony's acquisition of CBS's record division; General Electric's take-over of the US television network, NBC; the German multi-media group, Bertels-mann's, purchase of the Doubleday book company and RCA records; the Maxwell Communications Corporation's take-over of the New York publisher, Macmillan; and Rupert Murdoch's acqui-sition of a string of important communications concerns. These include the Twentieth Century Fox film interests; the major British publisher, Collins; Australia's biggest media company, the Herald and Weekly Times, and the Triangle Group of publications, which includes America's best-selling weekly magazine, *TV Guide*. By extending the activities of the leading media groups in such a visible way, these moves have breathed new life into long-standing concerns about concentration and ownership in the communications industries. To assess the significance of these developments, however, we must go beyond the immediate activity of bids, deals and buy-out, and analyse the longer-term movements which underpin them. As a first step we need to identify the key changes in the operating environ-ment of the leading corporations that are facilitating the current wave of expansion and shaping its direction.

Two processes have been particularly important in restructuring the corporate playing field: technological innovation and 'privatiz-ation'. The 'digital revolution' which allows voice, sound, text, data and images to be stored and transmitted using the same basic technologies opens up a range of possibilities for new kinds of activity and for novel forms of convergence and interplay between media sectors. At the same time, we must be careful not to overstress the importance of technological innovation or to assign it an autonomous and determining role in the process of corporate development. New technologies create new opportunities, but before corporations can take full advantage of them there has to be a change in the political context which extends their freedom of action. And here the major force has undoubtedly been the growing momentum of privatization initiatives over the last decade. Before we examine the implications of this movement for corporate structures and strategies in more detail, however, we need to answer the prior question of why these changes matter.

Media ownership and social theory

Part of the answer is that investigation of the emerging patterns of media enterprise and ownership, and the tracing of their consequences for the range and direction of cultural production, is not just a specialized topic in communications enquiry. It also helps to illuminate the general relations between structure, culture and agency in the modern world. This classic problem lies at the heart not just of media research but also of the human sciences more generally, and presents both the greatest challenge to anyone specializing in the social investigation of communications and the best opportunity to reconnect our particular concerns to general developments in the social sciences to the mutual benefit of both. The relations between structure and action have moved steadily up the agenda for debate within social theory, to the extent that they now constitute its central problem (for example, Bourdieu, 1977; Giddens, 1984). More recently, theorists have begun to examine the parallel issue of culture and agency (for example, Archer, 1988), but as yet there has been no systematic attempt to link these general concerns to a detailed investigation of the media system. This is a double loss, to social theory and to communications research.

The question of mass media ownership provides a particularly pertinent point of entry into the structure–culture–agency triangle for two reasons. First, the power accruing to ownership entails both action and structural components (see Layder, 1985). The potential control it bestows over production does not arise solely from specific exercises of power within the corporations directly owned or influenced. It is also a function of pre-existing and enduring asymmetries in the structure of particular markets or sectors, which deliver cumulative advantages to the leading corporations, and enables them to set the terms on which competitors or suppliers relate to them (see Mintz and Schwartz, 1985). Consequently, a close study of the interplay between the structural and action components of control within media industries helps considerably in illuminating the core issues at stake in current debates about the nature of power.

The second theoretical pay-off of analysing media ownership arises from the pivotal role that the communications industries play in organizing the symbolic world of modern capitalist societies and hence in linking economic structures to cultural formations. More particularly, they connect a productive system rooted in private ownership to a political system that presupposes a citizenry whose full social participation depends in part on access to the maximum possible range of information and analysis and to open debate on contentious issues. Since this dual formation of liberal democratic capitalism first emerged, sceptics have been asking how far a communications system dominated by private ownership can guarantee the diversity of information and argument required for effective citizenship.

This question is more pertinent than ever today when the modal form of media enterprise is no longer a company specializing in one particular activity, but a conglomerate with interests in a wide range of communications industries, often linked to other key economic sectors through shareholdings, joint ventures and interlocking directorships. Before we examine the ways in which this structure facilitates certain kinds of control over cultural production, however, we need to distinguish between different types of conglomerate.

Varieties of conglomerate

On the basis of their core activities we can distinguish three basic kinds of conglomerates operating in the communications field: industrial conglomerates; service conglomerates; and communications conglomerates.

Industrial conglomerates are companies which own media facilities but whose major operations are centred on industrial sectors. The Italian press provides a particularly good example of this pattern. The country's leading industrial group, Fiat, controls two major dailies: *La Stampa*, which it owns outright, and *Corriere della Sera* which it controls through its strategic stake in the paper's publisher, Rizzoli. The second largest group, the Ferruzzi-Montedison food and chemicals giant, controls *Il Messagero* and *Italia Oggi* in Milan, while the third main group, which is run through Carlo de Benedetti's master holding company, Cofide, has a controlling interest in the country's second largest publishing house, Editore Mondadori, which own 50 per cent of the best-selling daily, *La Repubblica*. Altogether it is estimated that over 70 per cent of the Italian press is controlled or significantly influenced by these three groups, with other major industrial companies accounting for significant parts of the balance. The widely read paper, *Il Giorno*, for example, is owned by the state energy company, ENI. Not surprisingly, this situation has led to allegations that press coverage is coloured by the owners' corporate interests. Critics include the broadcasting magnate, Silvio Berlusconi, who recently complained that 'Our newspapers are not written by journalists but by industrial competitors with special interests' (Friedman, 1988a: 32).

Berlusconi's own master company, Finivest, is a good example of the second main type of comglomerate, which is centred on service sectors such as real estate, financial services, and retailing. In addition to owning a national newspaper, a major cinema chain and Italy's three main commercial television networks, Berlusconi's interests include the country's leading property company; a substantial insurance and financial services division; a major chain of department stores, La Standa; and an advertising operation which accounts for around 30 per cent of the nation's billings.

In contrast to this highly diversified structure, the major interests of communications conglomerates are centred mainly or wholly in the media and information industries. Well-known examples include Rupert Murdoch's News International; the Maxwell Communications Corporation; and Bertelsmann. Until recently it was not unusual for communications conglomerates to own companies in unrelated industries. But lately there have been signs that the leading players are shedding these marginal subsidiaries in order to concentrate on expanding their core interests. In 1988, for example, Robert Maxwell disposed of his engineering interests, Associated Newspapers sold their North Sea oil division, and Reed International shed the paper and packaging division which had been their original base.

At the same time, the major communications companies have been making strenuous efforts to expand their core interests. These moves take several forms. First, there is a growing integration between hardware and software, prompted by a desire to ensure a supply of programming to service the new distribution technologies. Sony, for example, recently acquired the CBS record division, giving it a major stake in the international music industry to add to its already dominant position in the world market for compact disc players through its partnership with Philips. Second, there is a growing interpenetration between old and new media markets as major players in established sectors move into emerging areas which offer additional opportunities to exploit their resources. Newspaper and journal publishers, for example, have moved into the provision of on-line data services and broadcasting networks have branched out into cable programming. The rationale behind these moves is the desire for greater 'synergy' between the companies' various divisions so that activity in one sector can facilitate activity in another.

The rise of conglomerates as the modal form of media enterprise considerably increases the major players' potential reach over the communications and information system and makes the old questions of ownership and control more pertinent than ever.

Personal and impersonal possession

Changes in the organization of corporate enterprise have also been accompanied by shifts in ownership, though these are by no means uni-directional. Although there is a discernible trend towards the forms of impersonal possession outlined by John Scott (1986) in which the controlling interests in major corporations are held by other companies and financial institutions, older patterns of personal ownership, where effective control remains in the hands of the founding family or group, have also proved remarkably resilient within the communications industries. According to one recent estimate, for example, sixteen of the top twenty-four media groups in the United States 'are either closely held or still controlled by members of the originating family' (Herman and Chomsky, 1988: 8). They include both old-established companies such as the *New York Times* (the Sulzbergers) and Dow Jones and Co. (the Bancroft and Cox families) and newer arrivals such as Turner Broadcasting. At the same time, as the recent battles for control of the Springer press empire in West Germany and the Fairfax publishing interests in Australia clearly show, maintaining family or founder control can be a precarious and often expensive business.

The form of ownership is important since in combination with the structure and size of the company, it has an important bearing on the forms of control that proprietors want and are able to exercise. Although concern about the ways in which owner power may operate to curtail the diversity of publicly available information and debate can be traced back to the beginning of the modern media system in the second half of the nineteenth century, they are arguably more important than ever now, for three main reasons.

First, the fact that many of the leading communications companies command interests that span a range of key media sectors and operate across the major world markets gives them an unprecedented degree of potential control over contemporary cultural life. Second, as we shall see presently, the process of privatization has eroded the countervailing power of public cultural institutions. This is a significant loss, since at their best they embodied a genuine commitment to diversity and open argument, and at their minimum they filled a number of important gaps in commercially organized provision. Third, the privately owned media are becoming both more concentrated and more homogenized at a time when a range of new social concerns and movements, around ecological issues, women's rights and racial, regional and religious identities, are emerging in a number of countries. As a consequence, 'there is a growing gap between the number of voices in society and the number heard in the media' (Bagdikian, 1985: 98). What then are the powers of ownership? In what ways are proprietors able to shape the range and direction of cultural production?

The powers of ownership

Owners possess two basic kinds of potential control over the symbolic environment. First and most obviously, they are able to regulate the output of the divisions they own directly, either by intervening in day-to-day operations, or by establishing general goals and understandings and appointing managerial and editorial staff to implement them within the constraints set by the overall allocation of resources (see Murdock, 1982). Second, they may also be able to influence the strategies of companies they do not own in their roles as competitors or suppliers.

In the area of direct intervention, attention has mostly been focused on proprietor's efforts to use the media outlets under their control as megaphones for their social and political ambitions. As the more perceptive commentators recognized when the trend first became apparent at the turn of the century, the movement towards conglomeration offered additional opportunities for the abuse of power. It was no longer simply a question of an individual owner giving himself and his views free publicity. As Edward Ross noted in 1910, the growing integration of newspapers into the core sectors of capital threatened to create new 'no-go' areas for critical reporting on corporate affairs and to undermine the press's role as a Fourth Estate, keeping watch over all those institutions – whether governmental or corporate – with significant power over people's lives. As he pointed out:

> newspapers are subject to the tendency of diverse businesses to become tied together by the cross-investments of their owners. But naturally, when the shares of a newspaper lie in a safe-deposit box cheek by jowl with gas, telephone, and pipe-line stock, a tenderness for these collateral interests is likely to affect the news columns'. (Ross, 1910: 305)

Contemporary cases of such 'instrumental' abuses of power are not hard to find. In the summer of 1988, for example, Toshiba, one of Japan's leading contractors for nuclear power plants, withdrew a record protesting against the country's nuclear programme commissioned by its Toshiba-EMI music subsidiary. As is often the case in these situations, a political judgment was presented as a disinterested commercial decision, with a company spokesman claiming that 'this music is just too good to put before the market right now' (*Marketing Week*, 1988: 18). Direct interventions are also used to denigrate the activities of competitors. In March 1988, for example, the Fiat-controlled daily, *Corriere della Sera*, carried an abusive front-page story and editorial ridiculing the attempts of one of the company's main business rivals, Carlo de Benedetti, to take control of the leading Belgian holding company, Société Générale de Belgique. Although Fiat intervention was denied, it was clear that, however engineered, the story was designed to boost the company's position, and no one in Italy was surprised when the magazine *L'Expresso* produced a mock version of the paper's front page with the title altered to *Corriere della Fiat* (Friedman, 1988b: 115–16).

In both these cases we are dealing with industrial conglomerates defending their corporate interests. With service and communications conglomerates the dynamics of influence are somewhat different. Here the major impetus comes from commercial initiatives designed to maximize the 'synergy' between the company's various operations. When Silvio Berlusconi bought the Standa department store chain in July 1988, he immediately announced a programme of cross-promotion whereby his television stations would carry daily slots featuring the bargains on offer in the stores, thereby reducing the space available for other kinds of programming. When the publishing group Reed International acquired Octopus Books in 1987, it made no secret of the fact that it was looking to develop titles based on its substantial stable of magazines. Other publishing companies are actively exploring ways of making television programming for satellite distribution using the same editorial resources employed to produce newspapers and magazines (Handley, 1988). These are purely commercial decisions, but by promoting multiplicity over diversity they have a pertinent effect on the range of information and imagery in the public domain. In a cultural system built around 'synergy', more does not mean different; it means the same basic commodity appearing in different markets and in a variety of packages. But owner power does not end with these kinds of interventions.

As we noted earlier, as well as determining the actions of the companies they control directly, the strategies pursued by the major media owners also have a considerable knock-on effect on smaller competitors operating in the same markets and on potential take-over targets. The deeper their corporate pockets, the greater their potential influence. In the autumn of 1988, for example, in an effort to strengthen its defences against the hostile attentions of Rupert Murdoch who had built up a 20 per cent stake in the company, the Pearson group (whose interests include Penguin Books and the *Financial Times*) entered into an alliance with the Dutch publisher, Elsevier, who had been the target of another major media mogul, Robert Maxwell. Whether this tie-up is in the best long-term interests of Pearson or whether another partner would have been more advantageous is open to debate, but there is no doubt that this link will materially affect the company's future options.

The leading corporations' extensive power to shape the future of the communications and information system both directly and indirectly is not in itself new, of course. What is new is the rapid enlargement of these powers produced by a decade of privatization initiatives.

Dimensions of privatization

Since the term 'privatization' has acquired a variety of meanings in recent debates, I should make it clear that I am using it here in its most general sense to describe all forms of public intervention that increase the size of the market sector within the communication and information industries and give entrepreneurs operating within it increased freedom of manoeuvre. Two general features of this process are particularly worth noting. First, although such initiatives are usually associated with conservative administrations – most notably, the three Thatcher governments in Britain and Reagan's terms of office in the United States – they are by no means confined to them. The socialist government of Spain, for example, recently used its majority in the lower house to push through legislation authorizing three new commercial television franchises in the face of strong opposition from both conservative and left parties. More significantly, both the Soviet Union and the People's Republic of China have recently allowed commercial programme providers from overseas into their broadcasting systems. The second, and equally important, feature of privatization is its relative irreversibility. Although the popularity of specific initiatives may decline in the future and the original almost messianic impetus wane somewhat, there is little doubt that the previous balance between public and private enterprise has been tipped permanently in favour of the market in a growing number of societies. It is difficult, for example, to imagine any socialist or social democratic government capable of being elected in Western Europe in the near future, successfully re-nationalizing the key communications companies that have been sold off to private investors.

Privatization as I am defining it here is a multi-dimensional movement with four distinct components: de-nationalization; liberalization; the commercialization of the public sector; and the re-gearing of the regulatory environment. Each has important implications for the overall structure of the communications industries, for patterns of ownership, and for corporate strategies, which we need to trace, but it is important to separate them since they are not always pursued together.

Denationalization: from public to private ownership

Because denationalization involves selling shares in public companies to private investors, its most significant impact is on patterns of ownership. However, this varies depending on how the shares are placed. Where they are put out to competitive tender and awarded to a particular consortium, as in France under the conservative administration of Chirac, the advantage clearly lies with companies which are already well financed and positioned and who can use the opportunity to extend their interests into areas from which they were previously locked out. For example, the group that took over TF1, which had been France's major public broadcasting network, included the Maxwell media conglomerate, the Bouygues construction group and the major banking group, Société Générale (which also had important stakes in two other denationalized communications concerns: the Havas advertising agency, and the telecommunications and engineering group, Companie Générale d'Electricité).

In contrast, the British strategy of public flotation was expressly designed to create a 'popular capitalism' in which shareholding would be widely dispersed. To this end, shares in the most important communications utility to be sold to date, British Telecom, were underpriced in order to attract first-time investors. Not surprisingly, their value rose sharply as soon as they were traded on the Stock Exchange, and many small shareholders opted to sell and pocket the profit. In the two years between December 1984 and the end of November 1986, the total number of BT shareholders fell by almost 30 per cent from 2.1 million to 1.48 million, reducing the public's overall share to less than 12 per cent and leaving the bulk of BT's equity in the hands of financial institutions, many based overseas.

Overall, then, denationalization has operated to reinforce and extend the power of the leading communications, service and industrial conglomerates rather than to disperse it, or to create new sources of countervailing power. By the same token, liberalization has enabled them to extend their reach into new markets.

Liberalization

Liberalization policies are designed to introduce competition into markets that were previously served solely by public enterprise. Here the impact depends on the terms on which this competition is allowed to proceed. Broadcasting provides a good example. Britain was the first major European country to introduce a commercial television service in competition with the public broadcasting system, when the ITV network was launched in 1954. However, the private sector was carefully regulated to ensure a reasonable spread of ownership and to limit foreign programming to 14 per cent of the total output. Without these safeguards, moves to liberalize broadcasting serve to open up national markets to the major international corporations. The major shareholders in the new French commercial channels, for example, include the Italian television magnate, Silvio Berlusconi, who has a 25 per cent stake in La Cinq, and Companie Luxembourgeoise de Télédiffusion (which operates the Luxembourg-based television service RTL–Plus), which owns 25 per cent of the sixth channel, M6. In addition, the rapid expansion of commercial television paved the way for a sharp rise in the amount of foreign programming imported into the system since the proliferation of new distribution systems outstripped the supply of nationally originated material by a very considerable margin. This effect is noticeable even where broadcasting remains a public monopoly, as in Norway, where the decision to allow local cable systems to take advertising-supported pan-European satellite channels has already acted as a stalking horse for full liberalization by deepening the crisis of public broadcasting.

Commercializing the public sector

One response to this crisis is to commercialize the public sector itself. Faced with rising costs and government ceilings imposed on the income they derive from the public purse, this has become an imperative for many public institutions, but it is one which a number are now embracing with enthusiasm. It takes several forms. The first is to allow broadcasters to supplement their income by taking spot advertising, as the state broadcasting network RAI does in Italy. So far this option has been resisted in Britain, but as recent developments at the BBC show, audiences and indeed resources can be opened up to private enterprise in other ways.

In the spring of 1988, the BBC offered two new services to the corporate sector. The first provided for 100 new data channels for use by retailers and other service companies wishing to advertise to their customers. The second allowed a private company, British Medical Television, to use time after regular broadcasts had finished for the night to relay a programme with advertising from the major pharmaceutical companies to VCRs in doctors' homes and surgeries for later viewing. In return, the Corporation will receive a £1 million fee in the first year. As well as gaining access to transmission resources for the first time, private corporations are also gaining a foothold in programme production as a result of the Government's decision that the BBC should move rapidly towards a situation in which at least 25 per cent of its programming is obtained from independent producers. Although the independent sector has only been established for a few years in Britain, prompted by the launch of Channel Four, which buys in almost all its programming, there is already a movement towards concentration which senior figures in the industry expect to continue. As Charles Denton, the Chief Executive of Zenith Productions, one of the country's most successful television independents, told an interviewer: 'I think there will be a move to agglomeration, and to cope with the economic realities there will be some very complex cross-holding. When this industry matures, you will find maybe half a dozen, even fewer, large independents. And we intend to be one of them' (Fiddick, 1988: 21). Recent examples of this trend include Robert Maxwell's take-over of the creative consortium Witzend; the purchase of Goldcrest Films and Elstree Studios by the leisure group Brent Walker; and the acquisition of Zenith itself by Carlton Communications, one of Britain's leading facilities houses. These movements, coupled with the partial relaxation of the rules governing corporate underwriting and sponsorship for programming (particularly on cable), open the way for greater corporate influence over what appears on the domestic screen. This erosion of the traditional 'Chinese walls' separating programming from product or corporate promotion, which we now see in a number of countries, is part of a much wider re-gearing of the regulatory environment in which the communications industries operate.

Re-regulation: from public to corporate interests

This process is often called de-regulation. This is a misnomer. What is at stake is not so much the number of rules but the shift in their overall rationale, away from a defence of the public interest (however that was conceived) and towards the promotion of corporate interests. Communications corporations benefit from this shift at two levels. They not only gain from changes to the general laws governing corporate activity in areas such as trade-union rights but, more importantly, they have also gained considerably from the relaxation of the additional rules designed to prevent undue concentration in the market-place of ideas and to ensure diversity of expression.

One of the most important changes has been the general loosening of the restrictions on concentration of ownership. In Britain, for example, Rupert Murdoch's bid for the mid-market daily *Today*, was judged not to be against the public interest on the grounds that, although he owned the country's most popular tabloid paper, the *Sun*, and one of the leading quality titles, *The Times*, he did not have an interest in the middle range and that his acquisition would not therefore increase concentration – a judgment that conveniently leaves aside the question of concentration in the national daily market as a whole.

In the broadcasting field, changes to the rules limiting the number of stations a single owner can possess have led to a significant increase in concentration in both the United States and Australia. In America, in April 1985, the old 7–7–7 limit which had operated since 1953 was replaced by a new 12–12–12 rule which allowed one company to own up to twelve AM and FM radio stations plus twelve television stations, providing that their total audience did not exceed 25 per cent of the country's television households. This made network ownership a more attractive proposition (despite the steady erosion of their overall audience share by cable and independent stations), and all three became the subject of bids. ABC was merged with Capital Cities; NBC was acquired by General Electric; and CBS narrowly fought off a bid from Ted Turner. A similar relaxation occurred in Australia in November 1986 when Bob Hawke's Labour Government replaced the old two-station rule with a new arrangement which allows owners to have as many stations as they like as long as they do not reach more than 60 per cent of the national audience. Here again, the result has been a marked movement towards greater concentration of ownership as companies in the two major markets – Sydney and Melbourne – have branched out to build national networks. Between December 1986 and September 1988, twelve out of the fifteen stations in capital cities changed hands, leaving the commercial television system as a virtual duopoly divided between the media wing of Alan Bond's industrial conglomerate and Christopher Skase's Quintex Group (Brown, 1988).

Changes to the regulatory regime are not uni-directional, however. At the same time as they relaxed the rule on the number of television stations that could be owned, the Australian government imposed new restrictions forbidding cross-ownership of radio stations, television stations or newspapers in the same markets. This accelerated the shake-up in newspaper ownership already under way, though here again the major beneficiaries were the leading groups. At the beginning of 1987, Rupert Murdoch successfully bid for the country's largest press concern, the Herald and Weekly Times, bringing his total share of the Australian newspaper market to 59 per cent. In the United States, in contrast, the rules on cross-ownership have recently been relaxed, though not without a struggle. Senator Edward Kennedy, for example, appended a clause to the Federal government's spending authorization for 1988, tightening the restrictions on owning television stations and newspapers in the same city. This was directed expressly at Murdoch whose *Boston Herald* had been consistently hostile to Kennedy. Murdoch contested it, and in the spring of 1988 it was overturned by the Circuit Court of Appeals in Washington on the grounds that since it was clearly aimed at one person it violated constitutional guarantees of equal treatment. This ruling was in line with the general trend of recent regulatory thinking typified by the Federal Communication Commission's decision to lift the ban on local telephone companies owning cable systems.

The FCC has also been in the forefront of the drive to loosen the public service requirements governing commercial broadcasting so as to give station owners maximum freedom to make profits. One of the bitterest rows in this area has been over children's television, which during the Reagan years had become one more or less continuous advertisement for toys and other products both in and around the programmes. After a concerted campaign, a citizens' lobby was successful in getting a Bill passed in both the House of Representatives and the Senate, limiting advertising time during children's programmes to twelve minutes in the hour and requiring franchisees to show a commitment to education. However, in one of his last acts as President, Ronald Reagan killed the measure by the simple expedient of omitting to sign it, declaring that its provisions 'simply cannot be reconciled with the freedom of expression secured by our constitution' (*The Economist*, 1988: 50). This statement exemplifies the general view which sees corporate promotion as continuous with individual speech, a position neatly encapsulated in the description of advertising as 'commercial speech'. The cumulative result of these shifts, and the other dimensions of the privatization process I have outlined here, has been to strengthen and extend the power of the leading corporations and to pose more sharply than ever the dilemma that faces a liberal democratic society in which most key communications facilities are held in private hands.

Detailing the way in which our existing maps of the cultural industries are being redrawn by the twin processes of technological changes and privatization policies and tracing their consequences for the range and nature of cultural production is a key task for future research. By the same token, anyone interested in formulating alternative policies for communications urgently needs to grapple with ways of regulating the new multi-media concerns, both nationally and internationally, and with the problem of developing novel forms of public initiative and institution which avoid the over-centralized, unresponsive structures of the past and are capable of responding creatively to the new poly-cultural formations now emerging. This is perhaps the major issue facing those of us interested in the future of communications as an essential resource for developing and deepening democracy.

2

Communication Policy in the Global Information Economy: Whither the Public Interest?

William H. Melody

Information and communication developments have tended to erode heretofore separable areas of public policy, and to increase the probability of unforeseen implications arising in areas outside the purview of traditional policy analysis. Industrial policy, social policy and cultural policy are more integrated than they have been in the past. Each has significant implications for the others. The press, print, broadcast, library, telecommunication and computer industries are becoming more interrelated and interdependent, so that government policies toward one industry cannot help but have significant implications for others.

The difficulty to date has been understanding the many important dimensions of information and communication policy issues, particularly when it comes to assessing the long-term implications. There has been a tendency for governments to recognize only those immediate issues that have been thrust before them, generally in fragmented fashion, outside either a long-term or a systemic context. The great challenge for policy research is to explain the complex set of interrelations among policy areas that were previously thought to be reasonably discrete and separable, and thereby to provide a better understanding of the environment in which informed policy decisions must be made (Melody, 1989a).

The successful development of new information and communication markets for the benefit of all sectors of society will require major adaptations by both private and public institutions. If markets in tradeable information are going to work efficiently and equitably, they must be developed upon a foundation of public information that provides the education and training necessary for citizens to function effectively as workers, managers, consumers and responsible citizens. Determining the appropriate adaptations, both by the public and the private sectors, to the new information and communication environment is a crucial task for public policy.

Many individuals and organizations can benefit substantially from the rapid expansion of the information and communication sector, but at least some are likely to be disadvantaged, in both relative and absolute terms, especially if traditional public and social services are displaced, downgraded or made more expensive. To illustrate, a considerable portion of the information now accessible through public libraries is subject to commoditization and sale in private markets, where it would be accessible only through telecommunication-based information services. In recent years, many libraries have expanded access to a variety of bibliographic databases. But they have cut back their physical holdings of government reports and statistics, general research reports and studies, periodicals and even books. This has greatly facilitated research projects with the funding support to pay for computer searches and acquisition of the desired material. But most academic researchers, students, and the lay public can rarely afford to use computer searches, and are increasingly frustrated by the more limited access to hard-copy resources.

The telephone system is being upgraded to the technical standards of an integrated services digital network (ISDN) that is more efficient for the plethora of new information services required by sophisticated high-volume users. But it may be significantly more costly for small-volume users and users with only local telephone service requirements. This could make it more difficult to achieve, and for some countries to maintain, a universal basic telephone service (Melody, 1989b).

The characteristics of information markets create special problems associated with the transfer of computer and telecommunication technologies to developing countries. The market incentives are to sell new technology facility systems in developing countries to establish the infrastructure for both the domestic and international communication of information services. Given the established base of information in the technologically advanced countries, and their lead in establishing new information services, the information flows are predictable. Final consumer information, such as television programmes (often accompanied by advertising), is likely to dominate the flow from developed to developing countries. Specialized information markets that create value as a result of the monopoly of information are likely to generate a dominant flow of information about developing countries to developed countries and transnational corporations. These conditions may place developing country firms and agencies at an increased competitive disadvantage in their own countries because of an information deficiency about conditions there (Melody, 1985).

A major challenge for public policy is to find methods to ensure that developments in the information and communication sector do not exacerbate class divisions in society and that the benefits are spread across all classes. This requires new conceptions and operational definitions of the 'public interest' and of public services. It requires new interpretations of the requirements of social policy, and the design of new institutional structures for its effective implementation. It also requires a re-evaluation of the role of information and communication in participatory democracy and the public policies necessary to encourage its diffusion across all segments of society.

An increase in the quantity and diversity of information sources and communication opportunities seems to be upon us, as markets in this field have grown rapidly from national to global. The economy of the future has already been dubbed 'the information society'. But what of the public interest in the age of information overload and new communication opportunities? Is there still an important or even essential role for public interest policies, if the gap between theory and practice along the uncertain path to participatory democracy is to be reduced in the information age? This chapter explores these issues and suggests an updated interpretation of the public interest that is adapted to the changing information/communication environment.

Information, communication and participatory democracy

Participatory democracy requires a citizenry that is both informed and has a continuing opportunity to be heard in the market-place of ideas. For most of history, dictators and even democratically elected governments have attempted to bias and restrict the information made available to the public, while limiting and controlling access to the market-place of ideas. Indeed, this is perhaps the essential contradiction of democratic theory versus practice. For those in power, the practice inevitably falls far short of the requirements of theory. *Spycatcher* and Irangate are examples in two nations that have done much to further the cause of participatory democracy in the world today.

In democratic countries, the rights of citizens to be informed and have access to the market-place of ideas have been accepted as an obligation of national governments. These rights have been enshrined in a variety of laws, policies and regulations. The right to be informed has been reflected primarily in programmes in three areas: (1) opportunities for universal education of the population, ostensibly to promote learning and the ability to assess critically the changing world; (2) the widespread availability of public libraries as repositories of both historical and current information, and public access to information about the policies and practices of government and other dominant institutions in society; and (3) independent and widespread reporting and interpretation of changing local, national and international events by the mass media – primarily the press, radio and television.

Recognizing that it is technologically, economically and physically impossible for everyone to be read, heard and seen via the mass media, on an equal access basis, public policy has been directed to ensuring terms of mass media access that reflect the broad interests of the general public. These include: (a) requiring 'responsible' presentations and fair dealing by those in privileged positions of power who control access to the general public through the media; (b) safeguarding rights of reply and legal protection from libel for individuals and organizations that feel unfairly treated; and (c) taking positive steps to maintain a diversity of information sources and a variety of content from the mass media.

To facilitate direct intercommunication among the citizenry, interpersonal and interorganization communication networks have been encouraged through national public postal and telecommunication systems with a fundamental policy objective to provide universal service. Both the mass media and the post-telegraph-telephone (PTT) sectors of the economy have been recognized as being significantly different from other industries because of their importance to the preservation of citizen's rights to be informed and to communicate freely, conditions essential to political democracy. For the most part, these industries have been treated as 'business affected with a public interest', and subjected to special treatment under law and government policy.

The institutional mechanisms for implementing and enforcing the public interest in the mass media and PTT sectors have differed among countries and among industries within the same country, and have changed over time. When new technologies have led to fundamental changes in the structure of communication industries, a reassessment of public interest requirements in the light of the changed conditions is almost always necessary (Melody, 1973). In recent years, both major communication sectors have applied a number of new information and communication technologies and have undergone substantial structural change, challenging traditional public interest notions and the established mechanisms for implementing them.

The press

With the help of the Gutenberg press, the virtual monopoly over public information was wrested from the authorities (church and state) and the professional class (monks) in the late fifteenth and sixteenth centuries. Since then, a continuing struggle has taken place between the state and the 'independent' press with respect to the freedom of the press from state restrictions in providing information to the public. It was such a contentious issue in democratic Britain in the eighteenth century that the American revolutionaries established freedom of the press as a fundamental constitutional protection from government. The historic concern with the press has been government monopoly and control of information, not private monopoly and control. Given the techno-logical and institutional conditions of the day, a diversity of private supply (even at the local level) was the expected result that was borne out in reality.

In more recent times, such mechanisms as press councils and libel laws have provided a token of social responsibility and accountability of an increasingly powerful and concentrated private press to the citizenry it serves. But for most other purposes the press has been treated as any other industry. A diversity of supply has been assumed. Moreover, this diversity has been presumed to be protected in most democratic countries under the anti-monopoly laws govern-ing economic activity in general.

It has only been in recent times, with the rapidly diminishing number of newspapers and sources of news, that the problem of private monopoly and control of the press has arisen in an increasing number of countries. Diversity has been reduced substantially. Yet for most observers, the public interest has been seen essentially as preserving conditions of 'independent' reporting, not a diversity of information services and viewpoints. In fact, the line of analysis coming into fashion in recent years is that ownership domination is not the crucial issue. As long as there is editorial independence then common ownership involving the press with printing, distribution outlets, other media companies or major transnational corporations in other industries may provide economies of scale and scope. According to this view of information, quasi-monopoly of the private press may be efficient and effective as long as it is responsible and fair. Moreover, it is argued, there is ample competition with other media and other sources of information.

Helped considerably by the new computer and telecommunication technologies, the march to international oligopolization of the press as part of enormous multi-media transnational corporations is proceeding rapidly. National anti-monopoly laws seem inadequate to the task of addressing the broader public interest implications, or of fashioning appropriate policies to ensure that the public interest is served. It would seem inevitable that public policy soon will have to address the issue of public interest implications of the continued private monopolization of the press. If diversity is going to be sharply reduced, and barriers to access thereby increased, then the public interest responsibilities of the press must increase, and stronger mechanisms of accountability be established (Melody, 1976; Owen, 1975). But this can only be done in the context of the changing information and communication sectors of the economy, of which the press is an important part.

Radio and television

Radio and television were introduced long after the press had won freedom from direct government control in democratic societies. Radio and television required use of a public resource, the radio spectrum. Effective communication required at least a system of licensing and technical regulation that specified frequency, power and other characteristics of broadcast signals, and restricted entry to the industry. The underlying technological conditions meant that government had to be involved, either as supplier of the service or regulator of the private suppliers.

Different countries, each following its own traditions, adopted different institutional models for implementing the public interest. In many countries, government owned and operated 'public service' broadcasting entities were established. In the United States a model of government licensing and regulation of private broadcasters was adopted. Specific requirements for programming in the public interest were established. In other countries a mixed system was adopted. Under both the 'public service' models and the 'regulated private programming in the public interest' models of broadcasting, a policy of diversity of programme types in response to the diversity of interests in society (for example, news, public affairs, children's, religious programmes, etc.) was adopted as the responsibility of broadcasters. Under both systems a balanced programme schedule was required to be responsive to the diversity of interests in society and the broader public interest.

Research has demonstrated how the characteristics of media content are heavily influenced by the structure of the institutions that make up the total broadcasting system.[1] The major differences in programme content produced by competitive commercial and monopoly public service broadcasting are well known. But there is great variation within both the commercial and public service models. In the past, commercial broadcasting has not been totally ruled by profit maximization and often has provided some public service programming. Historically there have been limits on the extent to which commercialization is permitted to penetrate programme content. For example, there normally (but not necessarily on children's shows) has been an observable separation between the programmes and the advertisements.

Similarly, public service objectives are defined differently in different countries, and are constrained in varying degrees by cost and audience criteria. Some public service broadcast organizations emphasize a national public service while others emphasize a regional or local public service. Among those emphasizing a national public service, the BBC historically has interpreted its public service mandate, in the Reithian tradition,[2] as a paternalistic educational uplifting of the masses. In more recent times this view has been under assessment both within and without the BBC. The Canadian Broadcasting Corporation (CBC) mandate is to promote national unity, to develop a national consciousness and to interpret Canada for Canadians. The US Public Broadcasting Service's (PBS) primary purpose is to promote artistic, cultural, public affairs and related programming as a supplement to the United States commercial broadcasting system. Other countries have different models of public service broadcasting (Melody, 1987a).

In addition, the system of finance, the structural relations with production houses, the standards of accountability employed and other factors all affect programme content. These institutional constraints do not deny creativity and discretion so much as channel it in particular directions. Some of the most creative programming is channelled into advertisements.

New communication technologies, including CATV, direct broadcast satellites and VCRs are opening a variety of new options for delivering broadcast content and for implementing new methods of payment such as subscription and pay-per-view. In radio, new radio frequency and station allocations and pirate radio are expanding listener choice. International television broadcasting is expanding viewer choice. In the past, international broadcasting primarily involved exchanges among countries of national programmes produced for domestic consumption. This is now being superseded by programme production specifically created for global markets, often involving co-production among multiple countries and sometimes bringing together public service and private commercial broadcasters in co-productions (Collins et al., 1988).

Clearly the traditional distinctions between public service and private commercial broadcasting are being eroded. The former positions of privilege and power enjoyed by the dominant institutions in both systems are diminishing. For example, the BBC has a new potentially lucrative opportunity to enter global broadcast markets which will soon engulf the UK. But it would have to shift part of its programming away from traditional UK public service broadcasting. The CBC has been instructed by the Canadian government to direct its programming to global markets as a means of reducing its government subsidy. National governments everywhere are paying particular attention to the export potential of their public service institutions, including both education and mass media content.[3]

This apparent surfeit of new opportunity and choice that seems to be arising in the broadcast media could be interpreted as justification for a major relaxation, if not complete elimination, of public service and public interest obligations. However, greater choice does not necessarily mean greater diversity, adequate service to minority interests, or improved conditions of access to audiences for those desiring it. Clearly, the traditional conception of a quasi-monopoly public service broadcaster playing media den mother to the nation has been superseded by events. But the public interest responsibilities historically assumed by the national public service broadcaster remain. The challenge to future public policy is to establish workable institutional arrangements that will ensure that those responsibilities are met by the system as a whole.

Post–telecommunication networks

The communication systems that have provided the greatest opportunity for the population at large to participate as initiators of information exchange have been the postal and telecommunication networks. The opportunity to influence a mass audience is not present, but as media that permit, indeed require, active participation in the communication of ideas, they can provide – and historically have provided – a major stimulus toward participatory democracy. Monitoring the postal and telephone activities of particular individuals and organizations is a major concern of totalitarian governments, and a not insignificant one in many democracies.

Communication via post-telecommunication systems sometimes is viewed as not really important in affecting people's knowledge, beliefs and actions. The vast majority of messages are classified as commercial or social. But the vast majority of messages over the mass media are also commercial or social, and much less personal. Moreover, advertisers continue to find post-telecommunication effective vehicles for reaching markets of significant size. Winning the hearts and minds of people one at a time may be more effective than mass conversions–modern television advertising and the church of the airwaves notwithstanding. Even more important, participatory democracy is enhanced by increasing the numbers of people actively participating, and capable of applying their own critical assessments of mass media messages. It is enriched by an increase in the number actively initiating communication in the market-place of ideas, and by a reduced effectiveness of mass media propaganda of all kinds.

In almost all countries, the post was recognized early on as an important public service. Although the motives of national governments in extending the post were not the purest – for example, to facilitate taxation and military recruitment – the concept of a universal public service, accessible to all at a reasonable cost, was accepted in principle and implemented broadly in practice. It provided a major stimulus in the desire of many people to learn to read and particularly to write.

With the introduction of the telegraph (1844) and later the telephone (1878), most countries absorbed these new technologies into the national public service postal monopoly. In the United States, where they were invented and initially patented, private companies were established. After periods of vigorous – some would say destructive – competition, government regulation of territorial monopoly telephone companies was established at the state level (*circa* 1910), and was followed by creeping Federal regulation, culminating in the Federal Communications Act of 1934. It is debatable whether monopolization led to regulation, or whether the Bell System was successful in its campaign to get itself regulated as a means of eliminating its competitors by law rather than superior efficiency. Canada elected to follow the US, rather than the British model of telephone development, after a very intense debate in the House of Commons in the early 1900s.

The gap between theory and practice in the spread of universal telephone service has been significant. In North America, regulators were uniformly ineffective in getting the telephone companies to extend service to small towns and rural areas within their enfranchised territories. Near-universal service was eventually obtained by the establishment of municipal companies, co-operatives, small private companies, and in Canada, provincial companies. These developments were uniformly opposed by the private monopoly telephone companies, and sometimes by the regulators (Melody, 1989b).

Among countries adopting the public service model for telecommunication, Sweden was unique in that it established a telecommunication administration separate from its postal authority, and with very limited monopoly privileges. Sweden achieved universal service coverage some time ago. Those countries that incorporated telecommunication into the postal administration generally failed miserably in their attempts to achieve universal telephone service. Until a decade ago, household penetration rates in European PTT countries ranged from 10 to 70 per cent, with a general inferior quality of service and usually long waiting lists for basic connections. The most common explanations are: the inefficiency of long-standing bureaucracies; the use of telecommunication as a profit-maximizing money-spinner to subsidize the post, and general government coffers; and political resistance to committing funds for extending public service responsibilities beyond the post.

The ubiquitous telephone is an essential component of building and maintaining widespread political, economic, social and cultural networks in many democratic countries. In others, its absence is a significant barrier to participation by major segments of the population. According to the International Telecommunication Union, a majority of the world's population lives more than two hours away from the nearest telephone.

The renewed interest in telecommunication shown by national policy-makers in virtually all developed and many developing countries does not arise from a sudden recognition that universal service will facilitate participatory democracy and economic efficiency at the local and national levels. Rather, it is a recognition that the telecommunication infrastructure is becoming a crucial building block affecting the competitiveness and efficiency of the entire national economy in the evolving global information economy. This is prompting a fundamental institutional restructuring of the telecommunication sector in many countries (Melody, 1986a).

In many countries, progress toward the achievement of universal telephone service is being achieved by removing the dead hand of bureaucracy, exposing inadequacies of service coverage and adopting commercial efficiency standards. In only a few years after privatization, British Telecom (BT) has increased its household penetration rate from about 65 to 80 per cent. However, charges for connection and local use have increased significantly and the overall quality of service outside the major central business districts has declined. Whether BT will push its household penetration rate beyond the point of profit maximization, and whether the new regulatory agency, Oftel, is capable of enforcing social policy objectives such as universal service in the new telecommunication environment, remain to be seen. Given the pressures upon the telecommunication network as a cornerstone of national industrial policy in many countries, the public interest in a social policy of universal telephone service may be difficult to achieve. Yet in the 'information society', increasingly dependent on the telecommunication system, the need for universal service is likely to become even more important. The historic models of public service or regulated private telecommunication monopolies have generally been ineffective, and clearly are not applicable for the future. But the public interest needs are increasing in importance.

The information society

The growing significance of new electronic information and communication networks has brought to the foreground a recognition of the overwhelming importance of information and communication in society. The characteristics of information generation and dissemination affect the nature of markets and the structure of industry, as well as the competitiveness of firms, and the prosperity of regions and nations. They affect the internal structure of organizations, ranging from corporations to government agencies, political parties, universities, trade unions, libraries and volunteer groups. The implications of the changes now taking place in the information and communication sector are made all-pervasive precisely because they affect the characteristics of essential information and communication networks both for individuals and organizations.[4]

Because of its pervasive penetration of economic and social institutions, the newly forming information and communication sector is not easily separated from other sectors. Essentially it consists of microelectronics; computer hardware, software and services; telecommunication equipment and services; the mass media and a plethora of new database and information services, as well as the more traditional forms of information and communication such as print, library and postal services. Stimulated by continuing major technological change, this sector has experienced a rapid rate of economic growth in recent years. Moreover, the direct economic effects are compounded by the fact that major parts of this sector provide important infrastructure services, or facilitate functions that affect the operation and efficiency of almost all other industries, as well as government agencies and most other institutions.

Information gathering, processing, storage and transmission over efficient telecommunication networks is the foundation upon which technologically advanced nations will close the twentieth century as so-called 'information economies' or 'information societies', that is, societies that have become dependent upon complex electronic information and communication networks, and which allocate a major portion of their resources to information and communication activities. This sector may become even more significant to the development of national and international economic growth than any of the major transport expansion eras of the past, including canal, rail or highway.

Moreover, the implications go much beyond national considerations. The expansion of the information and communication sector serves to integrate the domestic economy more easily into the international economy by means of efficient international information and communication networks. As international economic integration is expanded, the impact of domestic public policies is reduced. Control over the domestic economy by national governments is weakened. These developments are forcing governments to recognize the need for a full range of international trade policies, addressed not only to direct trade in information and communication equipment and services, but also to acknowledge the implications of global information and communication networks and services for other industries. For example, these considerations are central to current discussions at the International Telecommunication Union (ITU) as well as GATT (ITU, 1989).

The international banking and finance industries have already been restructuring their organizations, and methods of operation, in the light of enhanced opportunities for transferring money and data instantaneously around the world. Many transnational corporations have been able to improve their organizational efficiency and control by centralizing more decisions at their world headquarters, while maintaining flexibility in decentralized production. This has raised the possibility that significant decision-making power, as well as research and development and information services activities, will be removed from 'national' subsidiaries that in some cases have been reduced to the status of branch plants.

Medical, tax, credit and other detailed information relating to citizens and institutions of one country is being stored with increasing frequency in another. This raises important public policy questions in a number of areas, including for example, the terms of conditions of access to information, privacy of personal information, and the scope and limitations of national and regional sovereignty. It raises questions as to the vulnerability of a country's economic and political decision-making systems to losses of essential information because of breakdowns in crucial information and communication networks that occur outside the country.

Significant changes in information and communication networks require a reinterpretation of traditional notions of public information (for example, news, libraries, government reports and statistics), private information (for example, strategic corporate plans and forecasts) and the terms and conditions for access to such information. In more and more circumstances, information itself is becoming a marketable commodity. There are now many thousands of databases in the world selling a variety of information to clients over modern telecommunication networks, and the number is growing rapidly. Proposed changes in copyright laws now under discussion in several countries would permit a further expansion by strengthening legal property rights to information.

Continuing growth in the information and communication sector is opening opportunities in a wide variety of information and communication markets, trading in both public and private information. Although these markets are adding value to international trade they are very imperfect markets. Their growth raises important questions, both of government regulation of monopoly power in national and international markets, and of government policy with respect to access by the public to traditional types of public information.

The public interest in the information society

Over thirty-five years ago the Canadian economist and communication scholar Harold A. Innis observed, 'enormous improvements in communication have made understanding more difficult' (Innis, 1951: 31). We would be hard put to demonstrate that the quantum leap in communication technologies, and the vast increase in communication and information transfer that now takes place using these technologies, have led to an increased understanding of human and social affairs. Communication opportunities have increased significantly for most organizations and many individuals. The volume and variety of communication over these new systems has increased dramatically. But these improvements in communication have also contributed to an increase in the complexity of economic and social relations, introduced new elements of uncertainty, had negative effects for some people, increased class disparities and in certain instances debased our information and communication currency.

Adjustments to a society in which new information and communication systems will play a more central role will require changes to existing laws, policies and regulations. These changes can either promote or retard adjustment patterns and can have very differential effects across sectors of society. It is not a simple matter of removing regulatory barriers and restrictions. It is a matter of assessing the implications of existing laws, policies and regulation, developing new policy options and assessing their short- and long-term implications. In the information society, policy direction will become more important. Therefore, it is essential that it be informed and that it encompass the broad public interest.

To begin the process of redefining the public interest in the information society, it is necessary to return to the essential functions of information and communication in modern participatory democracy, that is, to provide opportunities for citizens to be informed and to be heard. One might expect that in an information society, an increasing percentage of the population would be more informed and exercise more opportunities to initiate communication. An extrapolation of trends examined in this chapter indicates that, barring public policy intervention, the opposite may be true.

The diversity of sources, both within the different media and across the media, is being significantly reduced. The diversity in broadcast programming that now arises from a variety of different national industry structures, ranging from national public service to commercial, is gravitating towards a much more homogeneous international structure responding primarily to the interests of global mass-market advertising. For public service broadcasters, the increasing absolute costs of programming (which will be driven up further by high-definition television), the increasing opportunity costs of foregone commercial revenue, and the pressures for international co-production for global markets are already directing them ever closer to commercial programming standards. This is a privatization of purpose, if not ownership. Indeed, without public policy intervention, the television broadcast media could become little more than a global electronic billboard (Melody, 1988).

The decline in the quality of postal services throughout most of the world in recent years is expected to continue. In many countries important communication cannot be left to the post. The telecommunication system is being converted to Rolls-Royce Integrated Services Digital Network standards, but it may also require Rolls-Royce costs for the basic telephone service needed by everyone. For the most part, new global information and communication services will only be used by the better trained, educated, informed and economically comfortable segment of society. These people will not be affected by the reduced public services noted above. They will have better alternatives.

An overriding issue of social policy, it would seem, is to ensure the maintenance of existing public information and communication services to those dependent upon them during the transition to the electronic information society. An even more important requirement will be to enhance education and training programmes, so that an increasing portion of society obtains the skills and income necessary to benefit from the new opportunities. The public interest requires that the diffusion of the new opportunities be planned and implemented at a pace which minimizes the losses imposed on those who cannot benefit from them, and is accompanied by programmes to help the potential victims of change become beneficiaries of it.

Yet, on the basis of current trends, it would appear that neither national public service suppliers nor national regulatory authorities are likely to be very effective in implementing public interest objectives. Both are likely to lose sight of domestic public interest requirements in the wake of national concerns about international competitiveness and new export opportunities in expanding global markets.

Information/communication as a public utility

Historically, certain industries have been recognized both in custom and law as 'business affected with a public interest'. These are businesses that supply services under conditions where the public is dependent upon reasonable and non-exploitative treatment by a business monopoly. Inns, wharves, bridges, canals, grain warehouses, railways, electricity, gas, water, telephone and other services have all qualified in the past or do so at present. Each supplier was or is in a position of monopoly dominance in supplying an essential service to the general public. Because of this monopoly of an essential service, the businesses are 'affected with a public interest'. They are required by law to make their services equally available to the public under fair, reasonable and non-discriminatory prices and conditions.

Although the concept of business affected with a public interest was initially developed in English common law, its application over the last century is generally traced to a landmark decision of the US Supreme Court in the case of *Munn* v. *Illinois* (1877):

> When, therefore, one devotes his property to use in which the public has an interest, he in effect grants to the public an interest in that use, and must submit to be controlled by the public for the common good, to the extent of the interest he has thus created.[5]

The concept of business affected with a public interest has found its way into various codes of law in many countries. It provides the direct basis for public utility regulation and government public service provision (including telecommunication and post) in most countries. It is an indirect basis for regulating broadcasting.

Perhaps the most distinguishing characteristic of the information society is the increasing dependence of institutions and people on particular kinds of information and communication in order to function effectively in their economic, political, social and cultural activities. Although one could easily demonstrate that this always has been so – even in Greek city states and aboriginal communities – it is clear that the very different and more complex economic and social relations in the information society create a very different set of information and communication dependencies. In the information society this is governed increasingly by electronic communication networks which determine both access to information and the range of actual communication networks to which people and organizations have access. The types, structures, timing, selection and interpretation of information are unique, as are the needs to initiate communication in a timely and skilled manner in a variety of circumstances.

In the information society, access to information and communication would appear to be the most essentially public utility. It would be a logical extension of national law and policy to declare the international media and telecommunication conglomerates to be international public utilities subject to international regulation. But this would overlap with the jurisdiction of national authorities as well as some existing international agencies, for example, the ITU. It would require new international law to be effective. Given experience in other areas, including the interminable debates over devising international law for the oceans and for space, this does not appear to be a promising option for the foreseeable future.

It would seem that the global information and communication industries may have outgrown the national institutional mechanisms for ensuring that the public interest is seriously considered in their policies and practices. Could this mean that in the information society, the volume of information directed at passive recipients will increase substantially (especially entertainment and advertising), but that the population as a whole will be less informed and less capable of participating in the conduct of their own societies?

Public interest research

Perhaps the major deficiencies of public policy formulation generally are an inadequacy of substantive research and analysis on the public interest implications of policy options, and an absence of effective advocacy of concrete policy actions that would reflect the public interest. In the market-place of competing evidence, analysis and ideas, public interest advocacy has suffered. Regulatory authorities and national public service suppliers all too quickly become 'judges' and 'authorities'. Rather than seek out evidence on public interest implications, and give it great weight in the face of advocacy from powerful vested interests, they have tended to wait for public interest implications to be thrust before them under conditions where they cannot be avoided. This is illustrated well by a comment from a former chair of the Independent Broadcasting Authority, who explained that 'The public interest is what I say it is. And I was appointed because I know.'[6]

Whatever the institutional form by which public interest considerations are brought into the policy process, it will be ineffective unless there is a solid base in public interest research. It then must be followed up by advocacy of the practical implications for action. From where might this come?

In a democratic society, public policy should be responsive to the quality and quantity of evidence and argument advocated for particular positions put forward by various interests. In these debates, there are two primary perspectives that require representation, but which in most cases are absent. One is the perspective of those groups in society that may be significantly affected by the policies adopted, but which do not have a sufficiently organized financial vested interest to mount a representation, for example, disabled users of the public telephone service, children's interests in television or probable victims of technological change. This perspective is necessary to ensure that in the final balancing of interests that underlies most policy decisions, consideration of the interests of important segments of the public are not omitted.

The second perspective is that of society as a whole, focusing directly on the overall structure of benefits, costs and consequences for society. This perspective would examine those consequences that lie outside the normal realm of special interest decision-makers, and would include an evaluation of economic externality, and social and cultural consequences of policy options (Ferguson, 1986).

Public interest groups exist in many areas of society to advocate the special interests of neglected publics, for example, consumer associations, environmental groups, children's television advocates, etc. However, with severely restricted funding and inadequate research, effectiveness is limited. To the best of this author's knowledge, there is no public interest group advocating the information rights of the uninformed, or the right to have effective communication access to those denied it. Part of the problem, of course, is that it is very unclear what precisely should be advocated, given the underlying lack of research, evidence and policy analysis.

Perhaps more than any other policy area, information and

communication policies require an overall systemic analysis. They have enormous external consequences for the viability of political democracy as well as economic and social relations of all kinds. But what institution in society is likely to be in a position to undertake continuing research, policy analysis and effective advocacy of the public interest in information and communication?

Academia and the public interest

Academic researchers are in a unique position to provide a substantial contribution to policy deliberations from a systemic perspective in at least two important respects. First, the absence of a close connection with particular institutions that have a direct vested interest in the immediate results of policy considerations provides an essential detachment. This permits academic researchers to address the long-term societal implications of the issues more thoroughly, independently and continuously even than the policy making agencies. Second, by training and vocational practice, the perspective of academics should be more compatible with the exercise of research on long-run implications for society than that provided by any other institutional environment. For many aspects of policy issues, independent academic research can provide an assessment of issues which examines aspects of reality that elude special interest research and the normal analytical horizons of policy-makers.

Due in part to the absence of a significant body of such research, at the present time there is no conceptual or descriptive map by which one can assess the size, structure and implications of information and communication in the information society. Without this essential background information, neither policy decisions by government nor market decisions by corporations are as informed as they should be, or could be.

Academic research has much more to contribute to policy issues than might at first appear. Across the social sciences in particular, there is a substantial amount of fragmented research on a variety of information and communication issues. An assessment of its significance for policy requires that it be pulled together, integrated and examined from a systemic perspective. This knowledge then needs to be interpreted in the light of the major policy issues under debate. For the future, if more effective research co-ordination is established, the knowledge gained can be cumulative rather than fragmentary.

Moreover, if the scope of this interdisciplinary research enterprise is extended to include implications for policy, and supported by strong programmes of dissemination to policy maker and lay audiences (as well as the research community), the benefits will begin to penetrate the social system more effectively.[7] Within the framework of this new model of policy research, it should be possible to develop a much clearer understanding of the role of information and communication processes in the information society and their implications for policy.

The areas that require priority research attention are fundamental ones. The current state of knowledge on information availability and use by different sectors of society is extremely weak. Basic descriptive and statistical data are fragmented. Considered assessments of the public information needs of different sectors of society, and the terms and conditions of access necessary to meet these needs are required as benchmarks for public policy. Information indicators could be developed to measure, for example, relations between citizen needs, availability and uses of public information; the accessibility and use of public information by major segments of the population; and the rate of diffusion of essential public information throughout the population. Indeed we know from existing research that only a small proportion of minority cultures, and the poor of all cultures know their rights as citizens in democratic countries. If all the sick and elderly knew enough to claim all the benefits to which they are entitled, public health systems would be swamped and bankrupted in a few months.

In certain respects, the function of post-industrial economies in their present form depends upon major sections of society not having sufficient information, skill and knowledge to exercise their rights fully. As society becomes more information- and communication-intensive, these class distinctions based upon information disparities are likely to increase. But research on information processes, disseminated widely and advocated in policy arenas, could do much to promote both information and social equity in society. A corollary of this line of research is the documentation of public information deficiencies and their economic and social implications.

Parallel types of research are needed in respect of communication processes, especially those communication processes necessary to obtain access to essential information. This goes much beyond such questions as the availability of a universal telephone service, which is a precondition to electronic communication. It addresses questions of actual use, knowledge about how to acquire relevant information via the telecommunication system, and the extent to which useful information is actually obtained. If 20 per cent of the population is barely literate, does this indicate anything about their ability to find their way through a government bureaucracy using the telephone? The research needed here is neither on physical network connections, nor on idealistic rights to communicate. Rather, it is on the benefits obtained from actual communication, the barriers to access and the policies that encourage or prevent effective communication and the realities of information transfer.

Research is also needed on guidelines for making sense out of an environment of information overload. Effective understanding, followed by rational action requires an ability to filter, synthesize and interpret information. For many in society, including all business and political leaders, effective comprehension requires that information be screened, assessed and summarized before it is even examined. In a society of information overload, this new role of information interpreter is becoming ever more essential to rational decision making. Research is needed, to understand the processes at work; to define the most appropriate ways for interpreting public information for the public; and to devise operational programmes for implementing public information interpretation services.

It may well be that in future the new role of interpreting important information to the public could best be filled by public libraries. Given the trend of the public press, its interpretive role for the future is more likely to decline than expand for the public at large. Libraries could become advice centres on public information, including not only the location of relevant information and how to access it, but also what the information means and what action might be considered by citizens exercising their rights. (This, of course, would be vigorously opposed by the legal profession.) An extension of this role could be an information ombudsman. The primary functions would be to break down barriers to public information, and to advocate the public's information needs in relevant policy debates.

Several countries have established an information commissioner to deal with specific complaints by citizens that government agencies are withholding information from them that should be accessible. This is primarily the role of an *ad hoc* ombudsman and is concerned with the release of information by national government agencies to specific individuals and organizations. An unfortunate effect of U.S. 'sunshine' laws, which require open access to discussions by government policy makers, has been to make bureaucrats more, not less, protective of their information.

What is being suggested here is a much more proactive ombudsman role that examines in a systematic manner the information needs of the general public and the best ways of ensuring that they will be met. It is a step toward stimulating national governments to develop a national public information policy that would apply not just to government agencies, but also to major corporations and other influential institutions in society. The standard for judgement would be, what does the public need to know in order to function most effectively as a responsible citizenry in a participatory democracy?

A research strategy on information and communication policy is likely to find that such questions arise as important components of policy issues in many areas. Policy makers in seemingly unrelated areas may be unaware of the information and communication implications of the policy options they are considering. For certain kinds of policies, for example, the introduction of major new communication technologies such as ISDN or high-definition television, an information/communication impact statement might be a required consideration in the policy formulation. For other policies, for example, the environment, public health and so on, information reporting and communication requirements are likely to be an important aspect of effective policy implementation.

A key factor influencing the actual information/communication implications of policy decisions of all kinds will be the information/communication diffusion processes throughout society. This is a subject about which academic research already has something to say. But much more is known from the far more extensive research on the diffusion of material technologies, than about the diffusion of information, or of communication opportunities.

It is comforting to believe that there is a single policy authority and a carefully specified policy issue to which one's research and analysis can be directed. It is the policy authority's responsibility to seek out and consider the public interest in its policy processes. But when an authority is designated, for example, the FCC, IBA or Oftel, it represents only one of several loci where important policy decisions in the field are made. In the United States, for example, the Congress, executive branch, courts, state governments, one or more industries, foreign firms and governments, international agencies and potentially other institutions may exercise influence in the dynamic mosaic of policy development and implementation. Moreover, the formal policy-making authorities tend to have quite narrow remits defined by industry or technological boundaries, in comparison to the much broader agenda of information and communication processes in society. In addition, as indicated above, the authorities seldom go looking for public interest considerations. To a significant degree, only the research itself will expose the breadth of key policy decisions that affect public information and communication opportunities and uses.

Just as the model of the paternalistic national public service operator is becoming less relevant in the information society, so also is the model of beneficent national public interest regulation. Both were imperfect mechanisms acquiring increasing imperfections as time passed and society changed. Policy formulation in the information/communication sector is becoming more diffused. The structure of the policy-making process is not easily identified, assessed or influenced. Indeed, the policy process, access to it and diffusion of policy information is itself an important area for research. It could assist greatly in keeping the doors of the policy arena open, and the public more aware of its rights in the policy formulation process.

The policy research being suggested here would find its way into policy at local, state, national, regional and global levels in a variety of ways. Researchers would not be alone in seeking to place the knowledge gained from their research before policy-makers. Such knowledge will almost always find institutional support somewhere, ranging from public interest groups and government agency staff to specific firms and industries. Virtually all important policy issues are contested by several very different interests reflecting a variety of perspectives. In most instances, at least one of these is likely to find a common interest on any particular issue with the policy implications of knowledge gained from independent academic research. For academic researchers, there is a challenge to interpret the policy implications of their research in light of the policy issues being examined, and to disseminate their research results in a form that will be most easily understood by those involved in the policy debates.

It should not, of course, be expected that academic research is going to yield magic answers to the formidable issues of public policy in the information society. In fact, there are likely to be few issues in which all the research will clearly point to a specific policy solution. The contribution of the research is to inform the policy-making debates, to raise the knowledge level of the discussion, to ensure that information and analysis relating to the long-term, systemic and public interest implications are included in the debates, and to attempt to guide the policy debates in the direction of the most relevant issues. A major contribution of this research is likely to be the elimination of policy options that could have negative consequences for the general public, but substantial beneficial consequences for a large vested interest. Rarely will it point unequivocally to a precise optimum policy. Moreover, the greatest influence of the policy research is more likely to come from its integration into the on-going activities of the many organizations involved in the policy process, than from occasional injections of purportedly definitive policy research studies.

Some researchers may be concerned that on-going interaction

with organizations involved in the policy process runs the risk of biasing the research. Indeed, it does. But probably less so than the risk of bias that arises from a much lower level of information and knowledge about the real issues and problems, a very superficial understanding of the policy-making processes and a naïve belief that detachment, innocence (and sometimes ignorance) avoid biases. More direct involvement is likely to force the exposure of judgements and hidden valuations so that their consequences can be assessed. The independence of policy research, and indeed all social science research, must ultimately be preserved by awareness and sensitivity of the problem of bias, which always exists in one form or another.

Researchers must have sufficient confidence that they can maintain their intellectual independence when they bring their contributions into the market-place of ideas on public policy. The knowledgeable, independent views that have merit for application in public policy must be those that have stood the test of critical review of the evidence and analysis by those who disagree. Is this test any different from the test that academic research has always used in seeking the truth (that is, a critical review by knowledgeable peers), except perhaps that the public policy arena may provide a more rigorous application of it? Certainly a claim of independence arising from limited knowledge about the issues and non-involvement in the process cannot expect to carry much weight in a participatory democracy.

The academic social science research community is a major institution in modern society. One of its fundamental purposes is to develop information and knowledge about the changing structure of society. This academic research community is uniquely placed to extend its activities to policy research from a public interest perspective, particularly on the implications of changing information and communication structures in society. It is uniquely placed to be the best advocate of the policy implications of its public interest research. No other institution in society is so well structured to research and advocate for the public interest. Should the research community take this responsibility seriously, the contributions of research can more directly influence the course of events in the world. The public interest can become a major, rather than a fringe, force in policy-making, and the academic research community can fulfil its own potential in participatory democracies.

Notes

1 For a comparative perspective see Noll et al. (1973); Owen et al. (1974); Cave and Melody (1989).

2 The classic statement attributed to Lord Reith was 'few members of the broadcast audience know what they want, and fewer still want what they need', reflecting the ethos of the BBC under his leadership.

3 For comparative perspectives on these issues, see Mattelart et al. (1984); Wedell (1983) and Commission of the European Communities (1984).

4 For an examination of social science research and training developments in this area in the UK, see Melody and Mansell (1986b).

5 See *Munn* v. *Illinois* 94 US 113, 126. For discussion of related issues, see Melody (1971).

6 Personal interview with the author.

7 Indeed, this new model for social science research in the field is being adopted by major new academically based research programmes in several countries. Examples are the Programme on Information and Communication Technologies (PICT) in the UK, and the Centre for International Research on Communication and Information Technologies (CIRCIT) in Australia; see Melody (1987b).

3
Regulating Communications Media: From the Discretion of Sound Chaps to the Arguments of Lawyers

James Michael

Regulating the communication of information is as old as blood feuds over insults, and regulating the media of communications is as classic an issue as deciding whose turn it is to use the talking drum or the ram's horn (with the establishment of a system of access by rotation an important regulatory decision in itself). In very abstract terms, the regulation of communicating information is a series of answers by society to the questions of who should know what, and when, and how and where. 'Should' must be broken down into communications that the law forbids, requires or allows. Regulating the media of communication is mostly deciding who has access to a medium and what information may (or must, or must not) be communicated on it. A further distinction is between the 'prior restraint' of communication by censorship and the subsequent punishment of those who have communicated forbidden information. Although the distinction originated in eighteenth-century England, it is almost completely ignored in English law today. In the United States, however, the near-absence of prior restraint is considered to be the essence of freedom of expression.

There is very little in human behaviour that is completely free from 'regulation' of one form or another. If there were no acts of government forbidding or requiring certain acts by broadcasters at all, there would still be powerful influences determining what is or is not broadcast, for example. Law is only one influence, and not necessarily the most important one. Quite apart from rules about what may, must or must not be communicated (by voice, in print or by electronic means) there are important rules about who has access to or control over various media of communications. These may be silent as to the content of what is communicated, but they are almost always adopted on the assumption that control of a medium determines (or at least influences heavily) the content communicated. Rules about the nationality of broadcasting licensees or newspaper owners and rules about monopoly ownership are all based on the assumption that ownership determines content. Such rules are nearly as overt about what is communicated as straightforward prohibitions (or requirements) about content. Other forms of 'regulation' may be equally (or more) effective while remaining covert. Before the BBC's licence fee was linked to the cost of living, criticism of broadcasting from a government with the power to refuse an increase in a licence fee could have been considered as a form of 'regulation'. (But it is always difficult to prove a negative, and particularly difficult to prove why a programme was not made.) Such indirect and covert regulation is only partly dealt with by law in some US Supreme Court decisions striking down laws which have a 'chilling effect' on freedom of expression; and this chapter is concerned with regulation by law.

It is written because changes in the legal regulation of communications media are certain to come in the near future. When the much-postponed White Paper on Broadcasting in the United Kingdom was finally published in November 1988, it at least made clear that regulation of British broadcasting in future will be divided between bodies to hand out commercial franchises (the Independent Television Commission and the Radio Authority) and a Broadcasting Standards Council to regulate sex and violence content. The chapter concentrates on broadcasting, but considers broadcasting as only one of the many increasingly interrelated media of communication. International comparisons will refer more to the United States than to other countries.

Apart from considering general arguments about what 'regulation' is and why it is done, the specific case addressed here concerns the future 'regulation' of communications media in the United Kingdom. A preliminary answer is that an important part of deciding what that regulation is to be should be a close examination of how it is done in other countries (although Sir James Fawcett, QC, once said that the usual British response to a description of how things are done in other countries is to say, 'How funny'). Quite apart from any voluntary incorporation of foreign practice is the influence of regulation from the European Community and the Council of Europe.

Why study regulation?

Why are we (or perhaps should we be) interested in the regulation of communications media? Legal 'regulation' is new to the United Kingdom, but only in its form. Such regulation is not new in the sense that it controls behaviour that previously was uncontrolled; it is the institutions and substantive rules controlling communication that are changing. The previous 'regulation' of communications media was mostly by monopoly state ownership, supplemented by the granting of near-monopoly franchises. With the exception of print, mass communications media in Europe have mostly been treated as natural monopolies with a large measure of direction from central government. What is often called 'de-regulation', both here and in other countries, is usually the distribution of what was a monopoly over a medium of communication to several competitors. This does not necessarily mean that the content of what is communicated will become less regulated. If anything, the British tendency is for increased economic competition to be accompanied by increased regulation of the content being communicated.

The classic process of regulation in the United States (and many other countries) involves an industry that is not regulated at all, a growing consensus that the industry is doing something wrong or not doing something right, public suggestions from those with the ability to accomplish legislation that legal regulation is desirable or necessary, with replies from the industry that self-regulation is preferable to legislation for a variety of reasons. The end of the cycle (which can be repeated for the same industry from time to time) may be formal regulation by legislation (by a combination of several devices) or self-regulation, or a combination of the two. The process in the United States began with the creation of the Interstate Commerce Commission at the end of the nineteenth century to regulate an industry that had become dominated by a private monopoly. Broadcasting and telecommunications in the United Kingdom are approaching regulation by agency from administration of monopolies; print is approaching (or being threatened with) regulation by statute (for example, a right to privacy) and possibly by agency (as under the right to reply Bill). Whether 'regulation' is defined in the narrow sense which requires a specialist regulatory body or in the broader sense of new rules, most of the media of communicating information are likely to be subject to changes in regulation in the near future. This is partly because of the classic circumstances outlined above, partly because of a political decision to transfer publicly owned media to private ownership and partly because of changes in technology.

Although British broadcasting is already very restricted, if not regulated, the near-classic pattern of threat, self-regulation, then formal regulation, seems to be particularly applicable to broadcasting. When senior (and recently appointed) television executives make speeches criticizing television and suggesting more self-regulation, and when this follows public criticism of broadcasting by ministers, some form of greater regulation is almost certain to follow. The question for those in broadcasting and concerned with it is what the changes will be rather than whether there will be any. 'Regulation' required by the transfer from public to private ownership applies particularly to telecommunications. 'Ownership' itself, whether public or private, is a form of regulation in the sense that the general law says what an owner may or may not (and often must or must not) do with what is 'owned'. It is a common misconception to assume that 'ownership' provides complete freedom to use or dispose of what is owned. It is more useful to think of ownership as providing a 'bundle of rights' in the sense of things that the owner is entitled to do with the property (Veljanovski, 1987).

The traditional method of regulating the media of communication in the United Kingdom has been by government ownership or by licensed monopolies. The postal service is a prime example of the first (and we have recently been told that it will not be transferred to private ownership because it is 'the Royal Mail'). Soon after its invention the telephone was assimilated into the system of regulation by government monopoly used for the post. The regulation of broadcasting did not follow the pattern exactly. Although broadcasting was assumed to be a natural monopoly, its regulation was not by the same model of government 'ownership'. The reason was partly because of the nature of regulating communications media and partly political. The regulation of communications media may be characterized as 'common carrier' or 'content' regulation. 'Common carrier' regulation concentrates on who is allowed, forbidden or required to communicate information, with little regulation of the information actually communicated, which is 'content' regulation. The regulation of telephone service is largely as a common carrier, while that of newspapers is largely of their content. But the distinction is rarely absolute: it is an offence to communicate obscene or threatening telephone calls, and publishing a newspaper which does not comply with various statutory requirements (such as including information about the printer) is also an offence.

The regulation of postal and telephone service by government monopoly was essentially common carrier regulation, if only because general regulation of content was technically impossible. (Until the Interception of Communications Act, 1985, was forced on the British government by the European Court of Human Rights, the standard government justification for telephone and postal interception without judicial warrant was that the Royal Prerogative authorized interception of the Royal Mail.) A medium of communication to the general public, like broadcasting, obviously makes content regulation more of an issue because the content is available to the public for inspection and objection. Content regulation of broadcasting by government monopoly is always tempting, but has drawbacks both in terms of political ideology (if freedom of expression is an ideal) and effectiveness (credibility may be lost). The initial British solution was to create the 'independent' British Broadcasting Corporation (out of the Company), with emergency powers retained by government (followed by a half-century of tolerant explanation to foreigners who assume that it must be government-controlled if it is not privately owned).

The political decision to transfer government-owned monopolies to private ownership almost certainly will lead to some form of 'regulation', and in the case of privately owned communications media that will probably be regulation by specialized agency. But the political decision to 'privatize' (or to 'liberalize' in the form of greater competition) has certainly not been taken with a view to increasing the variety of content communicated. The effect of decisions taken and being taken is likely to increase the number of competitors among broadcasters, but to restrict the content of what is broadcast even more. Competition is to be for audiences and advertising revenue; the content of programming used for that competition will be within the same or even more restricted limits.

The technical reasons for regulation are closely connected with the increasingly international character of communications media. The essence of cable television is actually quite old (and followed on from the 'cable' radio that preceded the wireless); it is the combination of fibre optic, satellite, and computer technology that makes information from 'unregulated' (or differently regulated) foreign communications media increasingly available here. If this were not combined with a political decision for greater European integration the resulting regulation probably would be an attempt at prohibition similar to that imposed on offshore radio broadcasters. Instead, the regulation is likely to be an attempt (or perhaps two) at formulating and enforcing common European standards.

Why regulate at all?

And why regulate communications media in particular? Regulation is a form of influence on the exercise of freedom. It is only one form of influence and freedom is (without references to Sartre or the Grand Inquisitor) a matter of degrees rather than absolutes. An absence of regulation may well result in a lesser degree of freedom by deferring to other economic and social influences.

The regulation of communications media often follows the pattern of regulating other industries. But there are differences because of the particular cultural and economic characteristics of information, the 'product' of the industry. The first, and standard, reason for regulating communications media is technical, and applies particularly to broadcasting. It is true that the broadcasting frequency spectrum is limited, and that unrestricted broadcasting might result in chaos in which no signals could be received. But very few countries have ever restricted the regulation of broadcasting to the minimum required to avoid signal interference (the United States and Italy at various times have probably come closest). Instead, most countries treat not only the frequency spectrum as a limited public resource, but also the audience available. One of the classic questions of regulation of communications is how far those resources can, or should, be divided.

It is fairly commonplace to observe that many of the calculations about broadcasting regulation can be applied to print. The newspaper-reading market for London can 'support' only one evening paper in the same sense that the television audience can 'support' only one regional commercial television channel. But if that is the case, why not have a rational system of licensing newspapers instead of leaving it to the market?

The answer in Britain is as much a matter of history as logic. The licensing of the press was abolished at the end of the seventeenth century, and it was the absence of such administrative 'previous restraint' that Blackstone thought was the essence of freedom of the press. Although the nineteenth-century tax on newspapers was not direct censorship of content, it was an informal system of limiting both publishers and readers to those who could afford to pay.

Some other countries have gone some way towards treating print similarly to broadcasting, although few Western countries license newspapers in the same way as broadcasters. Sweden uses a system of taxation on advertising revenue which is redistributed to minority circulation publications. France effectively requires periodical distributors to act as common carriers for all publications. The Netherlands relates the allocation of broadcasting time to print circulation: the membership of organizations for purposes of such broadcast allocation is determined by the circulation of their programme bulletins (which is an additional reason for publication of such programme information to be in breach of copyright).

Why not leave it to the market? If it is so difficult for the legislators and regulators to agree about quality and how much it should cost, why not limit regulation to allocating frequencies and signal strength, with perhaps a bare minimum of content regulation such as forbidding the knowing broadcast of false fire alarms? Recently the United States has come very close to doing just that, with the weakening of the 'fairness doctrine' (required for programming overall) as the most recent development. (At last report, civil libertarians were divided over the fairness doctrine.)

One answer is to argue that if diversity of information communicated is desirable as an end, the market is not necessarily the best way of achieving it. Even in measurable common carrier terms of providing universal broadcast service, market competition will not necessarily be an incentive to reach remote areas. It is commonplace that broadcasting competition for audiences in the United States, and the delivery of those audiences to advertisers, affects the content of programmes. The effects are many, but they include limitations on subject matter in programmes and occasional cancellations. The cliché is that there are more television channels available in the United States than the United Kingdom, but less variety.

It is probably true that the communications media in the United States are freer from legal restraint than in any other country in the world. But that does not necessarily mean that the widest range of ideas and information is communicated to the widest possible audience. The influence of advertisers, the race for the largest possible audiences, even responsiveness to organized public opinion can all restrict what is broadcast.

It has been suggested that freedom of expression is tolerated in the United States because ideas are considered by an essentially anti-intellectual population to be unimportant. The activity which is regulated by a society is that which the society deems to be important, and toleration of marginal activity is easy. (It is tempting to use regulation as an index of national character. British near-pornographic telephone messages were tamed by self-regulation after threats from the newly formed Office of Telecommunications [Oftel]. The French equivalent on Minitel are charged at a higher rate.)

Another argument is that regulation of communications media (and perhaps other forms of regulation) may be counter-intuitive: a measure which appears to liberate communication may have the opposite effect over time, while a restriction may ultimately increase the flow of information. The best illustration of this is copyright law, which clearly restricts communication of information in a certain form to those who have permission from the copyright holder. But the (assumed) purpose is to provide sufficient financial incentives for writers and others to produce works which ultimately can be circulated freely. (Perhaps there should be a research project comparing the production of new books in copyright-free and copyright-tight countries.)

Economic regulation

Much 'regulation' by specialized agencies is aimed at the prices of goods and services to the public; this is often accompanied by regulation of the quality of such goods and services, but the two are not always given equal emphasis. There is a substantial literature about the relationship between price and quality regulation, usually in terms of a trade-off between acceptable levels of risk (often accompanied by insurance provisions) and affordable prices.

The regulation of communications media is also largely economic, but the relationship with quality regulation is even more difficult. So long as regulation is of common carriers, the quality of service provided is at least measurable. 'Universal service' is often a goal of common carrier regulation (and can apply to the regulation of systems for the transport of goods as well as communication of information; it is perhaps useful to remember that military 'lines of communication' include transport), sometimes as a matter of social policy, sometimes because such universality is considered necessary for an efficient system. The number of households on the telephone or able to receive broadcast transmissions (or cabled or with satellite receivers) can be counted. Similarly, the technical quality of service provided can be measured, as in the percentage of public telephones out of order, crossed lines, or transmission interruptions. Most trade-offs between the charges and the technical quality can be calculated.

It is in the regulation of content quality of the communications media that the issues become less calculable. It is possible to make some calculations that may have some indirect effect on the quality of what is communicated, however. In completely commercial broadcasting, if the number of licences were limited only to avoid technical interference, the immediate result would be very many broadcasting stations chasing a limited amount of advertising revenue. Unless they were subsidized from other sources or achieved a dominant position in the market, the broadcasters would be limited to inexpensive programmes.

One of the reasons for resistance to proliferation of broadcasting in Britain is that quality costs money. (This is not disputed here, although it does assume that there is consensus about 'quality'; assuming that, it should also be admitted that some such programmes can be produced cheaply and that there is expensively produced rubbish.) An important question in deciding whether there is to be a fifth television channel is whether there is enough potential advertising revenue to support it.

It is perhaps worth emphasizing that the content regulation of communications media is usually much more visible than economic regulation. Many more people are probably aware of the dispute between British Telecom and Oftel about the Talkabout service than about interconnections with Mercury. And the dispute over 'the secret society' is probably even better known than the pegging of the licence fee (which affects individuals directly), and certainly better known than calculations about a fifth channel.

But within the limits of content regulation most broadcasters are essentially concerned with finance, or matters directly related to finance. For the commercial broadcaster content is simply a means for the delivery of audiences for advertisers. Public service broadcasters are keenly aware that they must keep a reasonable percentage of viewers to justify the licence fee, and of the increasing need to generate income by foreign sales and co-productions and to cut costs by buying in programmes.

The bridge between the less visible economic regulation and content regulation is advertising, which is closely related to political and religious broadcasting in the sense that all three are often intended (although not religious programmes in the United Kingdom) to persuade. Until recently the regulation of broadcast advertising in this country has been fairly simple: commercial advertisements are limited in time and content by the IBA; political advertising is not allowed and party political broadcasts are rationed; religious advertising and proselytizing programmes are not allowed.

Three circumstances are likely to make the regulation of commercial broadcast advertising more difficult (and may also affect political and religious broadcasting). The first is the pressure for money. Public service broadcasters doing international co-productions may, wittingly or unwittingly, find themselves involved in advertising by product placement. US children's programmes written around toys (such as 'Thundercats') may be bought in. The second circumstance is the penetration by satellite and cable of programmes from countries with different regulatory schemes (regulation by Council of Europe treaty or European Community directive is actively being planned). The third circumstance will be the readiness of broadcasters to argue, especially at the European Court of Justice and the European Court of Human Rights, that 'commercial speech' (that is, advertising) should be as free as other speech.

Law and regulation

'Regulation' in the broad sense extends beyond specialist agencies to legal rules generally, including those concerning what usually is called 'private' law (such as contract) as distinct from 'public' law (such as broadcasting legislation). In one sense, all law is regulation, but the word 'regulation' is usually used in a more limited sense to mean the enforcement of rules by some government body which often makes rules as well as enforcing them.

An instrumentalist (or utilitarian) view of law considers it as one of several methods (including the market) of achieving a desired end. A more ideological approach is the libertarian one, which asserts that any law restricting human freedom is to be viewed sceptically, and to be allowed only if it clearly produces more desirable behaviour than the absence of such a law. The libertarian approach is particularly relevant to the regulation of communication technology because the 'right to receive and impart information' is considered to be a fundamental human right in instruments such as the European Convention on Human Rights. The effect of this is that the legal restrictions on the distribution of video cassettes, for example, are likely to require greater justification than restrictions on the distribution of more mundane consumer goods.

It is probably true that restrictions on the communication of information are often more difficult to justify by a utilitarian calculus than restrictions on the distribution of other goods and services. A requirement that electric fires should not be sold unless they meet certain standards can be justified (or not) in fairly concrete terms of probable costs of testing and enforcement, which can be measured against the probable cost of personal injury and property damage in the absence of such 'regulation'. The cost of a requirement that video cassettes should not be sold or hired unless they meet certain contents standards can be calculated, but the social consequences of not restricting such circulation are, at the very least, not so easy to calculate.

One important consequence of the distinction between criminal and civilian is in the enforcement of rules. Assume that there is a clear rule with clear consequences for breaking it, as in 'Thou shalt not reproduce copyright material without permission'. (As it happens, the law of copyright in the United Kingdom was largely a matter of civil law until the 1970s, when criminal penalties were drastically increased, both in severity and in the intensity of their application.) Assume also that the law says clearly what people who reproduce copyright material without permission should be forced to do. There still remains the question of who can (or sometimes must) begin the process of establishing that the rule has been broken and requiring some penalty or compensation. In simpler cases of purely civil wrongs, enforcement is left up to those whose private interests are being harmed. In the case of offences which are purely criminal, enforcement in most countries (but not in England and Wales) is left to public officials.

The criminal/civil dichotomy can roughly be defined as protecting interests which are public and private. In the regulation of communication the line is not always an easy one to draw, and the distinctions are not always easy to understand. To take one distinction which is not technology-bound, there is a crime of libel, the object of which is essentially to stop disturbances of the peace caused by libels (despite the 1936 case of *Wicks*), and there is a civil wrong of libel, the object of which is the protection of individual reputations. It is usually easier to demonstrate that a private interest in tangible property is interfered with than it is to demonstrate that a private interest in information is being abridged. And to complicate matters further, the human rights aspect of communication means that a right to receive and impart information (or perhaps to restrict it in the interests of the public) is likely to be asserted as a right of citizenship, rather than a right of ownership.

The distinction between public and private interests in information is not limited to the difference between criminal and civil law. In the *Spycatcher* case the British Government asked courts in several countries to forbid publication of a book co-written by a former member of a security service. The civil injunction was sought by arguing that it was necessary in the public interest and that it was also necessary to enforce the obligation of confidentiality that any employee owes to an employer. The attempt to ban the book was finally rejected by the House of Lords in October 1988, almost entirely because the book was published internationally and available to anyone in the United Kingdom who ordered it from abroad. The most far-reaching effect of the case was a ruling that a preliminary ban on publication of one newspaper (or broadcaster) is a ban on anyone who knows, or should know, of it. The rule was applied at the beginning of April 1989 when the *Observer* printed a leaked report from the Department of Trade and Industry: a court order quickly obtained against that paper stopped repetition of the information by anyone else.

In the autumn of 1987 the British Government obtained a preliminary injunction against a BBC radio series on the grounds that former members of the security services had taken part and were identified as such. One effect of this was to forbid the identification of Kim Philby as a former member of a security service. (This is not an exaggeration, but the rules applied by BBC lawyers to a television broadcast in which the writer participated.) The injunction was later modified, then dropped entirely, and the series was broadcast in its entirety. The case is particularly relevant to the doctrine (or the near-absence of it in English law now) that freedom of expression means the absence of prior restraint. The preliminary injunction was granted (in even wider terms than requested) because the Government had an arguable case that former members of the security services had breached their absolute obligation of secrecy. It later became obvious that the Government went to court because the BBC refused to provide transcripts on request before the broadcast. The legal proceeding enabled the Government to obtain the transcript by court order. The case may thus provide a model for future efforts at government previewing (or hearing) of broadcasts; it has also diminished the role of the non-legal D-Notice Committee, which had been consulted by the BBC and had not objected to the broadcast.

Although the US courts have taken the proposition that freedom of expression means no (or very little) prior restraint more seriously than in the United Kingdom, freedom of expression is not absolute in the United States. In some respects freedom of expression in the United States is as restricted as in the United Kingdom, and perhaps even more so. Although the United States has no equivalent to the catch-all section 2 of the Official Secrets Act, it does have an Espionage Act that is a rough equivalent to section 1 of the Official Secrets Act. No Briton has ever been convicted under section 1 for communicating information through the press to the public (although three people were once charged). In the United States Samuel Morison was convicted of espionage for providing a satellite picture of a Soviet shipyard to a journal (in London) for publication, and his final appeal to the US Supreme Court has not yet been decided. Even the Official Secrets Act does not go as far as the US Intelligence Identities Protection Act of 1982, which makes it a crime to identify members of the security services.

Although *ad hoc* civil actions and criminal prosecutions are a form of regulation, the term is more often used to describe a more established administrative procedure. The Broadcasting White Paper makes it almost certain that control over British broadcasting will be through the authority of an Independent Television Commission, a Radio Authority, and a Broadcasting Standards Council that will have much more power than the one already established.

Regulation by agency and separation of powers

Much of the literature on regulatory law is from the United States, and much of that is devoted to explaining how the regulatory agencies grew (mostly, but not entirely, during the New Deal of the 1930s). The explanation is thought to be necessary because of a model of government functions, separation of powers, which is considered to be inherent in government. But the assumption that the functions of making, enforcing and interpreting laws are clearly separate and to be carried out by different people is fairly specific to Western countries in the nineteenth and twentieth centuries. It is an old, and probably oversimplified, story that the separation of powers in the US Constitution was based on the writings of Montesquieu, who in turn had misunderstood the provisions of the English Bill of Rights and Act of Settlement (particularly the disqualification from Parliament of those holding an 'office of profit' under the Crown).

The functional justification of the doctrine is that of checks and balances, based on an assumption that concentrated power is likely to be abused. Historically, this theory is fairly recent, particularly in Britain. The independence of the judiciary from the Crown in deciding disputes was not established until the seventeenth-century case of *Prohibitions del Roy*, and the requirement that Parliament participate (let alone be supreme) in law-making until the *Case of Proclamations*. The early mixture of judicial and administrative functions is still seen when magistrates become licensing justices during 'brewster sessions'.

So in Britain, there are rather fewer eyebrows raised when a single agency is given power to interpret, enforce and even, to some extent, make law than in the United States. There, the establishment of bodies like the Federal Communications Commission was seen as a curious, if necessary, breach of the rule that the three functions of government should not be mingled. To complicate matters further, most of these agencies had a function that did not fit easily into any of the traditional categories: licensing.

'Licensing' is a rather general term to describe the granting and enforcement of a limited monopoly. In one sense it is administrative, approving and renewing permits and investigating to see if their conditions are being complied with (roughly what the Home Office did with much radio and cable broadcasting until very recently). In another sense it is adjudicative, particularly in deciding between rival claimants for licences, and perhaps considering arguments by those who oppose a particular licensee without a commercial interest of their own. And in creating a body of subsidiary legislation to go with the licences it is legislative.

The British approach to all of this is still essentially administrative. Separation of powers has never been taken to extremes in this country, and there has always been an aversion to the 'judicialization' of administration. It is far from being facetious to suggest something approaching constitutional status for Pope's couplet: 'For forms of government let fools contest; whatever's best administered is best.'

The British preference for discretionary administration over legalistic procedures can be seen as a reflection of a culturally cohesive set of administrators (or ruling class, if that is preferred). Elaborate rules need not be written down for those who already know what is done and what is not. Such a style of regulation is not, however, divorced from the substance of the rules which are followed, or the effect on the structure of the activity regulated. Bluntly, the style lends itself to regulation by the granting of monopolies, subject to fairly vague conditions, with the sanction of withdrawing the monopoly being imposed almost entirely at the discretion of the regulators.

Much of the history of regulatory law in this country has been in the occasional assertions by the ordinary courts that they have some authority to supervise the actions of administrators, often followed by legislative efforts to 'judge-proof' new systems of administration in order to make it clear that the decision of the authority or minister is absolutely final (frequently followed in turn by a judicial declaration that a decision is not really final if it is a decision that no reasonable authority or minister could have taken). In legal taxonomy 'regulatory law' (which is only just achieving recognition) is largely a division of 'administrative law' (which has achieved recognition only in the past twenty-five years).

Despite the common law doctrine that any contract which interfered with competition by restraining trade was against the public interest, it has long been assumed that many of the means of communicating information are natural monopolies, or at least that the public interest is best served by treating them as monopolies. This seems to be particularly true of, although not limited to, the post and telegraph systems in the sense of being common carriers. It has not been true of those means of mass communication such as newspapers which have not been treated as common carriers. The distinction essentially is that the common carrier is placed under an obligation to accept all traffic, but is not responsible for its contents (with exceptions for dangerous or indecent contents, in the case of the post and telecommunications).

One consequence of the privatization of telecommunications and consequent regulation by the Office of Telecommunications has been a step towards making common carriers responsible for the content of information communicated. A preliminary summary of this paper said: 'In concrete terms one example [of the blurring of distinctions between telecommunications and broadcasting] is whether Oftel should forbid (and whether it can) certain types of multi-party conversations using British Telecom facilities; another is whether the BBC and IBA should regulate the content of interactive teletext.' Since then the 'Talkabout' service has been withdrawn by

BT after Oftel proposed more stringent regulation and similar 'chatline' services offered by commercial operators have also been banned by British Telecom.

There are, of course, practical and technical reasons for treating some of these media of communication as monopolies. A postal (or telephone, or broadcasting, or perhaps even railway) system that is devoted to national service must have a degree of what will appear to be cross-subsidization. A telephone system linking Manchester and London, for example, could not be called a national communication system. (This is, of course, directly relevant to differential tariffs and compulsory interconnections.) Technically, there are of course good reasons for allocating a limited number of radio frequencies. But there never were real technical reasons for limiting national radio channels to four. One problem of regulating communication technology today is that the technical reasons for the monopoly (or duopoly) model are disappearing. The reasons for choosing new systems of regulation (including de-regulation) are increasingly those of economy, of cultural values and of politics.

The changing regulation of 'broadcasting'

The discussion of 'regulation' so far has been focused on regulation of the communication of information, but has not been limited in examples to those traditionally classified as 'broadcasting'. The main reason for this is the cliché that the boundaries between media of communication – in particular, those between broadcasting and telecommunication – are rapidly disappearing. One current illustration of this which has particular implications for British broadcasting is the plan by London Weekend Television (LWT) to counter any opposition to its proposed staff cuts by producing regular programmes from the Netherlands. Even assuming that the Dutch broadcasting authority (NOS) wanted to 'regulate' such 'broadcasting', they would have no jurisdiction. Although an NOS licence would be required for an LWT outside broadcast unit, satellite links are hired out by local PTT offices (*The Guardian*, 11 April 1988: 21). This example, although only a contingency plan, illustrates two of the major trends with which the future 'regulation' of 'broadcasting' must cope: the convergence of electromagnetic broadcasting and other media of communication, and its international character.

Until very recently the regulation of broadcasting internationally has been limited to the allocation of frequency spectra for broadcasting by the International Telecommunications Union. Apart from that the regulation of broadcasting has been almost entirely a matter of national law. Radio broadcasts which crossed borders sometimes have been felt to require regulation, but this has usually been done by criminal legislation which can make it an offence to receive such broadcasts or, as in the United Kingdom, to assist foreign broadcasters. The purpose of such regulation has been to maintain broadcasting as a protected national market for both producers and broadcasters for economic and political reasons.

The technology of television broadcasting which facilitated this national approach is changing. The economics of television are becoming more international generally, and the pressure for a common European market is being applied to broadcasting as it is to other industries. And the economic pressure to reduce national European boundaries is closely allied to the political institutions of the European Community and the Council of Europe.

Satellite broadcasting allows broadcasters based outside a nation's regulatory control to penetrate national TV broadcasting space. So long as satellite broadcasting was confined to low power, countries could control reception by controlling cable systems and large satellite receiving antennae. With the advent of Direct Broadcasting Satellites direct access to the domestic consumer cannot be controlled except by laws almost as intrusive as making listening to foreign radio broadcasts an offence.

The existing system of national television industries is closely related to the maintenance of national audio-visual industries, which is not done purely for reasons of national economy. At its most extreme, the production of programmes in a national language may be subsidized in order to promote a sense of national identity. The compulsion to produce 'national' programmes is not necessarily diluted when two adjoining countries share a language, with Canada and the United States as the clearest example (the 'regulation' by promotion is almost entirely defensive on Canada's part). Protection of such markets by limitation on the broadcasting of programmes produced in other countries is becoming increasingly difficult to justify. In crude terms, US programme-makers can recover their costs and then some from the US market and then sell them at very competitive prices to European broadcasters. European producers, fragmented into national markets, find it difficult to recover production costs domestically and to sell programmes abroad. Advertising markets are similarly fragmented (and not available at all for broadcasters in some European countries).

The technological changes and the economic pressures both suggest strongly that broadcasting in future will be, or at least may be, regional rather than national. If that is to be the future, then it must be reflected in regulation, if only to gain the consent of countries to allow the reception and re-transmission of foreign signals.

It is not necessary to accept the theory that regulatory bodies are usually 'captured' by the industries they regulate to recognize that regulation is often sought rather than opposed by an industry. Common regulatory standards accepted by several nations at least avoid the expense and uncertainty of negotiating individually with each country. 'Harmonization' of national standards about anything obviously opens a wide range of new standards. Common European standards of broadcasting could, hypothetically, include a common ban on all advertising. (Largely because the majority of European countries allow some advertising, that is not at all likely, although British broadcast advertising of cigars might be banned.)

The regulation of broadcasting in the United Kingdom in the near future is thus likely to be heavily influenced by whatever 'regulation' is introduced by European institutions. The purpose of such Euro-regulation is to cope with technology, to produce a European broadcasting market that can compete internationally, and to promote greater European political and economic co-operation. For these reasons this chapter attempts to speculate on the form and substance of European regulation rather than on the British Broadcasting Bill.

Broadcasting regulation from Europe

Some rough definitions are necessary first, with apologies to those for whom this is elementary, and perhaps insufficiently precise. 'European institutions' here means the European Community and the Council of Europe. The European Broadcasting Union is influential in lobbying these institutions, but does not itself have law-making power.

'Regulation' in the European context can take the form of 'rules' with varying degrees of effect. Probably the least binding would be a declaration by an *ad hoc* meeting of ministers from Council of Europe countries. The most binding would be a regulation from the Commission of the European Community, which would be directly enforceable in domestic courts. A Community directive, which initially would require national legislative implementation, would be slightly less binding, although parts of it might be directly enforceable in domestic courts.

There are two types of influence which European law may have on national laws: the first is to provide a way by which national restrictions on broadcasting may be judged to be incompatible with the Treaty of Rome or the Convention on Human Rights; the second is to provide a basis for Community 'legislation' to further a common market in information, or a new Council or Europe international agreement. The first requires someone to challenge the restriction before the European Court of Justice or the European Court of Human Rights. (It seems likely that both will apply the same standard; thus far they have been consistent in their interpretations, but there is always the possibility of conflict.) The second usually requires concerted action by both the officials of the Community or Council and some of the member nations.

The Committee of Ministers of the Council of Europe can propose conventions or other binding agreements or make recommendations to member nations. It is only if a member nation has accepted the provisions of a particular convention that it has binding force in international law. The most important of those for broadcasting now is probably the European Convention on Human Rights, Article 10 of which guarantees the right to receive and impart information. This is enforced by the European Commission of Human Rights, which receives and investigates complaints of violations, and the European Court of Human Rights, which decides such cases.

The emphasis of the Council is protection and promotion of human rights while the emphasis of the Community is on creation of a common market. There are, however, economic elements in activities of the Council of Europe, and human rights provisions in the Treaty of Rome. As broadcasting involves both human rights and economics, both bodies (or either of them) could take steps towards regulating it. This creates obvious possible problems of conflicting rules and duplication of effort. The process by which the institutions decide which will do what when is essentially political, with results legally binding (in various degrees).

When the two European institutions began taking steps concerning broadcasting in 1984 it seemed that the Community would take the dominant role. It could 'legislate' in the form of promulgating directives which members would be required to implement by national legislation (and which become directly enforceable in domestic courts if there is no implementing legislation). For 'legislation' the Council of Europe could only propose a new convention, which members would be free to accept or reject. As of October 1989 broadcasting is subject to a Community directive and a Council of Europe convention.

The Council of Europe has sponsored several separate agreements between member nations about broadcasting, perhaps the most important of which was the Agreement for the Prevention of

Broadcasts Transmitted from Stations Outside National Territories in 1965, which made life more difficult for the 'pirate' broadcasters in the North Sea. In 1982 the Committee of Ministers began publishing the 'Mass Media Files', and in 1986 they published a set of recommended principles for communication of television and radio by satellite. All of this activity has been quasi-legislative, but recommendations have no binding legal force. Decisions of the European Court of Human Rights interpreting the Convention are binding in international law, but there have been few challenges to national regulation of broadcasting thus far. In 1984 the International Chamber of Commerce published a persuasive opinion by two English barristers arguing (with considerable reference to US constitutional law) that 'commercial speech' was protected from restriction under Article 10.

In November 1988 the Commission found that the Swiss Government had violated the Convention by stopping Swiss cable networks from re-transmitting radio programmes broadcast by a transmitter in Italy. That case (*Groppera Radio*) is now before the Court. In another case now being considered by the Commission the complaint is that the Swiss authorities have refused to allow a company (*Autronic*) to receive Soviet satellite television programmes on a dish antenna.

The First European Ministerial Conference on Mass Media Policy, held in Vienna in December 1986, decided to 'assign the highest priority . . . to the rapid preparation . . . of binding legal instruments on certain crucial aspects of transfrontier broadcasting'. That means a Council of Europe Convention on Broadcasting, and is a significant shift from action by the Community to that by the Council of Europe.

The most important Community law on broadcasting is the directive following the 1984 Green Paper, 'Television without Frontiers'. The directive was approved in October 1989. The proposals that broadcasters reserve some programming time for Community programmes were changed from enforceable rules to goals.

The European Court of Justice has already decided several cases on the status of broadcasting under the Treaty of Rome. In 1974 the Court decided that a domestic broadcasting monopoly was consistent with the Treaty, but that a monopoly which discriminated on the basis of nationality against other EC nationals would violate the Treaty. A Community country could not restrict the right to receive broadcasts from other member states and to re-transmit them. In the 1980 *Debauve* case the Court made it clear that this applied to transmission by cable and satellite. But in that case the Court ruled that national rules prohibiting advertisements on cable or broadcast television did not violate the Treaty so long as they did not discriminate on the basis of the advertisements' national origin. In the *Coditel* case, also in 1980, the Court ruled that the holder of copyright in a film could stop its re-transmission by cable when it was broadcast on television. ('Le Boucher' was broadcast in Germany and transmitted by cable in Belgium. The agreement for Belgian rights prohibited television broadcasts until forty months after the first cinema showing.) In both the *Debauve* and *Coditel* cases the Court ruled against the submissions of the EC Commission (which happens sometimes) and against the opinion of the Advocate-General (which happens very rarely). The Court has recently ruled against Dutch limits on advertising.

The Council of Europe Convention on Transfrontier Television, now open for signature and ratification, is intended to create common standards for television between member states. Countries accepting the Convention may be as strict or lax in regulating domestic broadcasting as they like (within the important limits of the Human Rights Convention); but the restrictions imposed on 'imported' television are those required by the Transfrontier Television Convention. These include limits on sex, violence and racial hatred in programming. There are also affirmative requirements about the independence of news and current affairs programmes, and a transfrontier right of reply. But almost all of the controversy in negotiating the Convention was about advertising.

The Convention adopts the proposal that advertising messages must be clearly separated. Although it also establishes rules about sponsored programmes, it does not attempt to regulate sponsored events transmitted by broadcasters. The clearest message for countries thinking about signing the Convention is that those Council of Europe countries which still prohibit broadcast advertisements would be required to allow broadcast advertisements from other countries complying with Convention rules. The provisions about the content, frequency and length of advertisements were the most hotly disputed, with the United Kingdom arguing that its system of commercials during 'natural breaks' was superior to the more detailed restrictions supported by the Federal Republic of Germany.

In a brief television comment, Margaret Thatcher gave her own definition of 'regulation', saying that it should be concerned with limiting broadcast sex and violence rather than with advertising.

Conclusion

The outlines of future broadcasting regulation by European institutions are at least as clear as those of British regulation, about which we will learn more when the Broadcasting bill is published. It seems reasonable to predict that a consequence of both developments will be an increase, if not quite a proliferation, of radio and television broadcasting outlets. The shape of domestic regulatory authorities is likely to be more independent of the government of the day, but not necessarily free-standing. The style of regulation will probably be planned to be 'light-handed', but the increase in broadcasting competitors may well lead to challenges in court by way of judicial review.

The central thesis of this chapter is that overt 'regulation' of most communications media is likely to increase in the near future. This will involve a change in substantive rules and in institutions, as a change from administration of monopolies; it will not necessarily mean that there will be greater freedom in the content of what is communicated or that any notional greater freedom will lead to any greater variety. The language of formal 'regulation' is not familiar in Britain, and it is inevitably legalistic: it is a shift from administration by the discretion of 'sound chaps' to the resolution of disputes about legal rules. If Britain is to become more like other countries in the way it regulates communications media, perhaps more research into how they regulate can provide lessons from their mistakes. But then, was there ever an essay that called for an end to research on a subject?

PART TWO

CHANGING MEDIA PROCESSES

Politics and Power

4

Rethinking the Sociology of Journalism: Source Strategies and the Limits of Media-Centrism

Philip Schlesinger

Despite two decades of productive work in media sociology, the relations between media and sources have remained under-conceptualized. This chapter examines current orthodoxies in the sociology of journalism and suggests how we might move beyond them: at issue is the excessive *media-centrism* of much existing research.[1]

My central concern is to highlight the implications of a major lacuna in the existing literature; namely, the failure to look at source-media relations from the perspective of *the sources themselves*. I then move on to sketch a model in terms of which a rigorous sociological investigation of this topic might develop.

Occasionally, a sociology of sources has been advocated as a theme of central importance. For instance, in his major study of US news organizations Herbert Gans notes:

> My observations on source power suggest that the study of sources deserves far more attention from news researchers than it has so far obtained. To understand the news fully, researchers must study sources as roles and as representatives of the organized or unorganized groups for whom they act and speak, and thus also as holders of power. Above all, researchers should determine what groups create or become sources, and with what agendas; what interests they pursue in seeking access to the news and in refusing it. Parallel studies should be made of groups that cannot get into the news, and why this is so. And researchers must ask what effect obtaining or failing to obtain access to the news has on the power, the interests, and the subsequent activities of groups who become or are represented by sources. (Gans, 1979: 360, n. 3)[2]

This is an ambitious programme of work which Gans himself (not unwisely) relegated to a footnote. Over recent years, some of these themes have indeed been taken up in a piecemeal fashion, but it is now surely time to make such a research orientation both explicit and programmatic. Currently, apart from the study of the institutional and discursive fields of crime, law and justice out of which this chapter has developed, I know only of work by Richard V. Ericson and his colleagues (1989) in Canada which is posing questions about source power along lines similar to those pursued here.

Once one begins to analyse the tactics and strategies pursued by sources seeking media attention, to ask about their perceptions of other, competing, actors in the fields over which they are trying to exert influence, to enquire about the financial resources at their disposal and the organizational contexts in which they operate, to ask about their goals and notions of effectiveness, one rapidly discovers how ignorant we are about such matters – and this despite the undoubted importance of the contribution that production studies have made to the field.

One reason for this is that media sociology has largely, although certainly not exclusively, focused on how media organizations, especially those producing news, have made use of sources of information (a term which one is well advised to define broadly, so as to include, for instance, disinformation and 'economies of the truth'). In short, as I shall demonstrate in the discussion which follows, media sociology has been far too *media-centric*. We need to assess the costs and benefits of this. At the very least it is plain, as Ericson et al. observe at the conclusion of their recent study of Canadian news organizations that

> Grounded inside the newsroom, . . . research . . . has a tendency to depict news-media power as virtually boundless. Grounded in source organizations, . . . research . . . adjusts this picture. Journalists face the bounds of powerful sources who mobilize strategically to variously avoid and make news. While the news-media institution is effectively closed to most citizens, and a powerful force in society, a limited range of sources can pry it open and sometimes harness its power to advantage. (1987: 364)

The key issue at the heart of the study of sources is that of the relations between the media and the exercise of political and ideological power, especially, but not exclusively, by central social institutions which seek to define and manage the flow of information in a contested field of discourse. Inevitably, at the core of such an interest are the organs of the state and the ways in which these compete among themselves and with other more or less institutionalized sources of information. Any sociology of information management – which is surely central to the workings of the 'information society' – has to take due account of what the sociology of journalism can tell us about the nature and scope of source power.

It might erroneously be supposed that posing questions about non-official sources somehow runs counter to a notion of dominance in the exercise of media power, that it implies adherence to a pluralist conception of social organization. This could only be justified on the most facile understanding of the debate about dominance versus pluralism in the media.

John Westergaard, who does adhere to such a rigidly dichotomous view, takes the line that certain ways of posing questions are exclusively pluralistic:

> with regard to its methodology and underlying conception of the phenomenon of power, the pluralistic model takes a resolutely 'behaviourist' approach. Power, so it is asserted, is manifest in the outcome of active conflict and competition among contending groups and individuals. The locus of power at any given time can, and can only, be established by reference to the visible results of visible contests for influence over 'decision' making. . . . It defines power by reference to activities which can be systematically watched. But . . . only a fraction of the reality of power in fact is so observable. Excluded from such a conception of power is power that is effective without any active exercise of pressure – covert as well as overt – because it is not actively opposed'. (1977: 98–9)

Now, it is certainly well founded to argue that a purely empiricist conception is lacking in the theoretical sophistication necessary to take account of the 'hidden faces of power' and that it is apt to ignore the broader constraints within which competition may unequally take place. However, it is something quite different to dismiss as of no interest the potential value of empirical knowledge gained by observation. By that token, to pose questions about competition for space in the media by non-dominant sources is to pose a 'pluralist' question. Certainly, it is typically pluralists such as Gans (1979) and Blumler and Gurevitch (1977, 1986b) who have evinced curiosity along these lines, but there is no reason at all why such questions should not be posed *from within a theory of dominance* with the beneficial effect of making such theories broader in explanatory scope.

This has not happened because all too often research in the field has pursued an unnecessarily exclusionary logic, in which there are two closed, competing paradigms along the following lines:

> The pluralists see society as a complex of competing groups and interests, none of them predominant all of the time. . . . Marxists view capitalist society as being one of class domination; the media are seen

as part of an ideological arena in which various class views are fought out, although within the context of the dominance of certain classes; ultimate control is increasingly concentrated in monopoly capital. (Gurevitch et al., 1982: 1)

However, as the authors of the above characterization themselves accept, it over-simplifies for pedagogical purposes. Denis McQuail, largely echoing these terms (1987: 58–9, 85–7) also acknowledges the analytical usefulness of such a polarization; nevertheless, he does point out that '[b]oth models are ideal-typical in the sense of accentuating and exaggerating certain features of media and it would obviously be possible to offer intermediate models in which the features of both could be found together, as they almost certainly are in reality' (1987: 85).

Indeed, there does appear to have been a growing recognition of the way in which the empirical findings of Marxism and pluralism 'are not so far apart as is usually supposed; both agree about the nature and degree of power that can be attributed to the media, albeit that they express this in different terms' (Gurevitch et al., 1982: 7).[3] Curran et al. are also right to point out that, although Marxists and pluralists have shared a common concern with 'the interaction between media professionals and their "sources" in political and state institutions', it is nevertheless the case that in analysing 'the production process in the media . . . competing interpretations are provided by rival perspectives, although the evidence deployed by both is similar' (1982: 20–1).

However, so far, I would contend, such competing analyses of source activity have been highly media-centric. This may be illustrated by considering two main approaches: the structuralist concept of 'primary definition', and the empirical sociology of journalism. After a critical assessment, I suggest some necessary steps in developing an analytical model for the study of sources.

'Primary definers': the structuralist conception of sources

One important point of departure in recent debate about the power of sources has been the analysis by Stuart Hall and his colleagues in *Policing the Crisis* (Hall et al., 1978). Among other themes, this study has posed questions about the construction of ideology in a capitalist society where social democratic practices are eroding and an 'exceptional' form of state is being developed. This is an argument which Hall has gone on to develop in his subsequent work on 'Thatcherism'. A large portion of *Policing the Crisis* is focused on analysing the 'social production of news', and draws upon Hall's earlier studies of the workings of the media.

For present purposes, I shall focus on how the role of sources is conceptualized by means of the concept of 'primary definers', one widely employed in a spirit of uncritical emulation, with little attention being paid to its deep flaws. The analysis of Hall et al. offers a very clear instance of the way in which adherence to a theory of dominance may entail some crucial blind spots. In *Policing the Crisis* the social role of the media is integral to a theory of ideological power which draws upon a Gramscian conception of the struggle for hegemony between dominant and subordinate classes in capitalist societies. According to Hall et al.: 'It is this structured relationship – between the media and its [*sic*] "powerful" sources – which begins to open up the neglected question of the *ideological role* of the media. It is this which begins to give substance and specificity to Marx's basic proposition that "the ruling ideas of any age are the ideas of its ruling class"' (1978: 59; authors' emphases).

Hall et al. argue that media accounts are grounded in '"objective" and "authoritative" statements from "accredited" sources'. These sources are the representatives of major social institutions which are 'accredited'

> Because of their institutional power and position, but also because of their 'representative status': either they represent 'the people' (MPs, Ministers, etc.) or organized interest groups (which is how the TUC and CBI are now regarded). One final 'accredited source' is 'the expert': his calling – the 'disinterested' pursuit of knowledge – not his position or representativeness, confers on his statements 'objectivity' and 'authority'. Ironically, the very rules which aim to preserve the impartiality of the media, and which grew out of desires for greater professional neutrality, also serve powerfully to orientate the media in the 'definitions of social reality' which their 'accredited sources' – the institutional spokesmen – provide. (Hall et al., 1978: 58)

The argument, then, is that media give access to those who enjoy 'accreditation'. This is a resource limited to certain social groups which enjoy a special status as sources in virtue of their institutional power, representative standing or claims to expert knowledge. As a consequence of what they conceive as professional practices of ascertaining source credibility, the media are structurally biased towards very powerful and privileged sources who become 'over-accessed':

> The result of this structured preference given in the media to the opinions of the powerful is that these 'spokesmen' become what we call the *primary definers* of topics . . . [which] . . . permits the institutional definers to establish the initial definition or *primary interpretation* of the topic in question. This interpretation then 'commands the field' in all

subsequent treatment and sets the terms of reference within which all further coverage of debate takes place. Arguments *against* a primary interpretation are forced to insert themselves into *its* definition of 'what is at issue' – they must begin from this framework of interpretation as their starting point. (1978: 58; authors' emphases)

This is a very strong argument indeed.[4] Taken at face value its import is that the structure of access *necessarily* secures strategic advantages for 'primary definers', not just initially but also subsequently for as long as a debate or controversy lasts. It also asserts that counter-definitions can *never dislodge* the primary definition, which consistently dominates. Primary definition, then, involves a primacy both temporal and ideological.

The assumptions just discussed are open to various criticisms. First, the notion of 'primary definition' is more problematic than it seems. The broad characterization offered above does not take account of contention between official sources in trying to influence the construction of a story. In cases of dispute, say, among members of the same government over a key question of policy, who is the primary definer, or (and it goes against the logic of the concept) can there be more than one?

Second, the formulation of Hall et al. fails to register the well-established fact that official sources often attempt to influence the construction of a story by using 'off-the-record' briefings – in which case the primary definers do not appear *directly* as such, in unveiled and attributable form. Such an approach is plainly a function of the *method* used namely, that of using newspapers as data without examining processes of production behind the finished product.

A third point concerns the drawing of the boundaries of primary definition. Do these shift, and if so why? In the example of Hall et al., reference is made to MPs and ministers. Primary definition, presumably, is intended to include all consensually recognized 'representative' voices. But plainly the structure of access is skewed even in Hall's terms, with some members of the political class at times enjoying much more access than others. So not all of these 'representative' figures can themselves be treated as having equal access. Unfortunately, there is nothing in Hall's formulation of primary defining which permits us to deal with such inequalities of access among the privileged themselves.

Fourth, there is the unconsidered question of longer-term shifts in the structure of access. Writing in the late 1970s, it may have been obvious to talk of the CBI and TUC as major institutional voices. But with the disappearance of corporatism under Mrs Thatcher's successive governments these voices (especially the TUC, but also the CBI) have become less and less prominent, displaced first by the voices of monetarism and then of privatization. The structuralist model is *atemporal*, for it tacitly assumes the permanent presence of certain forces in the power structure. But when these are displaced by new forces how are we to explain the dynamics behind their emergence? The notion that primary definers are simply 'accredited' to their dominant ideological place in virtue of an institutional location is at the root of this unresolved issue.

Hall goes on to locate the media within the power structure:

> The media, then, do not simply 'create' the news; nor do they simply transmit the ideology of the 'ruling class' in a conspiratorial fashion. Indeed, we have suggested that, in a critical sense, the media are frequently not the 'primary definers' of news events at all; but their structured relationship to power has the effect of making them play a crucial secondary role in *reproducing* the definitions of those who have privileged access, as of right, to the media as 'accredited sources'. From this point of view, in the moment of news production, the media stand in a position of structured subordination to the primary definers. (Hall et al., 1978: 59; authors' emphasis)

So the media are seen as a subordinate site for the reproduction of the dominant ideological field.

This now brings us to a fifth objection, which is that the model of reproduction of Hall et al. deals with the question of the media's relative autonomy from the political system in a purely *uni-directional* way. The movement of definitions is *uniformly* from power centre to media. Within this conceptual logic, there is no space to account for occasions on which the media may take the initiative in the definitional process by *challenging* the so-called primary definers and forcing them to respond – as, for instance, in investigative journalism dealing with scandals inside the state apparatus, or when leaks by dissident figures force undesired and unintended official responses, or when accidents occur and official figures are caught on the hop (cf. Molotch and Lester, 1974). At times, too, it is the media which crystallize slogans or themes which are subsequently taken up by the primary definers because it is in their interest to do so (cf. Elliott and Schlesinger, 1980).

The assumption of uni-directionality of definitional flow also carries over into the vexed area of media effects:

> Concentrated media attention confers the status of high public concern on issues which are highlighted; these generally become understood by everyone as 'pressing issues of the day'. This is part of the media's *agenda-setting* function. Setting agendas also has a reality-confirming effect . . . it inserts the language of everyday communication *back into the consensus.* (Hall et al., 1978: 62; authors' emphases)

That the primary effect is invariably that of reinforcing the consensus via uni-accentual linguistic mediation is open to question. Hall et al. do themselves explicitly recognize this when they note that the tendency towards ideological closure is at times challenged by a counter-tendency that depends 'on the existence of organized and articulate sources which generate *counter*-definitions of the situation'. How effective this may be 'depends to some degree on whether the collectivity which generates counter-ideologies and explanations is a powerful countervailing force in society; whether it represents an organized majority or substantial minority; and whether or not it has a degree of legitimacy within the system or can win such a position through struggle' (1978: 64).

According to the primary definition thesis, counter-definitions are bounded by tight parameters, as those with alternative views (such as official trade-union spokesmen, in the example suggested) 'must respond *in terms* pre-established by the primary definers and privileged definitions' (1978: 62). I have already commented on the assumption of necessary temporal priority that this formulation makes. It also rules out any process of *negotiation* prior to the issuing of primary definitions. Moreover, there is a further conceptual weakness revealed by this specific example, for the notion of primary definition shifts significantly here. In the formulation quoted earlier, trade-union spokesmen figured as primary definers; now they are classed as 'counter-spokesmen' or mere 'definers'. This shift reveals a crucial conflation between, first, the media's use of routine, privileged official or quasi-official sources and, second, a process of primary definition understood as successful domination of the agenda: the two are not identical (cf. Molotch and Lester, 1974: 104–5).

The model given by Hall et al. is one in which primary definitions are conceived of as commanding the field and as producing a dominant ideological effect. While this offers a coherent critique of various forms of pluralism, an uncritical adherence to this model involves paying a price. For this structuralist approach is profoundly incurious about the processes whereby sources engage in ideological conflict *prior to or contemporaneous with the appearance of definitions in the media*. It therefore rules out asking questions about how contestation over definitions takes place *within* institutions and organizations reported by the media as well as the concrete strategies pursued as they contend for space.

Furthermore, it may be demonstrated that access for 'alternative' viewpoints differs as between the press and television, and indeed as between different newspapers. Hall tends to reduce all to a uniform variation upon a theme. No analytical framework is presented which permits us to analyse the degree of potential openness available in different media sites or through different forms of output and the scope that these might offer for alternative views (cf. Schlesinger et al., 1983). The whole approach to the activities of alternative sources is not based on any analysis of the workings and objectives of such groups but is deduced from a reading of newspaper content. It is one thing to denounce the politics of exclusion and another to analyse its dynamics.

Although Hall's approach clearly fails to deal with a number of conceptual difficulties, there is still undoubtedly a strong case for arguing that the way in which journalistic practice is organized *generally* promotes the interest of authoritative sources, especially within the apparatus of government and state. That is a paramount finding of much of the contemporary sociology of journalism, which will be discussed below. However, because Hall's approach to 'primary definition' resolves the question of source power on the basis of structuralist assumptions, it closes off any engagement with the dynamic processes of contestation in a given field of discourse. Although it has the advantage of directing our interest to the question of definitional power, it offers no sociological account of how this is achieved as the outcome of strategies pursued by political actors. They do not need strategies because they have guaranteed access by virtue of their structural position. Because this model is blind to the question of source competition, it follows that those dismissively lumped together as 'alternative' are of virtually no interest at all. But as we shall see, empirical research shows that their views and arguments may be incorporated pre-emptively into so-called 'primary definers' definitions', thereby both modifying them and at the same time indicating that the boundaries between sources are not always as impermeable as the charmed circle conception of primacy would imply.

The empirical sociology of journalism

The empirical study of news production is probably the most fully elaborated single area of media sociology. But whereas the conceptual basis of the structuralist approach to sources has been fully spelled out within the framework of a theory of contemporary capitalism, the development of theorizing about sources over the past two decades by exponents of empirical research on journalism has tended to be more *ad hoc* and tied to the particular purposes of the study in hand. As noted earlier, one of the fullest programmatic statements in the literature is actually a footnote to a major empirical study. Consequently, a critical assessment has to proceed differently in this case, and rather than offer a detailed exposition of a single, given position, I shall present a synoptic overview of the main tendencies to be found.

First, most accounts analyse the role of official sources in government and administration, and there is widespread agreement that these play a crucial role in defining and shaping the media agenda through interaction with the news production process (cf. Villafañé et al., 1987). It is broadly characteristic of studies of source activity to concentrate on a single institutional area. Thus, for instance, in the case of the political system, British studies such as Seymour-Ure (1968), Tunstall (1970) and Cockerell et al. (1984) have focused on the Westminster-Whitehall lobby system, whereas in the American context, Sigal (1973, 1986) has studied the relations between reporters and officials in Washington.

This pattern of attention has been followed for source-media relations in areas other than political reporting. Thus, in British work the lobby model as central focus has been applied to other areas of institutional activity – quite rightly, because that is how things work. Hence, for instance, there are studies of the relations between the Metropolitan Police and crime reporters (Chibnall, 1977), social policy reporters and the Department of Health and Social Security (Golding and Middleton, 1982), the media and the military and the police in partial engagements or counter-insurgency warfare (Adams, 1986; Hooper, 1982; Morrison and Tumber, 1988; Schlesinger et al., 1983: Curtis, 1984).

Second, despite this well-founded recognition of the crucial role of the state (in the form of government departments and the wider political class) as the major producer of information, the empirical sociology of journalism for the most part shies away from endorsing a straightforward notion of primary definition. Without doubt, analogous notions are to be found in the literature but the pressure of detailed analysis of source activity has tended to result in a more complex appreciation of divergences *within* the official camp. The question of alternative views (even if they fall into quite a restricted ideological range) necessarily surfaces as a matter of importance, as does a recognition of the fact that official status does not necessarily *automatically* ensure credibility. As Sigal (1986: 22) observes, 'The convention of authoritativeness may assure a hearing in the news for those in authority, but it is no guarantee of a "good press" so long as other sources are willing and able to talk to reporters.' Hence:

> If the voices of government by their ability to dominate the news, get to define the issues that are potentially salient, opposition voices frame the lines of cleavage over which policy battles are fought and thereby help define which outcomes are politically practicable. The press, in

amplifying some voices and muting others, in distorting some messages and letting others come through loud and clear, affects the nature of opposition and hence of governance. The press does not do so on its own: groups differ in their ability to make their voices heard and to direct and shape their messages for the public. (Sigal, 1986: 37)

It is precisely this latter point which the concept of primary definition devalues. Clearly, assumptions have to be made about the measure of relative pluralism in the polity (which can be analysed both structurally and conjuncturally). If we are to take seriously notions of hegemonic ideological domination, on the surface it would appear that we need to make a choice between the pole of determinism on the one hand and that of free competition on the other. As I shall argue below, that is not the choice at all.

In the present context, though, it is worth illustrating the *simplisme* of a forced choice between determinism and autonomy by reference to Golding and Middleton's work, which clearly derives from theoretical premises closer to those of Hall than those of Sigal. Golding and Middleton (1982: 121) recognize the 'monumental importance of the apparatus of the state, and particularly of government and senior civil servants, in defining the amount, timing and overall direction of social policy news' – the state thus acting, in their words, as a 'prime defining source'. Yet engagement with the empirical realities of source activity produces an awareness of the significance of non-official sources, in particular of pressure groups which

> serve a twin function. On the one hand they act as research agencies, able to point out the inconsistencies or evasions in official versions of policy. On the other hand they provide hand-wringing reactions to the iniquities of government policy that can be used to 'balance' a story. (1982: 119)

Built into the empirical sociology of journalism (even where its assumptions are broadly Marxist) is the potential for opening up a distinctive problematic: that of the social organization of non-official sources and the ways in which they achieve (or fail to achieve) their impact. As Gans has noted, this has not so far been accomplished, and as I argue here we need to begin to conceptualize this question quite explicitly since, as we shall see, it offers points of connection with other areas of social analysis.

A third point concerns the *methodology* of empirical studies of how sources act, an issue that has attracted almost no critical attention at all so far. The available approaches fall into two: the internalist and the externalist. These are not mutually exclusive by any means, but treating them as distinct alternatives helps bring out their separate logics.

Internalists produce their analyses of source behaviour either by interpreting what sources do by a reading of media content or by deriving conclusions from accounts given by practitioners of journalism of their interactions with their sources, or by combining both. There is nothing wrong with this, but it has shortcomings. If we restrict ourselves to what appears in the media this plainly does not tell us much about the process whereby it comes to be there. (This is a particular defect of the analysis of Hall et al. of primary definition.) Furthermore, if we restrict ourselves to *journalists'* accounts of how they have dealt with sources, the optic is largely limited to how *the media* organize their information strategies.

These limitations can be circumvented by taking an *externalist* approach. This implies a thoroughgoing analysis of the strategic and tactical action of sources in relation to the media. Such work exists already, for instance, in the form of *post hoc* reconstructions of particular exercises in news management or censorship. Such evidence is usually based upon a mix of journalistic reflections on experience, revelations in the press based on leaks or the subsequent coming clean of participants, and the release of official documents much after the event. In short, for externalist accounts involving substantial reconstruction from diverse sources the passage of time is a great help, especially so where the weeders of public records or the feeders of shredders have lacked foresight.

My argument is that, in addition to using internalist evidence, we need to extend the scope of externalist evidence. At one level, the method for doing this is simplicity itself. It involves interviewing and observing those organized to influence the discursive fields of a determinate universe of coverage. In advocating this additional empirical enquiry, it should be clearly understood that any researcher is open to the same problems of incompleteness and interpretation as occur in using other methods. And indeed, serious problems of access could arise. For instance, as Gandy (1980: 114) has rightly pointed out, the attempt to reconstruct source strategies does come up against the limits of secrecy. In such cases, it is obviously necessary to have recourse to the normal research strategies of internalism by, for instance, using content analysis or network analysis. The central point for present purposes, however, is that *an expansion of empirical scope has necessary effects on the type of theory of sources we can employ.*

This brings me to a fourth point, which is to note how existing theory has evidently been closely allied to the scope of empirical research. The explicit use of models to address the question of sources has been unusual, a rare example being Jeremy Tunstall's work on the Westminster lobby (1970) and on specialist correspondents (1971), another being Herbert Gans's (1979) study referred to above. In addition, Molotch and Lester (1974) have also attempted to develop a relevant account of news as 'purposive behaviour'.

In both of his studies Tunstall suggests (very briefly) that some modified version of exchange theory be applied:

> The interaction of any journalists with news sources can be seen as an exchange of information for publicity. . . . An exchange between a journalist and political source takes place within two sets of occupational norms. On the side of the journalist are occupational norms stressing the anonymity of sources, the importance of mutual trust, and an expectation that sources are motivated by self-interest. On the side of the politician-source, there are *presumably* occupational norms to the effect that journalists are potentially helpful as well as potentially dangerous, and that publicity is a significant political resource. . . . Frequently the relationship is strongly dyadic, an encounter, usually face-to-face, between two individuals – although it is also part of a wider exchange process between two groups, or occupations, or two organizations. (1970: 43–4; emphasis added)

This, then, proposes that we analyse source–media interaction in terms of a confrontation between two underlying normative structures rooted in particular sets of relations between individuals. We should note the presumptive nature of what is said about politicians' action. In a subsequent formulation, Tunstall significantly modifies this by moving towards the idea of a *field of interaction*, although without fully arriving there, and then retreating to a position of radical indeterminism:

> At the organizational level a number of source organizations, which compete and cooperate with each other, confront a number of news organizations, which also compete and cooperate. . . . The routinised provision of information . . . is clearly not a simple exchange between an individual source and an individual specialist. There is a strong *collective* element here. (1971: 185–6; author's emphasis)

This clearly shifts us towards the notion of a structured field, although Tunstall's insights into the role of collective action in the flow of information are once more restricted to the ways in which journalists' work is structured: 'Source attempts to stop a particular specialist from getting information are wholly ineffective – because his competitor-colleagues are likely to help him, and because some other news sources may become friendly' (1971: 170). Elaborating his reservations about the notion of exchange of publicity for information, Tunstall observes that this cannot possibly account for all the variables involved:

> Most exchange models suggest structured interaction, balance, careful calculation of interest, the gradual development of norms of exchange

behaviour. Such exchange models ignore the instability of news, the loosely structured (or chaotic) character of the social interaction, and especially the lack of time for care, gradualness or full communication about the dispositions of different parties relevant to the rapidly changing 'current' story. (1971: 202)

This move in the argument oddly echoes journalists' occupational ideology, which stresses indeterminacy and unpredictability and cuts across the empirical analysis actually offered. Nevertheless, despite undermining his own model, Tunstall does pose relevant questions for the future: 'What kinds of control do sources have over journalists' and 'To what extent are these contested?' (1971: 203). The first question clearly points towards an externalist approach, whereas the second refers to the ways in which journalists contest source control. However, there is also an externalist dimension to this latter question, which concerns the ways in which sources themselves contest one another's control – which is precisely the question for which we need to develop a model.

For his part, Gans observes that 'the source–journalist relationship is a . . . tug of war: while sources attempt to "manage" the news, putting the best light on themselves, journalists concurrently "manage" the source in order to extract the information they want' (1979: 117). This characterization presupposes an instrumental approach to the handling of information in which each side pursues strategies in the furtherance of its goals. Gans sees the media as passive on the whole, so the strategic advantages lie with sources. This point is reiterated by others (cf. Golding and Middleton, 1982; Sigal, 1986). Gans identifies a number of factors which he considers shape source–media relations, the nearest he comes towards developing a model.

Most basic is the *incentive* to get information into the public domain, the other face of this being the desire for secrecy. A second factor is *power*:

> While in theory sources can come from anywhere, in practice, their recruitment and their access to journalists reflect the hierarchies of nation and society. The President of the United States has instantaneous access to all news media; the powerless must resort to civil disturbances to obtain it. (1979: 119)

It is normally sufficient for the powerful to 'create suitable news' rather than 'bully their way into story lists'. The converse practice, the negative exercise of power, is to refuse access which in Gans's terms is 'the primary form of censorship' (1979: 120). There is no real distinction between the first and second factors proposed: they collapse into the proposition that information management and secrecy are a function of power.

A third factor, Gans suggests, is the importance of economic resources to those who act as sources: the fact that they are not generally paid entails an implicit class bias both in terms of self-selection as an information provider and in the media's selection of given individuals or groups. This links into his fourth point: namely, the way in which social and geographical proximity act as selector mechanisms: lack of social contact screens out most would-be sources, whereas the geographical concentration of news-gathering brings about routinization of media search procedures. Like Sigal and Hall, Gans concludes that the media's stress upon 'authoritative and efficient sources' leads to a 'cumulative pattern that determines availability and suitability' which 'makes the public official the most frequent and regular source' (1979: 145). This point plainly recognizes the fact of structured access which is central to the structuralist approach. Nevertheless, this is perfectly compatible with Gans's commitment to pluralism and his recommendation that 'multiperspectival' news be adopted as an antidote to present exclusions.

The arguments propounded by Molotch and Lester, despite their ethnomethodological terminology, are close to those of Gans. They see the activity of sources (which they call 'promotion') as focused upon bringing the priorities of media production in line with their needs for publicity or secrecy. The greatest potential success in doing this, they argue, occurs in the case of 'routine events', as opposed to 'scandals' and 'accidents', which are by definition unpredictable and therefore less controllable by those in power.

Once again, the key notion of structured access comes up. Those who enjoy 'habitual access' are usually

> high government officials, major corporate figures, and, to a lesser extent, certain glamorous personalities. Such people must be concerned with keeping their podia alive [*sic*] and organizing the news so that their goals do not suffer in the continuing competition to create publics. . . . Intra- or inter-group competitions notwithstanding, habitual access is generally found among those with extreme wealth or other institutionally-based sources of power. . . . Routine access is one of the important sources and sustainers of existing power relationships. (Molotch and Lester, 1974: 107)

The main competition from outside the centres of power comes from either those who attain access via 'disruptions' (a catch-all category too broad to be illuminating) or 'directly' (from inside the media themselves, when investigating or campaigning). The central importance of scandals and accidents, it is argued, lies in revealing the hidden face of power normally 'deliberately obfuscated by those with the resources to create routine events' which are recognized as having strategic purposes (1974: 109, 111).

The empirical sociology of journalism, therefore, plainly shares insights with the structuralists about the strategic advantages that political and economic power secure for sources. But on the whole it holds back from characterizing this as primary definition because of its recognition – nowhere fully developed – of the *active pursuit of definitional advantage* required by those seeking access to the media. Sources have to engage in goal-oriented action to achieve access, even though their recognition as 'legitimate authorities' is already usually inscribed in the rules of the game. This contrasts with the structuralist notion of 'automatic', accredited access resulting in primary definition. In short, the empirical sociology of journalism repeatedly appeals to a non-articulated concept of strategic action.

Empirical studies, however, have largely failed to investigate the forms of action adopted by non-official sources. Although the pressure to develop a more all-encompassing account is obviously at work in the sociology of journalism, the failure to push research beyond present limits has resulted in a dearth of sustained investigation into unofficial source competition or into the internal organization of the media strategies of pressure groups. On the few occasions where this is mentioned, it tends to derive from journalists' accounts rather than those of the groups themselves. Consequently, there are theoretical and empirical grounds for examining the actual behaviour of sources. But what should be the theoretical approach?

Developing a model

The impetus for rethinking the question of sources has come from the research process itself, in which the need to find an appropriate conceptualization has accompanied the engagement in empirical work. In investigating the institutional field of crime, law and justice the focus has been wider than the conventional concentration upon law-enforcement bodies and the judiciary as the only sources that matter. The aim has been to discover more about the organization of pressure group and lobbying activity in relation to the media in various areas such as prison reform, civil liberties, police accountability, the criminal justice process and so forth.

It would be agreeably simple if sources could be categorized as either 'official' or 'non-official' and matters left there. However, the fieldwork undertaken has revealed greater complications. For instance, some groups in the field of prison reform, such as the National Association for the Care and Resettlement of Offenders (NACRO), are directly funded by the Home Office and are sometimes expected to take up positions at variance with current policy. How is this kind of source to be characterized? Clearly, it is within the orbit of the state but retains some autonomy. Even if in some sense it is para-statal it would be unduly reductive to assimilate it to a single, overarching category of primary definition. Similar problems arise when the activities of state employees in the field, such as the Police Federation or the Prison Officers Association are observed. In some circumstances, such groups often behave just like other trade unions attempting to improve their bargaining position. Once again, while recognizing their proximity to the state apparatus proper, it is reductive to obliterate distinctive positions over current policy.

However, as has been made clear, there is no developed externalist model of analysis that makes pressure groups' media strategies a central concern. My objective has been to develop an analysis capable of handling the activities of non-official sources in a way that treats them neither as theoretically irrelevant nor simply views them from the media-centric standpoint of news processors. At the same time, one recognizes the compelling evidence for the centrality of the state as a source of definitions, not least in a study focused on the problem of social and legal order.

Consequently, it is necessary that sources be conceived as occupying fields in which *competition for access* to the media takes place, but in which material and symbolic advantages are unequally distributed. But the most advantaged do not secure a primary definition in virtue of their positions alone. Rather, if they do so, it is because of successful *strategic action* in an imperfectly competitive field. It is important, therefore, to chart the ways in which sources pursue their goals when contributing to what Gusfield (1981) has called a 'public culture' in which oppositional and alternative views are not excluded. Thus, while we may certainly accept that the state dominates institutional news coverage, this does not render irrelevant questions about differently endowed contending groups in the building and modification of political agendas.

Some of Pierre Bourdieu's insights seem particularly relevant here, in particular his notion of an 'intellectual field'. This conception has a very general scope and has been applied to a wide range of cultural practice, with obvious applicability to media production and consumption. I have employed this notion elsewhere in analysing the disposition of positions in the debate over political violence and the media (Schlesinger and Lumley, 1985). According to Bourdieu (1971: 161), an 'intellectual field' may be understood as 'a system of social relations in which creation as an act of communication takes place'. Bourdieu argues for the material determination of cultural production but in a way that takes account of how 'forces of determinism' become 'a specifically intellectual determination by being reinterpreted according to the specific logic of the intellectual field, in a creative project' (Bourdieu, 1971: 185). This position (which is non-reductionist) implies that cultural institutions and actors do not possess complete autonomy from fundamental processes of social production, yet they nevertheless operate according to practices inscribed with a distinctive cultural logic. Each intellectual field is structured in terms of 'themes and problems' which cannot be escaped, and according to this conception, is made up of contending intellectual alignments engaged in a struggle to 'impose their cultural norms on a larger or smaller area of the intellectual field' (Bourdieu, 1971: 175). At the centre of such conflicts is the incessant effort to impose an orthodoxy of interpretation upon cultural products or attitudes. The most relevant feature of this sociology for present purposes, then, is the struggle of classes, or fractions of classes for symbolic dominance.

The institutional arenas of the criminal justice process which act as a focus for the competing activities of state, para-state and non-official bodies variously relate to a number of overlapping intellectual fields concerning justice and the law, social order, criminality and imprisonment, and so forth. In this kind of framework, the supposedly 'pluralist' question of how various organizations contend for space in the media seems hardly inappropriate. Posing this scarcely necessitates our ignoring 'the implicit pre-set terms of the contest for influence' as some would have it (cf. Westergaard, 1977: 100). On the contrary, we can fully accept Bourdieu's view that the field of argument 'is demarcated against the background of the field of *doxa*, the aggregate of the presuppositions which the antagonists regard as self-evident and outside the area of argument' (1975: 34), which in turn is a function of concentrations of power.

One signal advantage of this position over that of Hall's conception of primary definition is the centrality of the notion of strategic action, of the idea that cultural actors compete using their various forms of capital as resources whereby they might in future increase their capital: 'transformations of the structure of the field are the product of strategies for conservation or subversion whose orientation and efficacy are derived from the properties of the positions occupied within the field by those who produce them' (Bourdieu, 1975: 27). Bourdieu divides positions in an intellectual field into the dominant (who pursue 'conservation strategies' in respect of institutions and publications in which they have a stake) and the new entrants (who either pursue 'succession strategies' of trying to stay ahead in the established game by limited innovation, or the much riskier 'subversion strategies' of tilting against the system).

Clearly, these are rather schematic notions of the strategies available and it is an open question whether in any given empirical analysis this categorization would exhaust the field. The main value of Bourdieu's schema, however, lies in conceiving of dominance as a continual struggle for position involving the mobilization of resources in a process of change. Putting it differently, *primary definition becomes an achievement rather than a wholly structurally predetermined outcome.* In this sense, sources may be seen as 'political entrepreneurs' in which an attempt is made to use available resources to maximum effect within a shifting framework of constraints (cf. Padioleau, 1982: 23–31). The aim of such political entrepreneurship is to affect the various audiences concerned with the policy process by means of influencing the political agenda, to shape the interpretation of current issues, and to respond to events in which a source may be somehow involved.

In any model, we require some ideal-typical yardstick as a starting-point for analysing actual behaviour. A plausible starting-point is to ask to what extent source action conforms to *an instrumental-utilitarian calculus* according to which information is tailored for media consumption. Such assumptions throw into relief sources' internal media strategies and their own criteria of effectiveness. I suggest that such an ideal type would involve at least the following conditions:

1 that the source has a well-defined message to communicate, framed in optimal terms capable of satisfying news values;
2 that the optimal locations for placing that particular message have been identified, as have the target audiences of the media outlets concerned;
3 that the preconditions for communicative 'success' have been assured so far as possible by, for instance, cultivating a sympathetic contact or fine-tuning the timing of a leak;
4 that opposition has been neutralized or anticipated (for example, by astute timing or discrediting).

In attempting to assess source strategies, the role played by resources is crucial. First, there is the extent to which any given source is *institutionalized.* In the context of the present study of crime, law and justice, the most advantageous locations in this respect are occupied by the apparatuses of the state (such as the Home Office and the Metropolitan Police) because these are a 'consecrated' locus of permanent activity for which the routine dissemination of official information is important. Within the same institutional field, in competition for space in the media are long-term pressure groups – such as the National Council for Civil Liberties (NCCL) and the Howard League for Penal Reform – which, however, do not enjoy fully secure material bases. At the other end of the continuum are the least institutionalized actors, arising from very specific conjunctural circumstances, consisting of *ad hoc* issue-oriented groups or groups whose base of support is narrow and weak (such as victim support groups and police monitoring groups). I have already noted the further complexity brought about by relatively autonomous state-funded groups and professional associations of state employees.

Second is the *financial base* available to a given actor. As media strategies have become increasingly perceived as important to political actors, the surplus within an organization directed towards symbolic media-oriented action becomes a crucial determinant of effectiveness. Oscar Gandy has pointed out that there is an economic relation between news sources and reporters:

> Information subsidies of journalists and other gatekeepers operate on the basis of simple economic rules. Journalists need news, however defined, and routine sources are the easiest way to gain that information
> . . . success in providing information subsidies to one's chosen targets is closely tied to the resources available to the subsidy giver. (1980: 106)

State organizations and large corporations are those best endowed with such information subsidies, and it may plausibly be argued that such advantages permit media coverage to be influenced significantly. Gandy proposes that we apply the tools of cost-benefit analysis in evaluating the 'productivity' of information subsidies. He also suggests that we 'plot the movement of subsidised information from its sources to a variety of targets at different levels of the policy system' in order to uncover 'the existence of *strategies* which characterize certain actors or classes of actors in the policy process' (1980): 113–14).

On the latter point there is surely sufficient evidence for saying that media strategies do exist without the need for any sort of inductive argument based upon a study of diffusion, although that would not be uninteresting in itself. As for applying cost-benefit analysis, despite its heuristic value, we would be well advised to be cautious. The reason for this is the difficulty of establishing unambiguous criteria of success in the realization of communicative goals, and indeed, in ranking such goals themselves. Even where, say, the Home Office and the police have invested in developing a media and public relations strategy, this has come up against internal budgetary limitations: monitoring is incomplete and so consequently is evaluation. While television may be seen as the most powerful medium, the most easily collected and assimilable material comes from the press.

Obviously, in the voluntary sector, with perennially shaky finance and dependence on low-paid idealists, the position is much more vulnerable. It then becomes sociologically very interesting to see what kind of investment is made in a media strategy and its related expectations. Criteria of success may be vaguer still, and targeting ambitions much more restricted. As with official sources, we may find a curious juxtaposition of strong beliefs in television's power coupled with actual ignorance of what is screened.

In the case of pressure groups, the question of competition arises in a further context. Where a given institutional arena has to be covered on the basis of scarce resources divided among competing groups in a 'social movement industry' strategies of 'product differentiation' become highly relevant (Zald and McCarthy, 1980). However, strategies of co-operation also become salient: where political goals coincide (as, for instance, in relation to a piece of legislation) a combination of several groups may occur in respect both of lobbying and media strategy.

The relations between social movements and media have been largely unexamined, but there is some evidence of the way in which media coverage may exaggerate existing internal contradictions. Todd Gitlin (1980) has analysed the anti-Vietnam War campaign in the United States using a model of movement media interaction, drawing attention to the way in which the media developed frameworks of interpretation of the New Left which were continually adjusted. He has demonstrated the impact the media had on the internal workings of the student left, in particular how in seeking sources they made celebrities out of unknowns which in turn fed back into leadership struggles with destabilizing effects. Gitlin also analysed how the New Left entertained illusions about the ways in which their media strategies might affect the political agenda.

A further resource is *cultural capital* in the shape of legitimacy, authoritativeness, respectability and the contacts which these bring. Such cultural capital derives from the location a source has in the institutional field. The credibility factor plainly links in directly to the perception of sources within the media and the rules of thumb for handling them. Official sources may not always have to be believed, but they do have to be taken seriously. Non-official sources therefore have to acquire credibility by dint of quite developed media strategies, in which the aura of expertise is plainly important. Such institutional questions link in directly to questions of how various forms of discourse are used by sources in targeting their messages.

These are some of the considerations relevant for a model of source activity. At root, what makes such an investigation worth while is the fact that it yields sociologically interesting results. Let me offer some brief examples. Anthony Giddens makes much of the point that 'human beings reflexively monitor their conduct via the knowledge they have of the circumstances of their activity' (1979: 254). The activity of sources, within a context of unequal competition for access, conforms well to this observation. There has been a developing process of source sophistication. For instance, in the case of pressure groups, lessons have been learned from the example of the Child Poverty Action Group's effective media strategy and have been applied in the criminal justice area. Groups may go in for competitive profiling: for instance, HM Customs deliberately competing for television coverage with the police, and the Prison Officers self-consciously changing their profile by learning from others' mistakes. A second instance of such reflexivity concerns the ways in which the *anticipated* strategies of others are incorporated into on-going media strategies: the Home Office, for instance, will engage in second-guessing NCCL, a process which raises further questions about the nature of primary definition. Linked to this is the way in which *responses* to others' interventions in the field are part of some source strategies, with attempted control over timing being particularly important. Nor is it necessarily the case that all strategies are aimed at the public in general. Some messages may be as much private as public, as is well brought out by Sigal (1973: ch. 7) in his discussion of 'informational press manoeuvres'. An example from our own study is the case of HM Customs showing its mettle (via television) to the Home Office as part of an argument for extra resources.

Concluding remarks

The above are merely a few synoptic observations about some of the things to be learned about source strategies. Such work inevitably takes us into broader questions about the nature of information management in society by a variety of groups in conditions of unequal power and therefore unequal access to systems of inform-ation production and distribution. This type of investigation cannot avoid being focused on the apparatuses of the state, which do, as theorists of dominance rightly say, enjoy privileged access to the media. However, that does not mean that we should ignore the activities of other sources as this unnecessarily deprives us of empirical knowledge of how the battle for access is conducted. For those who consider this concern an arid exercise in micro-politics, one can only observe – not least in the increasingly censorious British context – that the conditions of survival of alternatives are crucial to the survival of any public sphere at all.

I would further like to suggest that a technicist obsession with the workings of the 'information society' that exclusively gives privilege to economics and formal legal questions of regulation simply will not take our understanding far enough. A wider political sociology of information seems ever more necessary when posing essential questions today about, *inter alia*, official secrecy, censorship, propaganda, and the political imperatives that lie behind the transformation of information and media law with such a potentially far-reaching impact on source-media relations.

Notes

This chapter draws on research on 'Crime, Law and Justice in the Media' funded by the Economic and Social Research Council (UK) in its 'Crime and Criminal Justice System' initiative, reference number E0625 0013. Prior to the ESRC's Cambridge workshop, earlier versions were presented at the annual meeting of Section 'N' (Sociology) of the British Association for the Advancement of Science held at The Queen's University, Belfast in August 1987 and at a meeting of the Media Association of Ireland held at University College, Dublin, in March 1988. I am grateful to the respective chairmen of those meetings, John Eldridge and Richard Pine, for their invitations to speak and to the participants for their many helpful comments. My thanks go too to my regular interlocutors, Howard Tumber and Graham Murdock, for their valuable suggestions and stimulus and also to Marjorie Ferguson and Lcc Sigal for their supportive criticism of the previous draft.

1   The need for such a theoretical exercise has become clear in the course of studying a wide range of competing actors in the criminal justice field, in particular in considering the ways in which they organize themselves in order to have an impact on the media. The failure of current media sociology to deal with this has increasingly obliged me to think beyond existing paradigms.

2   In personal correspondence reacting to this chapter, Herbert Gans notes: 'Emphasizing the role of sources is the best way, or perhaps the only one, to connect the study of journalism to the larger society' (22 July 1988).

3   The reappraisal of pluralism ranges well beyond the concerns of this chapter and shortage of space precludes any further discussion. Cf., however, Crouch (1983) for an evaluation of the politics of current debate and Hirst (1987) for a searching re-analysis of some classic writing.

4   Nor has Hall altered it almost a decade on. In the opening essay in a critical collection aimed at giving an 'adequate understanding' of media power to those at the receiving end, he has put the argument in a less qualified, and therefore more revealing way:

> Some things, people, events, relationships *always* get represented: always centre-stage, always in the position to define, to set the agenda, to establish the terms of the conversation. Some others sometimes get represented – but always at the margin, always responding to a question whose terms and conditions have been defined elsewhere: never 'centred'. Still others are always 'represented' only by their eloquent absence, their silences: or refracted through the glance or the gaze of others. (Hall, 1986: 9)

Although Hall goes on to deny that we should draw conclusions about the monolithic nature of the media system, it is hard to resist the temptation.

5

Political Communication and Citizenship: The Media and Democracy in an Inegalitarian Social Order

Peter Golding

Questions about the just and effective workings of the democratic process may sometimes seem rather remote from the mundane enquiries of much research into mass communication. Yet behind much of the empirical work of media researchers lie fundamental questions about the role of communications institutions in enabling industrial democracies to achieve their own idealized image. The critical results of such enquiries often place research at odds with the more Panglossian or optimistic of practitioners. In the more simplistic and Utopian formulations of the role of the media democracy is like a political supermarket, in which customer-voters wander from counter to counter, assessing the relative attractions and prices of the policies on offer before taking their well-informed selection to the electoral check-out. The media play the part of consumer watch-dog, providing the means for the well-informed citizen to play his or her role to the full.

This conception has been at the heart of philosophy and ambition in public service broadcasting institutions. It was expressed best, if somewhat portentously, in the memoirs of Charles Curran, a distinguished Director-General of the BBC in the 1970s. As he wrote,

> The underlying assumption of the BBC is that of liberal democracy. . . . Broadcasters have a responsibility, therefore, to provide a rationally based and balanced service of news which will enable adult people to make basic judgements about public policy in their capacity as voting citizens of a democracy . . . the only practical guideline is to try and ensure that every view which is likely to have a lasting effect on public thinking is at some time reflected in the public debate on the air about any particular subject. (C. Curran, 1979: 106, 115)

This is a proud and large ambition. Yet research has time and again punctured the balloon of usually decent, though occasionally insincere, political posturings of this kind. The integrity of major figures like Curran is not in doubt. But the accumulated evidence of decades of research cannot all be dismissed as the pre-judged rantings of politically motivated academic dissidents, or the obscurantist negativism of an intelligentsia at odds with the more favoured world of the media professionals. The inadequacies of mediated information have been exhaustively catalogued by media research. However defensive or aggressive the response of media professionals, and however inflated the sometimes premature or even immature claims of researchers, there can be no serious doubt that such sources as news media significantly and consistently provide a partial and coherently weighted account of many areas of social and political life, whether of crime (Chibnall, 1977; Hall et al., 1978), welfare (Golding and Middleton, 1982), industrial relations (Glasgow University Media Group, 1976, 1980), terrorism (Schlesinger et al., 1983), race (Hartmann and Husband, 1973), local government (Goldsmiths' Media Research Group, 1987), or a range of other areas familiar to researchers in this field. This goes way beyond the arithmetic biases of electoral campaign coverage to cast fundamental doubt on the propositions of such major figures as Charles Curran.

The problem remains, however, to explain and make sense of such debates in a wider context. In this chapter I wish, first, to outline two approaches to this issue which I would assert to be, in different respects, fundamentally flawed. The first of these focuses on texts, and leans to an essentialism in its critique of the political character of media communications. The second leans to a technological determinism in seeing a wholesale solution to the failings of political communications in the promises of new technologies. Second, I wish to suggest that analysis of information institutions beyond the media, not least in government, need examination more fully to understand those failings, which in turn need to be set in the context of a more extensive analysis of inequalities of access to information. Finally, I wish to propose the concept of citizenship as a key element in the development of a more adequate analysis of the political role of communications institutions and processes.

Texts and technology: from essentialism to video-Utopia

In assessing the character of political communication, research has departed along two detours, neither of which have been ultimately productive in explaining or analysing political change. One broad approach is concerned to focus on texts–visual, written or filmic – in an attempt to discern the linguistic or cultural determinations exerted by artefacts on their consumers. This concern with symbolic rather than with material barriers to social and political behaviour and interaction is, of course, the distinguishing mark of cultural studies, and the root of much dissatisfaction with more traditional styles of structural sociology. It has been a powerful force within media studies, particularly in Britain.

One forceful and provocative recent attempt to sharpen this focus on symbolic barriers is provided by Fiske (1987). Fiske argues that there are two simultaneously operating spheres within which cultural entities circulate; the cultural economy and the fiscal economy. These two work separately and in different ways. The purpose of this distinction is to proclaim and demonstrate the continuing vitality of audience resistance, people making rather than just taking meaning, constructively opposing and withstanding the apparent persuasive or informative message of mediated symbols. This theme, of the interaction of active audiences with polysemic messages, has been a leitmotif of much work in the cultural studies tradition, and where empirically applied, has provided a much-needed corrective to the simplicities of some other traditions.

Nonetheless there are problems in maintaining this view. To support his notion of twin economies Fiske has to argue that resistance also comes in two categories, 'the power to construct meanings, pleasures, and social identities, and the power to construct a socioeconomic system' (1987: 316). The former, which he terms 'semiotic power', is the power domain within which popular culture mainly works. This large claim is in turn based on the presumption that audiences as makers of meaning in the cultural economy are not disadvantaged.

> This is partly due to the absence of any direct sign of their (subordinate) role in the financial economy which liberates them from its contraints – there is no exchange of money at the point of sale/consumption, and no direct relationship between the price paid and the amount consumed, people can consume as much as they wish and what they wish, without the restriction of what they are able to afford. (Fiske, 1987: 313)

Such a claim simply will not stand up to empirical scrutiny, as a brief illustration using data from Britain will demonstrate. In particular, it ignores the massive inequalities of access to cultural goods created by what Fiske rather cavalierly places on one side as the financial economy.

In booming Britain there is likely to be 'a steady growth in personal disposable incomes in the 1990s. The real spending power of the employed labour force in particular will grow as wages rise faster than prices' (Hamil and O'Neill, 1986: 313). That view from the Henley forecasting centre must be amplified by the undoubted and dramatic widening of the gap between both the employed and unemployed, and between the well-paid and those in low-income and often insecure or part-time employment. In 1984–85, the most recent year for which figures are available, the top 10 per cent received 26.5 per cent of net incomes, the bottom 10 per cent received 2.7 per cent of the same cake. Recent fiscal changes will have widened this gap (*Economic Trends*, November 1987: 94). The significance of this is its impact on access to cultural goods whose availability is increasingly determined by the market and the price mechanism. An examination of existing patterns of consumption makes this point clearly.

Table 1 *Average weekly household expenditure on service as a percentage of all household expenditure*

Year	%
1953/54	9.5
1960	8.9
1980	10.8
1986	12.9

Source: Family Expenditure Survey 1986, Department of Employment, 1987, Table 8

Household expenditure on services generally has been increasing steadily since the ending of post-war austerity, as shown in Table 1. This rise, however, has been disproportionately enjoyed by different groups in the population. As Table 2 shows, the value of services enjoyed by groups in the highest-income groups is several times higher than that available to lower income groups.

Table 2 *Expenditure on services by income quintiles, 1986*

Income group	Household weekly expenditure (£)
Top fifth	54.17
Second fifth	27.34
Third fifth	19.34
Fourth fifth	11.59
Bottom fifth	7.04

Sources: Family Expenditure Survey 1986, Table 6

We can see the significance of this by looking at the amount spent by different income groups on services in general and on communications resources in particular. Such analyses demonstrate the common pattern that the gradient for essentials, like food, is less steep than for services. The lower-income households consequently spend a far higher proportion of their incomes on essentials like food, housing, and clothes than do higher-income groups. In turn this leaves less disposable income for other categories of expenditure. The gradient of differential expenditure on categories like TV and video equipment, or publications, is therefore particularly steep, the highest-income groups spending very considerably more than low-income groups. The exception is in TV rental and licence fees, where the flat rate provides for a relatively equal spread of consumption. Cinema attendance is, of course, virtually irrelevant for all groups (see Table 3).

Table 3   *Average weekly expenditure of illustrative income groups on selected goods and services, 1986*

Household weekly income (£)	Average weekly expenditure (£) on					
	Services	Food	TV/video/audio equipment	Books/ nprs/mags	Cinema	TV/video lic./rent
80–100	9.46	24.02	1.19	1.85	0.04	1.66
150–175	19.82	32.32	2.82	2.49	0.09	2.16
200–225	19.87	35.68	3.71	2.55	0.07	2.01
275–325	27.99	43.51	4.82	3.27	0.14	2.33
over 550	73.75	71.94	11.59	5.95	0.28	2.50
All	23.89	35.64	3.37	2.79	0.10	1.98

Source: Family Expenditure Survey 1986, calculated from Table 5

The consequence of this pattern of economically differentiated access to media goods is demonstrated in Table 4. This shows ownership of basic communications resources among different income groups. Although television is almost universally available, albeit with varying degrees of technical sophistication and multiple ownership, even such a basic resource as the telephone is far from comprehensively available. As I have argued elsewhere in joint work with Graham Murdock (Golding and Murdock, 1986), those households without a telephone are disproportionately those whose alternative means of mobility and communication are most truncated. In 1986 36 per cent of low-income pensioner households lacked a telephone, as did 41 per cent of one-adult households with a single

Table 4   *Ownership of communications hardware among households in different income groups, 1986*

Household weekly income (£)	Percentage owning			
	TV	Phone	Video	Home computer
0–45	87.9	47.8	5.7	1.3
46–60	94.0	54.7	9.0	2.2
61–80	96.9	67.4	12.6	3.3
81–100	97.0	72.9	14.3	4.6
101–125	98.1	76.7	21.2	7.6
126–150	97.2	78.0	29.8	9.7
151–175	97.9	76.3	31.7	9.6
176–200	98.1	85.5	35.2	11.4
200–225	98.5	84.9	42.3	17.4
226–250	97.5	87.3	43.5	21.2
251–275	97.5	88.5	47.5	20.4
276–325	98.7	93.7	54.2	22.8
326–375	98.0	94.1	56.5	26.5
376–450	98.9	96.6	59.7	29.4
451–550	98.8	97.3	64.5	32.1
over 550	98.4	97.3	64.5	32.1
All	97.1	80.9	36.3	15.1

Source: Family Expenditure Survey, 1986, calculated from Table 3

child (*Employment Gazette*, 1987). The rapid growth in video ownership has been similarly unequal, as has the ownership of home computers (see Table 4).

Future trends in this pattern of unequal access are unlikely to follow the diffusion pattern of earlier 'white' goods such as cookers, washing machines or freezers, for three reasons. First, these goods became more widely owned in a period of economic boom, not now likely to be replicated, at least for a significant proportion of the population. Second, in the nature of communications hardware their ownership provides access to cumulative other goods in the communications market place, requiring additional and recurrent expenditure on software, add-ons, or the means of relating the various technologies to one another (Golding and Murdock, 1986). Third, the rapid development of new technologies or of alternative storage or retrieval hardware makes purchase of such goods a high-risk act of consumption, contemplated only by those for whom the costs of a mistaken reading of the technological winds will not prove irretrievable.

The Peacock Report on the financing of television in Britain provided a reasonably reliable estimate of the average expenditure pattern, at 1986 prices, of a 'basket' of media goods. This included newspapers, basic cable services, TV and video. Using and adapting this figure I have shown, in Table 5, the proportion of average weekly expenditure that this figure would comprise among different income groups.

Table 5   *Potential media expenditure as a proportion of household expenditure for different groups, 1986*

Income group	Average weekly expenditure (£)	Media expenditure as proportion (%)
Lowest fifth	62.90	25.7
Middle three-fifths	170.22	9.5
Top fifth	351.53	4.6

Sources: Household expenditure figures calculated from advance Family Expenditure Survey figures in *Employment Gazette*, Dec. 1987: 594; media expenditure calculated from figures given in Peacock Report (1986: Table 6.8, p. 53)

The difference between top and bottom is stark. Entrance to the new media playground is relatively cheap for the well-to-do, a small adjustment in existing spending patterns simply accommodated. For the poor the price is a sharp calculation of opportunity cost, access to communication goods jostling uncomfortably with the mundane arithmetic of food, housing, clothing and fuel. We have moved a long way from Fiske's cavalier claim that 'people can consume as much as they wish and what they wish' since 'there is no direct relationship between the price paid and the amount consumed' (Fiske, 1987: 313).

There is a great deal more to be done to develop sensitive and meaningful measures of the consumer economy for cultural and communication goods. But clearly, even on the limited evidence now available, these goods sharply differentiate between groups unequally located in the market economy. The implications for political communication are, or should be, obvious. Access to information is in a state somewhat removed from Millsian democratic ideals.

To give analytical priority to the barriers of symbol and cultural exchange can be an empirical aberration in an approach such as that just described. In the work of some recently influential theorists it becomes celebrated and made axiomatic. A most notable example is in the largely impenetrable nostrums of Baudrillard. There is inherent in any paradigm wedded to the study of texts a loose idealism, eliding the mundane mechanics of social structures and inegalitarian patterns of human interaction. However, it is the contention of some writers such as Baudrillard that this is a reflection of the world as now constituted. The growth of information systems, he contends, has evaporated meaning, providing instead 'a gigantic process of simulation' (Baudrillard, 1983: 98). Extending and distorting McLuhan, 'the medium and the real are now in a single nebulous state whose truth is undecipherable' (1983: 103).

This logic, if such it is, claiming that 'TV is the world', is lucidly summarized by one of Baudrillard's followers thus:

> the dominant mode of social power is no longer that of political economy (of production) but that of the operational structures of codes; within which commodity consumption is always and already 'programmed' as the spectacle. Accordingly, the functioning social logic has passed from commodity to sign, and the exploitation of social labour has been displaced by the excessive production of meaning and information. Hence the 'theoretical base' of the system of power has been transferred from Marxist political economy to structuralist semiology, information theory, and cybernetics. (Kuan-Hsing Chen, 1987: 72–3)

There are a number of claims, outrageous or absurd by turn, in this useful summary. The key observation in the context of this chapter is the axiomatic elevation of sign systems to the summit of cultural analysis. In part, this draws oddly on the notion of an information society, the undue translation of superficial statistics about the volume of bits of paper in the world or their electronic or photonic equivalent into grand summations of the state of the human condition. In fact, shifts in the occupational order have been, in the main, within industrial sectors rather than because of the growth of new, especially service, industries (see, for example, Gershuny, 1983: ch. 7). In part, it is a view which resonates with a faintly old-fashioned phenomenological rhetoric, and in its idealism has been, not altogether surprisingly, linked to right-wing political positions fairly readily (Kellner, 1987).

A recent example of the influence of this work is in the extensive survey of disordered capitalism provided by Lash and Urry (1987). Seeking to explicate the conditions which provide for the rise and dominance of 'post-modernism' they follow Bourdieu (though perhaps not far enough) in asserting the consumption of goods for their symbolic power. One is tempted to resurrect Lockwood's famous acerbic aside in the Affluent Worker studies that 'It is in any case sociology gone mad to assume that because people want goods of this kind they always want them as status symbols. A washing machine is a washing machine is a washing machine' (Lockwood, 1960: 253). There is something faintly cheering about such gritty materialism which contrasts sharply with many who prioritize the symbolic. Lash and Urry, for example, though far from culturally deterministic, follow Baudrillard explicitly along a number of byways, agreeing with

> the importance of the sphere of consumption for the constitution of individual and collective identity; with the idea of post-industrial domination through communications in the sphere of production; with the idea that in contemporary capitalism what is largely produced – in the media, a large part of the service sector, in parts of the public sector – consists of communication and information. (Lash and Urry, 1987: 289)

There are several fallacies which could be dissected here. The central thesis that consumption is of images and not of commodities is no more true of the modern era than of others. The thesis mistakes the form for the structure. It is the ad-man's view of society. But the world of work and consumption are both ever and always productive of images, symbols and contested bodies of iconography. That these are recorded and transmitted in more obvious profusion now is not an indication of a new order; this is to misread the tradition of analyses from Veblen to Bourdieu which these authors would claim as ancestry.

In both traditions of work analysed, using first Fiske and then Baudrillard, the realm of the symbolic is promoted to an invalid central position in the analytical explanation of the failings of political communication. This leans very much to an essentialism, eliding the more complex of social processes in which texts operate. The second area of work which I wish to examine here concedes the structural defects of present communications institutions and practices, but sees their rectification as the inevitable outcome of wise usage of the new communication technologies. What I term 'techno-Utopia' is analysis based on the presumption that a new political order of a majestic and, indeed, Athenian perfection can be borne by new communication technologies.

Some recent American research has moved rapidly along these lines, providing an empirical gloss to the visionary rhetoric of many commentaries on the new information age. Hollander, for example, suggests that video democracy will offer the opportunity to 'dispel voter apathy; to jettison the perils of special interests; to involve the citizen to an extent never before believed possible' (1985: 2–3). This will 'merge the spirit of ancient Athens with the technologies of the twenty-first century – Pericles with digital transmission' (1985: 3). The transformation of politics into direct democracy is exemplified, he argues, by the various experiments in interactive video, including the original QUBE system in Columbus (where the most popular request was for repeat showing of the feature film *Captain Lust*). Direct voting in local elections or referenda are but the first of new opportunities for electronic participation so that the citizen 'becomes filled with the joy of accomplishment and feeling of belonging' (1985: 136).

Streams of technological doxology in this style do not pass unquestioned. Arterton (1987), for example, offers a more sober assessment of the potential and achievements of 'teledemocracy'. As he concludes,

> any mechanism of communication that costs money to use will necessarily produce inequalities of access among social and economic groups. When these media become conveyors of political participation, differential access, both as to speakers and listeners, can become unduly restrictive from the viewpoint of a democracy. . . . Teledemocracy cannot be justified by rhetoric that suggests 'the people' are going to be empowered by technology. (Arterton, 1987: 203)

Despite such cautionary qualifications, however, research has too often been invited to celebrate rather than to construct a critique of the potential of new communications technologies. Curiously, such optimism mirrors the stark pessimism in Gerbner's work. In both the crucial focus on the technology produces a strangely truncated view of politics. For Gerbner,

> Television has taken the place of the medieval church in the historic nexus of power. Today it is not church and state but television and state that govern in an uneasy relationship of mutual dependence and tension. Television has also replaced political parties as the chief means of communication between leaders and voters. (Gerbner, 1986: 1)

Wober and Gunter have usefully catalogued many of the empirical doubts about Gerbner's work in other fields, and, reviewing empirical work on political 'effects' come to the predictable though sensible conclusion that 'evidence for coherent inculcation of particular ideologies is [not very] widely supported or convincing' (1988: 87).

Such debates seem to suffer from a restricted vision of the extent of the political, too often operationalized as the vote, the legislature, the referendum. Few voting studies offer the sophistication of such work as that in Himmelweit et al. (1985), where at least the social action being studied is explicitly defined by the duration and scope of election campaigns. But in Britain voting turn-out has persistently declined throughout the post-war period (from 84 per cent in 1951 to 73 per cent in 1983), and, as Crewe (1987) noted in assessing the 1987 election, 'Britain's most expensive, media-saturated campaign, appears to have had the smallest net impact on party support for decades'. In the media-saturated 1988 presidential election in the

United States voter turn-out only just crept above the 50 per cent mark. It is not clear, therefore, that this limited range of political behaviour offers the most profitable terrain for fundamental enquiry into the dynamics of political communication.

The obsession with techno-Utopia suffers, then, from two key deficiencies. On the one hand, the focus on technology produces a research agenda couched in the unreal terms of optimism which assert that what is possible is also probable and almost certainly desirable. On the other hand, the terrain of the political remains contained within the narrowest of boundaries, defined by political behaviour in electoral or party political terms.

It becomes necessary to move beyond the radical pessimism of much research which merely defines the political contribution of communications media as deficient or corrupt, and beyond the technological optimism which is its counterpoint. The further stage of explaining this contribution in relation to wider social processes requires a return to some of the fundamental questions of social and political research. In illustrating this claim I turn first to those sources from which media derive much of their material, and then briefly consider the notion of information inequality which emerges from the kind of data provided above on access to information resources.

From sources to audiences – the wider picture

In Britain, at least over the last few years, one has learnt to live with an administration that shows signs of not trusting its public. In this context one would have to take account of such developments as increasing secrecy in government departments, statutory controls over information provision and distribution by local government, and various aspects of the new legal framework for education. The relationship between the state and the media would seem to occupy a prominent position in this unattractive tableau, but has rarely been the focus for research concerns (see Golding, 1986a).

Not least among the developments in state information management is the growing tendency to the professional and positive presentation of government views via the media to the public. Sins of omission give way to a public relations industry of rapidly increasing dimensions. A major effort is now sustained by government in the provision of information. Much of this is, of course, the innocent provision of essential and pragmatic information to client or interested groups in the population. But there is more here than mere administration. Such contentious initiatives as privatization have been supported by massive promotional programmes; £71.6

million has been spent on corporate advertising, offer for sale advertisements, and agency fees for the nine major privatizations since 1979 (HC Hansard 18 Jan. 1988 WA Col. 473). As Hillyard and Percy-Smith suggest,

> A total of 1,200 civil servants are involved in the preparation and dissemination of official information. Departmental press releases are frequently treated uncritically as 'fact' by journalists who do not challenge the official version of events and are therefore used as channels for state propaganda. Because the state has a large contingent of press and information officers and considerable resources at its disposal which may not be available to other groups, it is well placed to feed the media with 'news' that is heavily biased in its favour. (1988: 125)

Franklin has noted that by 1987 the total government budget for advertising and information services had toppled Unilever from first place among Britain's advertisers (Franklin, 1988). Table 6 charts the scale of this exercise in British government public relations.

Table 6 *Budgets and staff establishments of government departments for public relations and information work, 1987/88*

Department	PR and info staff	Budget for PR and info (£m)
Central Office of Information	804	104
Trade and Industry	51	13.34
Health and Social Security	68	52.8
Energy	11	3.01
Northern Ireland Office	47	3.37
Environment	47	4.6
Education and Science	38	4.0
Agriculture and Fisheries	32	3.0
Employment	60	12.5
Manpower Services Commission	61.5	33.4
Cabinet Office	18	0.5
Treasury	11	0.63
Transport	17	5.47
Defence	215	1.77[1]
Foreign Office	19.5	0.55

Figures for PR and Information have been combined; in many cases one or other of these is the major part or even the whole of the total. Plus £5.55m for the Services.
Sources: Collated from a series of Hansard parliamentary written answers, vols. 124–8; see also Franklin (1988)

Analytically, how do we make sense of such trends in the delivery of managed information and its consumption by a population increasingly divided by the growth of economic inequality? Two areas of research which address these issues are work on 'information gaps', and the more general study of 'agenda-setting'. Extensive reviews of both these areas exist elsewhere, occurring regularly in such publications as the annual *Mass Communication Review Yearbook*, for example, and it is not my purpose here to duplicate these bibliographical surveys. None the less, one or two points should be made.

The notion of the information gap is inevitably simple, suggesting that the educationally and socio-economically advantaged are able to enhance their advantages via communications media, whose distribution and consumption are such as to ensure that such social division widen (Gaziano, 1983; Sauerberg, 1986). The term is variably applied to knowledge or information, but the general concept is consistent. A major industry of micro-studies has followed the original work of Tichenor et al. (1970) in charting the precise mechanics, timing and demographic niceties of this process. Inevitably veering to the positivist at times, frequently unimaginative in conceptualization, none the less this is a concept that has encapsulated a simple truth, and has focused research attention on a central dynamic of political communication processes.

Weaknesses in the field tend to follow from the unduly social-psychological conception of the mechanism by which the process occurs. Thus information gaps are seen to be due to the inability of lower socio-economic groups to absorb new material, rather than to the fabric of social institutions which make differentially available a sharply demarcated universe of symbols and interpretative frames. Equally, much of the research focuses on educational attainment as the key mediating variable, arising from an early and patronizing concern to root out the difficulties of the 'chronic know-nothings' (Hyman and Sheatsley, 1947). Not for the first time research finds itself colluding with victim-blaming (Dervin, 1980). None the less, the correlation between structures of material and cultural disadvantage which lies at the core of research into the knowledge gap deserves further elaboration and investigation; it is a mine that is far from exhausted, even if rather new veins need opening up.

Agenda-setting is similarly useful as an essentially simple concept that can too easily get lost in an avalanche of micro-studies of technically fascinating detail but conceptually numbing unoriginality. That the media set limits of political vision and discourse has become a starting-point for work in a variety of analytical styles. Essentially a description of a field of audience studies, agenda-setting research has suffered from an overdose of empirical attempts to refine understanding of the mechanics – the time-lag, degrees of definition and so on – of the agenda-setting process. 'Agenda-generating', as Himmelweit et al. term it (1985: 228) has been less well researched, despite the work of such writers as Oscar Gandy (1982). The task remains, then, to examine in more concrete detail the processes by which those with privileged access to sources of information distribution and construction 'work' – ideologically, politically, socially. Our understanding of those elite processes is primitive and under-explored, and much more work is needed to address the issues of agenda-building in the locales of powerful message and ideology creation which prefigure mediation through the communicative apparatus.

Tapping the mediation of political communication – evaluative and interpretative dimensions

Part of the task required is an examination of the terms by which political initiatives are constructed and conveyed. In lay terms the critique of political information is about bias, persuasion or evasion. More analytically, the research process has typically described in terms of categories the content of media accounts. Always the problem is to convey the adequacy or otherwise of this account calibrated against some 'extra-media' reality – itself the most exasperating and elusive of constructs.

The concern, implicitly if not explicitly, is to ascertain one particular vector of the content: evaluation. This is, however, but one dimension. There is another vector in the content; namely, the interpretative dimension. This distinction can be made clearer. The *evaluative* dimension addresses the question of whether the media account is pro or anti the policy issue or matter being described, the normal question being asked in posing questions of partisanship or bias. In empirical terms this question makes an early appearance in attempts to develop evaluation assertion analysis. The *interpretative* dimension asks what aspects of the policy are broadcast into the public domain, what is the issue seen to be about. This dimension can introduce indirect evaluation by linking a policy with preset responses to key issues. For example, as I have attempted to suggest in earlier work (Golding and Middleton, 1982), news and other accounts of social security work to produce a hostile response by linking descriptive and narrative chronicles of policy development to well-rooted folk myths, and to notions of work, laziness and dependence, rather than to issues of redistribution and collective responsibility.

The point being illustrated is that it is the more general frame of reference into which this policy initiative is translated that determines its reception, lodging it into a predetermined response set more permanently located in the political culture. For example, in news about welfare, if the issue is about regressivity and distribution, then responses are along familiar left–right lines. If the interpretation yields a translation into the criminality issue, then other chords are struck. I do not wish here to press one or other of these analyses, merely to suggest that this approach, seeking the interpretative rather than merely the evaluative dimension of political communications can produce at the very least suggestive analyses moving beyond the descriptive.

The 'so-what' question: citizenship and political communications

At the heart of political communication research must be enquiry into the contribution of information flows and media institutions to the exercise of democracy. I wish to suggest that this empirical concern is best encapsulated in the concept of citizenship. To what degree and in what ways are people denied access to necessary information and imagery to allow full and equal participation in the social order? Indeed this has more general application in the wider field of media studies, and can reasonably be argued ethically to underpin the purpose of much social research. I have reviewed earlier the extensive range of media research demonstrating the systematic deficiencies of media communications in providing an adequate account of social and political process (see Golding and Elliott, 1979: ch. 8). But such research illuminates only half the issue, exposing the failings of mediated barriers but leaving unexplored the painful and damaging effects of socio-economic barriers to political communications as a resource for citizenship.

Such a postulate requires that we reconceive audiences as citizens, confronted by two sets of barriers denying or qualifying full citizenship. The first set of barriers is largely socio-economic, erecting via demographic determinants (like race or gender) or economic determinants (employment and income) the denial of resources allowing for full participation in the social and cultural process (Golding, 1986b). The second set of barriers is mediated, and denies to all the full and adequate range of imagery and information assumed by ideal definitions of citizenship. Unlike Fiske's account, described earlier, these two are not distinct but intimately related, and compound rather than complement each other.

The concept of citizenship finds its most extensive and influential expression in the seminal work of T.H. Marshall. Arguing historically, Marshall (1963) suggests that citizenship, 'full membership of a community', evolves through three stages, corresponding to three aspects of citizenship. The civil element, comprising the individualistic freedoms of speech, property rights and contract, evolves first, largely in the eighteenth century. Political citizenship, the right to participate in the exercise of political power, crucially arrives for Marshall with the 1918 Act providing male universal suffrage in Britain. Social citizenship, the product of more recent progress, includes the miscellaneous range of provisions for economic security and welfare which Marshall feels to have been adequately bestowed by post-war developments.

Clearly there is much to contest in this account. However, at the core of the concept are important and pertinent insights. While complacent at the arrival of what he perceived to be an essentially socialist system of social organization, Marshall famously notes that it 'is clear that in the twentieth century citizenship and the capitalist class system have been at war' (1963: 87). Marshall, of course, retired from the scene before that war was to be re-engaged with such renewed vigour in the 1980s. The structure of available information and the inegalitarian distribution of imagery and data are the backdrop to this war, since 'what matters to the citizen is the superstructure of legitimate expectations' (1963: 103), a phrase calling to mind the similar observation by C. Wright Mills that the media are in the business of supplying 'master symbols of legitimation'.

Class structure, then, and the twin barriers to participation that I have outlined, are most powerfully construed as impediments to citizenship. That communicative competence and action, and the resources required to exercise them, are requisites for citizenship has been recognized by many writers (notably, of course, by Habermas, for example, 1979; for an illuminating discussion see Garnham, 1986). As Roche has recently pointed out, they are

> central to any conception of the social element of citizenship, particularly in contemporary conditions of social change towards social formations in which education and leisure will assume increasing importance in social life. . . . Politics of and policies for such things as free speech, access to information, access to education, mass communications etc. can be seen as crucial practical dimensions of citizenship and of social citizenship in particular. (1987: 380–1)

Conjoint with our understanding of citizenship is our definition of the sphere of the public. The fluctuating fortunes and uncertain future of public service broadcasting urgently require from research something rather more considered than we have been thus far able to provide, at least in disentangling the purposes of regulation from the bases of finance. How far public conceptions of broadcasting locate communications in an ideological field akin to education or health remains unexplored. We urgently require a philosophy of communications which locates and understands the role of communications processes and institutions in the public sphere. What is the nature of the goods produced by broadcasting and other communications services? Without the answer to that question the response to much communication research must indeed be 'So what?'

Conclusion

The lamentable but inevitable conclusion that must be drawn from research over the past couple of decades is that the communications media have failed democracy. If our ideal but none the less worthy intention is that citizens should be afforded an opportunity adequately to inform themselves about social and political process, then the media as currently constituted do rather less than serve this need. Why this should be so and how it arises are central to the concerns of research into political communications. In order to advance the contribution of research to these debates I have suggested that the key concept of citizenship distils the essential questions and concerns we should address.

This chapter has advanced essentially two arguments, one methodological, the other conceptual. My first argument has been to suggest that an undue emphasis on symbolic and cultural barriers or on technological opportunities will divert attention from what remain crucial barriers of access to communications and information erected by structures of social and economic inequality. We lack adequate or sensitive measures of the links between cultural opportunity and structures of socio-economic distribution, and mapping and calibrating these links remains an urgent task for research. The second point made is conceptual, a claim for the resurrection of the concept of citizenship as a critical bench-mark of enquiry in communication research. The partial and attentuated citizenship imposed by information poverty casts as large a shadow over social theory as any of the grand and ambitious questions posed by classic social science. The current failings and structured deficiencies of mass communications mean that at a local and national level our democracy puts its citizens in blinkers. Removing the mask is as much an urgent task for research as it is for political action.

6

Elections, the Media and the Modern Publicity Process

Jay G. Blumler

This chapter discusses an imperative that is increasingly shaping the more overtly political face of public communication in many competitive democracies. Curiously, though widely acknowledged at a certain level of awareness, this imperative is still intellectually neglected, lacking that form of focused and explicit definition which, when framed, could serve to identify significant trends and questions for research. Such neglect may explain why much current scholarship in political communication appears at one and the same time up to date but not very interesting. Absorption of the missing element might help to refresh it.

This thesis is developed in what follows, through first, a brief review of recent influences on election and political communication analysis; second, consideration of a process that is central to the making of much modern political publicity (though varying in its penetration into differently organized polities); and third, specification of certain research priorities that flow from the analysis.

Political communication research so far

It may seem churlish to sound even a faint note of disappointment over the present state of the art of research in political communication. Compared with the doldrums in which the study of mass media in politics seemed stalled in the 1940s to the 1960s, when the 'limited effects' model dominated, the field today is much invigorated.

In a spirit of counting our blessings, it could be pointed out that leading researchers have been quite responsive to relevant tides of social, political and communication change. Although much work still focuses (too narrowly, some would argue) on election campaigns, media scholars of otherwise quite diverse persuasions have in fact accepted a big expansion of the boundaries of 'the political'. The notion, for example, that even entertainment is or may be 'political' undergirds *both* the approach of Gerbner et al. (1979) to 'cultivation analysis', which alleges that television programming as a whole uniformly inculcates (false) images of reality, *and* the quite different view of television as a 'cultural forum', propounded by Newcomb and Hirsch (1984: 64–5), who maintain that, 'Conflicting viewpoints on social issues are . . . the elements that structure most television programs'.

There has also been a veritable renaissance of research into political communication effects, based on the premisses that media potentials for impact are greater on cognitions (that is, on people's impressions of what the political world is like) than on their attitudes; and that such influence does not necessarily lack ultimate attitudinal or behavioural consequence, since attitude change may result from the gradual learning through repetition and practice of new ways of looking at the world (Nimmo, 1970). And although there is some imbalance in the concentration of this very active line of enquiry on micro-level media effects on individual voters, broader opportunities have also been taken for studying political communication in macro-level system terms, implying structures, roles, relations and dynamics that are more abstract than and not subsumable into the personalities and motives of the individuals and groups acting within them (McLeod and Blumler, 1987). Such a systems perspective has paved the way in turn for a certain amount of cross-nationally *comparative* political communication analysis, based on the assumption that differently organized linkages between media systems and political systems will have specifiable and varying consequences for the kinds of messages that are presented to voters, what uses they can make of them, and how their political outlooks may be affected (Blumler and Gurevitch, 1975).

The now familiar context for all this flowering is rooted in two related transformations: in academe and in socio-political reality. On the one hand, communication scholars of many different stripes have come increasingly to see the mass media as amidst, not above, power forces – wielding power, subject to other powers, the object of power struggles (Blumler, 1987). Just as critical theorist Gandy (1987) regards information control through the mass media as a source of hegemonic social power, so too is empirical investigator Weaver (1987: 63) concerned to examine 'the question of the power of mass media – the power to shape political agendas, to determine which versions of reality are acceptable on a widespread basis, and to shape the values of a society'. As Turow (1989: xiii) points out, 'Telling stories on television [whether in factual or fictional genres] is, above all, a game of power.'

On the other hand, from the 1960s onwards, elite–mass relationships that were formerly more solid and enduring have weakened and been de-stabilized, 'de-aligned' in Ivor Crewe's (1983) term. Allegiances to major parties declined as did the voting loyalty of those retaining party identification; new and minor parties threatened the more established ones; demographic correlates of party preference were no longer so predictive; political socialization seemed less effective; voting turn-out was more problematic; popular attitudes to political authority and political talk became more wary, ambivalent and sceptical; electoral volatility was on the increase.

Many who have become aware of these trends, especially political scientists who work part-time on media topics, seem to share a common response to them. They will say that election campaigns may matter after all; the 'limited effects model' of media impact is out of date; the reinforcement thesis, holding that 'the mass media conserve but do not change the political attitudes and behaviour of the electorate . . . is moribund'; 'the media are now full members of the family of significant influences on voters' political attitudes and behaviour'; the political role of the media should be located 'in the context of personal communication'; the mass media help set the agendas of issues that people think important and will talk about with one another; and so on (Harrop, 1987: 45, 59, 60). Although all these formulations are true, they can also be impoverishing, fostering rather mechanical and repetitive approaches to research. What they lack is reference to some broader set of processes at work in the post-1960s world in which meaningful enquiries could be situated, thereby nourishing research creativity and cumulative development.

The modern publicity process

So, to that end, where might we start? The fluidity and fickleness of public opinion, the lack of stabilizing political and demographic props, the correspondingly greater significance of short-term information flows, all point to what Colin Seymour-Ure (1987) has termed 'the growing intrusiveness of media' in politics. This translates into a perception, shared among many influence-seeking political actors, of the greater centrality of the mass media to the conduct of political conflict and its outcomes. And that propels in turn the emergence of what, for want of a better term, may be called 'the modern publicity process', defined thus:

> The modern publicity process involves a competitive struggle to influence and control popular perceptions of key political events and issues through the major mass media.

From this definition two master propositions may be drawn. One concerns concomitants and consequences. As *'the modern publicity process' takes over, other sub-processes are likely to advance in its wake.* To itemize:

First, there is the need for would-be political actors to devote more thought, energy and resources to media strategies and tactics. As Seymour-Ure (1987: 20) has put it, 'any Leaders in the 1980s who do not actively try to manage their communication show either a blind spot about the intrusiveness of media into politics or a blind optimism about their public image'. The urgent saliency of the publicity arena for modern politicians and others seeking to influence their policies springs from two tap-roots. One is the assumption that publicity matters. It can bring one's priorities to the attention of broad publics and help to order theirs. It can cultivate influential images of what one is striving to achieve in politics. It can establish or cement one's political status. The other tap-root of high publicity consciousness reflects the evanescence of civic issues and concerns that is built into a more news-based polity. Often what is at the top of the news agenda today will be displaced by something else tomorrow. Consequently, as the news scene shifts, and as the spotlight moves from one topic to another, leading politicians and their advisers must be ready to get their messages out into the media. They cannot rest on past publicity laurels.

In fact, this sub-process runs quite deep. Because would-be opinion moulders are competing fiercely with one another for access to limited news-holes and for more favourable treatment within them (in the hope, initially, of setting the press agenda and through that of eventually commanding popular perceptions of key political issues and events); because they must tailor their messages to the requirements of journalists' formats, news values and work habits; and because this is thought to demand anticipatory planning, fast footwork and a range of specialist skills – for all these reasons a significant degree of 'source professionalization' has emerged from this imperative. By this is meant the deeper, more extensive and pervasive involvement in political message-making of publicity advisers, public relations experts, campaign management consultants and the like. Such 'source professionals' are not only assiduous and gifted at fashioning messages for media consumption; they also immerse journalists in what appears to be an increasingly manipulative opinion environment. Lacking ideology and partisan commitment in many cases, they are in a sense mutually interchangeable, and they over-represent news-making as a field of power struggle rather than as a source of issue clarification. In the process, leaders and activists who are less attuned to the media sphere are discredited as amateurs out of touch with the modern world.

Second, the modern publicity process has generated a more media-centric model of pressure group activity (Blumler, 1989). Until the 1960s, interpretations of the roles of pressure groups focused mainly on relations between organizations representing the diverse interests and causes of a pluralistic society and the agencies of government, in which news media publicity played little part. Direct and regular access to decision processes was the favoured goal, and prime avenues of influence included formal and informal contacts with legislators and officials, membership of advisory committees and the establishment of rights to be consulted over policy developments, provision of expert information in reports and testimony to policy enquiries, representation in party platforms and machinery, and offers of financial contributions and other favours. This view particularly featured a strong party system, into which group demands were channelled and within which interest group coalitions were formed.

Since the 1960s, however, several trends have heightened publicity-mindedness among groups and inserted media influences more formatively into their relations with government. The decline of the party system has undermined the traditional model at its core and given many groups incentives to cultivate media attention as an alternative channel of influence. As party abilities to impose their definitions on controversial issues have waned, groups have concerned themselves more closely with the agenda-setting power of the mass media, appreciating that, 'control over the definition of a problem is a major stake in the policy process' (Cobb and Elder, 1981: 400). When parties are weak, how group claims appear in media terms may also stand a greater chance of tilting the power balance on contested issues. As Lang and Lang have pointed out:

> Political posturing for the media has one major purpose, the mobilization of the public to be used as an ally when one side lacks the political resources to push through its viewpoint or policy or, conversely, when the other seeks to retain its advantage over potential challengers. (1983: 22)

Further, as the ideational foundations of society and moral consensus have become less assured, and the institutions that traditionally upheld them have weakened, the mass media have come to be seen as providers of an equivalent social cement. This has prompted more determined efforts by certain groups, perceiving the mass media as sites of symbolic conflict, to influence their ideologically relevant output. Many groups have become sensitized to the media as purveyors of stereotypical images of their identities, be they related to gender, ethnicity, class, age or sexual preference, which it is then in their interest to challenge and displace.

Moreover, pressure group emphasis on the publicity function appears to have developed an accelerating momentum of its own. In part, this reflects the spur of presumed competitive advantage. The less publicity-minded bodies are motivated to emulate their more active rivals, whenever the latter appear to have enjoyed some publicity success. And with more voices trying to get into the publicity act, competition for access to limited news-holes intensifies, making it yet more important for each group to get its voice heard in the right way.

Third, policy decisions are more liable to be influenced by how they will play in the arena of media-filtered mass *perceptions*. Leading political actors have almost to be split personalities – policy-makers and publicists without ever being quite certain which is more important and whether the two can be reconciled. Thus, the modern publicity process puts a high premium on getting the *appearance* of things right. Even something as globally significant as the Reagan administration's SDI programme may have been affected by its packaging as Star Wars. But a more amusing and down-to-earth example of this need can be found in the terms that Donald Regan, then Ronald Reagan's chief of staff, used in the autumn of 1986 just after the issue of arms sales to Iran surfaced into the American news:

> Some of us are like a shovel brigade that follows a parade down Main Street cleaning up. We took Reykjavik and turned what was really a sour situation into something that turned out pretty well. Who was it that took this disinformation thing and managed to turn it? Who was it that took this loss in the Senate and pointed out a few facts and managed to pull that? I don't say we'll be able to do it four times in a row. But here we go again and we're trying.

Fourth, political personalization is advanced because it is easier to project than the hard stuff of issues and policies. A leader-seeking media system promotes a leader-elevated political system. As Bryan Gould argued, following the British General Election of 1987, 'Labour had no option but to run a personalised presidential-style campaign; that is the nature of modern politics.' Leaders' effectiveness as publicists and media handlers then becomes correspondingly more important. With a strong reputation for this, a leader can be difficult to dislodge; without it, he or she becomes vulnerable. Hence, 'considerations of candidates' media performances increasingly affect the party electorates' choices of their own leaders' (Seymour-Ure, 1987).

Fifth, the mass media sometimes adopt a sort of umpiring role – defining the rules of the competitive publicity game, articulating and enforcing certain standards of propriety in competitive publicity-seeking. A good example is how the British news media came down like a ton of bricks on Denis Healey's head in the 1983 election when he incautiously alleged that Mrs Thatcher had 'gloried in slaughter' over her victory in the Falklands War.

Sixth, the modern publicity process may intensify conflict between opinion advocates and journalists, with the former seeing themselves as engaged in a competitive struggle not only with their political opponents but also with the press itself. In British election conditions, Blumler et al. (forthcoming) suggest that party attempts to dominate the television news agenda have become more self-conscious, assiduous and persistent, listing six tactics adopted by Labour and/ or the Conservatives which they noticed while attached for observation purposes to BBC Television News during the 1987 campaign:

1   putting forward only one or two top speakers on the hustings, to discourage the cameras from going to somebody who would not be voicing the party's chosen message for the day;
2   co-ordinating a leader's activities across the day, so that the same theme would be reflected in what she or he did or said at a morning press conference, at an afternoon walkabout and at an evening rally;
3   holding several press conferences on the same issue from different angles on a given day;
4   declining interviews and refusing spokespersons for appearances on subjects not on the party's chosen agenda item;
5   complaining – why are you proposing to take up such and such a subject instead of dealing with such and such? or you've been leading the bulletin on the ———— party's issues in the campaign so far, far more often than on ours;
6   putting the rival party on the defensive, by raising a series of provocative questions that should be pressed on it for journalists to take up.

Governments in power are particularly apt to assume that, in order to govern successfully, they must proactively set the public agenda, not just allow the press to set it and then react. In effect, this turns the adversarial model of press–government relations, which taught journalists to regard leading politicians as antagonists when seeking information and news, on its head. The modern publicity process implies that an adversarial attitude towards the media among holders of and contenders for political power is at least equally appropriate.

Seventh, the modern publicity process makes journalists uneasy about their roles and concerned at times to reassert somehow the significance of their own contributions. The dilemma is that journalism-steered-by-news-values converts all too readily in practice into news-management-for-politicians. A device journalists have developed for resolving this has been termed 'disdaining the news' (Levy, 1981), much indulgence in which Blumler and Gurevitch (1986a) noticed when attached to NBC News for nine days during the 1984 presidential campaign. In essence, this involves attempts by reporters to distance themselves from the propagandistic features of an event by suggesting in the story that it has been contrived, stressing how it has been crafted, and warning that it should be taken with a grain of salt. As an NBC producer explained:

> We should let everybody know what is going on – image projection and other ways of packaging campaigns – so that they will be in a better position to make up their own minds. . . . When Walter Mondale picks a red blinking telephone to alert people to the possibility that Gary Hart might panic in a nuclear crisis, somebody has got to say what the device of the red blinking phone is trying to do. (Personal interview)

A correspondent justified such an approach in these terms:

> There is a naïveté of people out there. They see a one-minute to two-minute story, cutting from one electric scene to another and can be taken in by them, . . . Many television news stories . . . can give a false sense of what the event is like. So if viewers are helped to recognise by a story of this kind that they're being manipulated, they can then analyse the situation and understand it even better. *If that is the way politicians want to run their campaign, then that is also the way in which we should report it.* (Personal interview, author's emphasis)

Intriguingly, Blumler et al. (forthcoming) report that in 1987, for the first time in a series of four election observation studies, they heard members of the BBC news team stress their obligation to open viewers' eyes to campaign management practices in terms strikingly similar to those voiced at NBC, for example:

> Thinking of the campaign as it is organised by the political parties, all we can do is point out that things do not happen by accident. It is not a mere whim for Kinnock to have chosen a red rose as the party's symbol, to have selected a certain passage of Brahms for repetition. . . . What we should do in this context is to point out the degree to which deliberate campaign management goes on and what the principal managers hope that the viewers will see and will not see. (Personal interview)

> Television is such a passive medium that people might often just sit before it and let the way in which the election is presented wash over them. . . . But we can see behind that and are in a position to show how that has got where it is. *It is important to show that the campaign is being fought in a way that campaign managers want it to be fought, which may not be in the interest of viewers and voters.* (Personal interview, author's emphasis)

Eighth, there are signs that the modern publicity process may be promoting an increased circulation of negative messages about political actors, events and decisions. A striking example is how negative advertising – political commercials sharply attacking opponents' past records, policy inconsistencies and character defects – has recently become a staple of electioneering in the United States in both congressional and presidential contests. Such a tendency certainly meshes compatibly with the dominant values of a news-driven polity: journalistic predilections for bad news; the need for brevity, making it easier in 30 seconds to pick holes arrestingly in one's opponent's credentials than to outline a convincing case for one's own candidature; and a scepticism that may make negative statements about politicians seem more credible than positive ones. The prospects are evident for inculcating detachment, confusion and mistrust among citizens.

Finally, we may note in all this a threatened subjection of public communication to Machiavellian perspectives of *realpolitik*. Not fully articulated yet, these nevertheless lurk in the woodwork of the modern publicity process. They presume, first, that group actors should not leave opinion formation to chance; second, that they are involved in a competitive struggle, not only with their political opponents, but also with the press itself in a battle over what version of political reality will be communicated to the public; and third, that sentimental notions like a free market-place of ideas, the social responsibility of the press and the role of the informed citizen in decision-taking should be discarded as illusory. Should such perspectives gain further ground, the democratic legitimacy of the public opinion process might become increasingly hollow, rather like a termite-infested timber, leaving a thin shell intact but eaten away from the inside and perilously near to crumbling.

After all this has been said, however, it must not be forgotten that 'the modern publicity process' is at bottom an abstraction, a definition coined to identify a variable process of media intervention into political life. And a second master proposition is the comparative observation that *such a process will tend to be more advanced in certain societies than others, depending on differences among them in how relationships between their media systems and their national cultures, economic arrangements and political systems are organized.*

In the United States, for example, the modern publicity process appears to have moved very close to the heart of national politics, while in Britain it does not dominate the political arena to quite the same extent. British politicians may often flirt with it, are drawn extensively into its milieu and even heartily embrace it at times, but, in a 'safe sex' spirit, they have not gone all the way to full consummation with it. If so, the triumph of the modern publicity process in Britain has probably been as if held back by certain braking mechanisms in its political communication system.

One such braking factor may be Britain's less than wholeheartedly populist political culture. Populism, or the principle of *vox populi, vox dei*, stresses the inherent desirability of satisfying mass demand and consulting mass opinion and is based on the assumption that a policy is right because it is popular. Of course British politicians must keep their popular tinder dry and will often seek electoral advantage from broad public support. But they rarely feel under a *principled* compulsion to do so. Presumably this helps to explain why, until very recently, Britain was almost alone among Western democracies in not having admitted the cameras into its main legislative chamber. The broader point, however, is that the relative weakness of a populist ethos reduces pressure on British politicians to court mass opinion through the mass media, compared with the almost incessant need to do so that is imposed on their counterparts in, for example, the United States.

A second braking influence on the modern publicity process in Britain stems from the strength of its parliamentary system. Because that system is normally organized and run on disciplined party lines, and the government of the day can usually count on voting support in the House of Commons, the current state of popular opinion on the issues of the day is rarely imminently crucial (although in the long run, of course, it will be decisive for electoral purposes). Consequently, there is less need for the Prime Minister and her colleagues continually to cultivate mass opinion through the news media in order to put the pressure of popular sentiment on a potentially recalcitrant legislature – as is often the case for the President of the United States.

A third braking factor may be the 'sacerdotal' orientation to the political sphere, including Parliament, of Westminster correspondents working for television and the press. According to such an orientation, major political developments and institutions deserve a prominent and regular airing through the mass media almost by inherent right and regardless of news-value calculations. The point is complex, for news organizations include many pragmatically minded reporters as well, who doubt the audience-holding power of many political stories, which they therefore consider should be obliged to fight their way into press and broadcasting strictly on their news-value merits. In fact, many British journalists seem torn between high respect for Parliament, as the symbolic core of British democracy, and hard-nosed perceptions of it as grist for their news mills. Nevertheless, much control over the content of political stories is in the hands of parliamentary specialists, who work and have their offices in the Palace of Westminster, depend on daily access to and interaction with MPs to do their job, and may still tend to regard Parliament as the keystone of the British political system and the repository of its central values. To the degree that such sentiments prevail, reporting will tend to accord with what parliamentarians themselves regard as their due and will not depend merely on what happens at Westminster and how that chimes with conventional news values (Blumler and Gurevitch, 1986b).

Finally, compared with other national press systems that are only barely accountable to political agencies (as in the United States), in Britain there are more elements of subordination of the media system to the political system. The Fleet Street press has become highly partisan in recent years (strongly favouring the Conservative Party, of course). There are many informal influences and ground rules that tend to privilege the political sphere and shelter it from the most crass of journalistic intrusions. There is the fact that British public service broadcasting was and is a creature of Parliament, inculcating among many of its practitioners some sense of responsibility for upholding the political system and some sensitivity to its leaders' communication interests and concerns.

In the last analysis, however, all these 'system conditions' of British political communication serve as little more than brakes – the force of some of which may be gradually weakening – on the accelerating momentum of the modern publicity process.

Research implications

What about research priorities in light of all this?

First, more scholarship is needed on the organization of *local* political communication systems. Their neglect by academics until recently is curious at a time when trends in the national electoral system (partisan de-alignment and the lack of uniform national voting swings) and in local media systems (the expansion of local radio and regional television and the growth of free newspapers) in aggregate suggest that local politicking could be growing in importance.

Second, more case studies are needed of what may be termed 'the politics of news-making', taking some area of controversy and examining the efforts, influences, relationships and norms that have shaped its media appearance, public reception and legislative or policy outcomes. A splendid model for emulation is the Lang and Lang (1983) analysis of influences on the development of the Watergate controversy in the United States.

Third, more studies are needed of roles at the cutting edge of 'source professionalization'. After all, leading campaign consultants and publicity specialists do have theories of political communication and are often in a position to apply them. So what are their most prevalent theories? How far are they shared across the profession as a whole, and what differences, if any, divide it? Do such theories meet any significant opposition within campaign teams? What normative restraints and controls have to be respected? How does publicity professionalism relate to more partisan influences?

Fourth, it is essential to recognize that political communication models are becoming more complex. The literature now includes many serviceable theories of political communication processes and effects, but they must not be bowdlerized. Agenda-setting theory is one excellent example. Although once upon a time this was only about the media content/audience reception interface, alleging influences from the salience of topics and issues in media coverage to the salience of the same topics and issues among readers, viewers and listeners, this is no longer the case. It has broadened out into notions of 'agenda-building', influences *on* the media agenda (Weaver, 1987), agenda-negotiation (McCormack, 1983), plus a much broader and more diverse impact than simply audience effects, as in work that is starting to examine the agenda-setting impact of media reports on interest group leaders, policy-makers and policy itself (as well as on audiences).

Fifth, though demanding both conceptually and practically, comparative political communication analysis looks like bearing fruit (Blumler, 1983) and deserves more commitment and encouragement. Experience of cross-national election studies suggests, for example, that indicators in media content can be devised of its relative subjection to what Mazzoleni (1987) has termed a 'party logic' or a 'media logic', shedding light, then, on differential contributions in different national systems of party forces or journalistic forces to campaign agendas.

Sixth, rich pay-offs may come from more work on how voters frame, decode and make sense of political news and the electoral process more broadly. So far a complex and sometimes baffling picture of the audience recipient of entertainment and news materials alike has been emerging from both European reception analysis and American work on people's information processing strategies, driven by developments in cognitive psychology. Some preliminary impressions are as follows: that many audience members are active meaning-makers but use different processing strategies in responding to the news; that images of what the mass media are like may play a part in this; and that often the news is 'reconstructed' in ways that might not be predicted from a straight reading of reports (Jensen, 1988).

Two impressions stand out here. One is how inadequate this makes traditional notions of communication activity and outcome appear – far richer than just 'selection', 'reinforcement' or 'conversion'. The other concerns the almost seeming perversity of the audience. The rich variety of what it takes from the material seems at odds with impressions based on content analysis of the highly constrained, patterned and repetitive character of much news output. It is almost as if more or less unitary content is being refracted by pluralistic mental frames. And this conveys in turn a quite urgent research priority: to examine how audience meanings may vary in response to *differences* in the more open or closed character of media materials – that is, the degree to which they may be constraining (or freeing) in the readings they make available (Blumler et al., 1985).

Conclusion: the power of mass communication

As pointed out in the introduction, scholars have increasingly accepted the idea that the organization of mass media lies at the heart of social and political power. Such a power perspective, however, can take various forms. A model particularly prominent in much British writing likens media influence to a set of weights thrown on to the socio-political scales, tilting them in favour of certain interests at stake in power struggles and against others. While not denying or challenging that view, the foregoing analysis rests on a different, more independent or distinctive, model of media power. It suggests that the modern publicity process could be likened to the near-irresistible force of a magnet, obliging those that enter its field to conform to its pull. This is then capable of altering the messages of opinion advocates, the issues and terms of political combat and public discourse, and finally the perspectives and choices of citizens themselves.

7
Culturalist Perspectives of News Organizations: A Reappraisal and a Case Study

James Curran

Culturalist interpretations of news organizations take different forms, and are situated within widely contrasting models of society.[1] But they have one thing in common, which makes it legitimate to discuss them as a single category of explanation: they are founded on the paradoxical claim that control of the media lies primarily outside the media.

Probably the majority of British journalists adhere to a culturalist interpretation of the media. This revolves, in its simplest and most pervasive form, around the image of the media as a mirror of society. Journalists are neutral and dispassionate mediators of information: the 'news' is determined by the pattern of events in the 'real' world.

This particular version of the culturalist argument has become a favourite punch-ball for overweight media sociologists, and need not detain us. A large number of studies show that the structures, routines and values of media organizations help to determine the selection and presentation of news (for example, Epstein, 1974; Golding and Elliott, 1979; Ericson et al., 1987). Powerful institutions and groups also play a strategic role in generating and presignifying the 'news' in the first place (Murphy, 1976; Chibnall, 1977; Tuchman, 1978; Gandy, 1980; Hess, 1984; Cockerell et al., 1984; Sigal, 1986).

There is another culturalist explanation with a large following among journalists: the neo-liberal hypothesis that 'sovereign consumers' control the media as a consequence of the free interplay of market forces. As John Whale puts it, 'the broad shape and nature of the press is ultimately determined by no one but its readers' because newspapers must reflect their readers' views and wants in order to survive in a competitive market-place (Whale, 1977: 85). This familiar thesis is vulnerable on several counts. First, print and broadcast journalists are often unrepresentative of their audiences, and are poorly informed about them (Burns, 1977; Gans, 1979; Tunstall, 1971). Second, most media markets are highly 'imperfect' and 'misrepresent' consumer demand because oligopoly, mass marketing strategies and high entry costs limit choice, while public preferences are distorted by advertising allocations (Murdock and Golding, 1977; Curran, 1980; Murdock, 1982; Bagdikian, 1987; Curran, 1986). Third, there is often a demonstrably large gap between editorial opinion and public opinion (Seymour-Ure, 1977; Dunleavy and Husbands, 1985; Curran, 1987; Curran and Seaton, 1988).

The debate around the neo-liberal culturalist perspective has been most fully articulated in historical research. Some British historians have argued, for instance, that state economic de-regulation and the development of an unfettered market reconstituted the press as an independent fourth estate representing the public (Christie, 1970; Aspinall, 1973; Asquith, 1975; Koss, 1981 and 1984). This Whiggish thesis has now been attacked on a broad front. It pays insufficient attention to the role and influence of press owners and the interests they represented (Lee, 1976; Boyce, 1978). It ignores the ways in which the political elite managed the news to their advantage (Brown, 1985). It views economic de-regulation of the press through contemporary, liberal preconceptions, whereas in fact it was largely conceived and implemented as a control measure (Curran, 1978). And it overlooks the way in which the market operated in practice as a control system which was considerably more effective than the direct legal repression which it replaced (Curran, 1977).

Neo-liberal culturalist arguments have not been taken up extensively in British media studies mainly because economics has played a surprisingly small part in the evolution of British media research. But they have been a central feature of government-sponsored reports. For example, the first Royal Commission on the Press (1949) offers a classic exposition of a neo-liberal perspective, laced with Leavisite disapproval. 'The failure of the press to keep pace with the requirements of society is attributable largely to the plain fact that an industry that lives by the sale of its products must give the public what the public will buy' (RCP, 1949: 177). In short, the shortcomings of the press are merely the shortcomings of society writ (or, rather, printed) large.

In contrast, successive inquiries into British broadcasting (1951, 1962, 1977, 1986 and 1988) have all attacked the Press Commissions' premiss that 'competition for numbers' produces media content that people want. The only partial exception to this is the 1986 inquiry, chaired by the neo-liberal economist Professor Alan Peacock, which argued that at some point in the future the maturing of the broadcasting market could create, in certain circumstances, the conditions for consumer sovereignty.

The culturalist thesis reappears in a more unformed state in a number of studies of media content. Thus Lowenthal (1961) assumed that the shift of American press attention from 'idols of production' to 'idols of consumption' in the period 1901–41 reflected a change in the core values and 'dream world' of American society. A more sophisticated variant of this approach is offered by A.C.H. Smith (1975) in a brilliant, if flawed, study which argues that certain British popular newspapers between 1935 and 1965 articulated the assumptions and outlooks of their publics (Smith, 1975). This alleged rapport between press and public is explained by Smith in terms of the insight and empathy of journalists:

> They must continually refer themselves to their readers' experience and, more broadly, to the experience of society on which they report and comment. It is a question of reciprocal structures: the images newspapers [*sic*] form of their readers, the imprecise notions they have, as rules of thumb, for figuring out what is happening in the society for which they write . . . But, in the end, most working journalists will come back to 'flair', just as all good editors will come back to 'news sense', by way of professional working rationalizations of their own daily practice. (A.C.H. Smith, 1975: 247)

This idealization of journalists as ventriloquists of their readers' collective voice, and of newspaper content as the structuring of social experience through the assumptions and subjective identities of audiences, is questionable on a number of grounds. It implies a much greater degree of homogeneity among mass audiences than exists in reality;[2] it suggests a greater degree of shared experience between journalists and large audiences than is now common;[3] above all, it pays insufficient attention to organizational influences on the editorial development of newspapers. However, this culturalist approach does capture one important element in the relationship between media and public, and accomplished textual studies in this tradition can provide illuminating insights into the way in which publications reflect or fail to reflect structures of popular feeling (Holland, 1983; Jeffery and McClelland, 1986).

A more persuasive and influential paradigm is advanced by Stuart Hall and researchers in the structural culturalist tradition. They argue that news content is decisively influenced by bureaucratic news-gathering routines oriented on powerful institutions and groups, the reliance placed on them as sources, and the taken-for-granted assumptions of the dominant culture that shape journalists' thinking. The news media are thus shaped more by the patterns of thought and power relationships outside the media to which journalists respond than by direct controls exerted within media organizations. As one influential essay put it, 'the media *accurately* reflect and represent the prevailing structure and mode of power. It is in politics and the state, not in the media, that power is *skewed*' (Birmingham CCS Media Group, 1976). A similar perspective is articulated more simply by another researcher in the same tradition: 'the practices of television journalism reproduce accurately the way in which "public opinion" has already been formed in the primary domains of political and economic struggle, how it has been structured in dominance there' (Connell, 1980: 140).

This paradigm is based on the premiss that underlying antagonisms within society generate challenges to the dominant order and to the ideas and assumptions that sustain it. The media are the site of a permanent ideological struggle between contending forces over 'the meaning of signs'. However, the dominant power bloc usually succeeds in promoting its definitions of reality through the media because, so the argument goes, access to the media is structured by the hierarchy of power in society. However, the more sophisticated versions of this perspective allow that changes can occur over time. Shifts within the power structure, and in the field of contestation in which the media are situated, can lead to space being given to definitions that are opposed to those that are dominant.

This structural culturalist approach is still dominant in British media studies. However, there is another important culturalist tradition which advances a similar perspective of the media but from the vantage point of a pluralist model of society. According to this perspective, the media reflect consensual, core values in societies where there is no fundamental and irreconcilable conflict of class interest. But the media are also arenas of contest between competing political parties, power centres and pressure groups, and media content is crucially shaped by competition between these interests (A. Smith, 1976; Tichenor et al., 1980; Harrison, 1982; Lang and Lang, 1983; Blumler and Gurevitch, 1986).

Relative autonomy of journalists

In culturalist research, journalists appear in many different guises and disguises: as disinterested professionals, accomplished ventrilo-quists, instruments of the market's hidden hand, stooges of the powerful (so called 'secondary definers') or bearers of consensual values. But common to all these different perspectives is the assumption that journalists enjoy a high degree of autonomy. Thus, John Whale's neo-liberal culturalist account stresses that the modern journalist is 'left to get on with the job' (Whale, 1977: 74). Similarly, the Marxist, culturalist analysis of Hall et al. emphasizes 'the day-to-day "relative autonomy" of the journalist and news producers' (1987: 57). Belief in the relative independence of journalists is thus a foundation stone of the culturalist faith, in all its denominational forms. It is the premiss on which culturalists' perception of media organizations as relatively free-wheeling agencies, free to adapt and respond to their external environment, is based.

This premiss is apparently well grounded in empirical research. Jeremy Tunstall found, for example, that most specialist correspondents have considerable freedom from editorial supervision because of their knowledge, reputation and network of contacts. They also tend to hunt in packs, share some information and form a group consensus about developments on their beat, which helps them to resist pressure from their employing organizations. Indeed, so great is their propensity to conform to the collective judgements of 'competitor-colleagues' that paradoxically, suggests Tunstall (1971), their independence poses a potential threat to the diversity of the press.

Tunstall's findings have been echoed, in various forms, by numerous other studies. Hetherington and his team concluded that news is the product of 'a series of individual decisions' to which 'most journalists and most broadcasters bring a strong sense of public responsibility' (Hetherington, 1985: 20–1). A study of broadcast producers by Tracey (1977) also emphasized their tactical autonomy. But perhaps the most striking testimony to the 'relative autonomy' thesis comes from two researchers, Peter Golding and Graham Murdock, who are ironically perhaps the most distinguished exponents of the view that ownership and control of the media are important and neglected influences on media content (Murdock and Golding, 1977: Golding and Murdock, 1979; Murdock, 1982). Their recent concrete studies of news reporting tell a different story. Thus, Murdock (1984) accounts for the way in which the 1981 riots were reported exclusively in terms of ideological influences and source availability, without reference to economic control of the media. In Golding and Middleton's admirable study of coverage of the welfare state, media ownership appears only as a residual, background influence chiefly significant in generating a demand for audience-oriented entertainment in social reporting. Their analysis, with its heavy emphasis on the individualist values of journalists and the key role of the state in mapping welfare reporting, is in fact a classic example of culturalist analysis. They also report without comment that 'most correspondents felt themselves ultimately the master in any conflict' with their news desks (Golding and Middleton, 1982: 132).

There are also a large number of scholarly studies of American media which document in great detail the considerable freedom that American journalists appear to enjoy in selecting and reporting stories (Tuchman, 1978; Gans 1980; Weaver and Wilhoit, 1986). This makes still more persuasive the relative autonomy thesis since the findings of British research appear to be corroborated by experience elsewhere.

As we shall see later, the empirical evidence is not without ambiguity. It is also worth noting that there are two voices of dissent. Schlesinger's penetrating study of the BBC argues that broadcasters' perception of themselves as being highly autonomous 'does less than full justice to the substantive controls which actually constrain production' (Schlesinger, 1987b: 162). A recent Canadian study (Ericson et al., 1987) also differs from most comparable ethnographic research in suggesting that there is sometimes considerable conflict between journalists and senior executives. The study also cites graphic evidence of the way in which some journalists adjusted their reporting to accommodate the demands of new editors. But the maverick findings of this research can be attributed perhaps to the particularities of the Canadian news media. The conventional wisdom about the relative autonomy of journalists seems, superficially at least, to be solidly founded. Predictably, it is embalmed uncritically in widely used textbooks on the British media (Tunstall, 1983; Curran and Seaton, 1988).

Media convergence

Seeming confirmation that journalists enjoy a considerable degree of autonomy is provided by the apparent congruence of the British press and broadcasting, even though the latter is publicly regulated and required to be bipartisan. If the two media really do offer similar definitions of reality despite the differences in their formal structures of control, this powerfully corroborates the argument that journalists are relatively free from hierarchical supervision, and respond, wherever they work, to a common set of influences in the external environment.

Certainly, it has become the convention among British researchers to assume that press and broadcasting offer similar definitions of society. Thus, Stuart Hall writes with characteristic eloquence:

> Nevertheless, regularly and routinely, day after day in the press, night after night on television, week after week in the journals, we find the same categories, the same repertoire of images, the same systems of representation, the same structure of presences and absences, stresses and weaknesses, the same explanatory frameworks, the same pictures connoting the same chains of association, the same plots and narratives, the same links and smooth transitions, tending to repeat and reproduce a certain definition of the world, in and amidst the infinite 'diversity' of

our great Britain media institutions, effortlessly to the end of time. (Hall, 1986: 11)

This characterization is supported obliquely by a number of studies which argue that broadcasting coverage is framed in terms of the culturally dominant assumptions within society. Perhaps the best-known of these are the important, pioneering investigations undertaken by the Glasgow University Media Group (1976; 1980; 1985), which concluded that TV coverage in a number of areas – industrial relations, management of the economy and the Falklands War – was structured in dominance.

But perhaps special reference should be made to a small Glasgow University Media Group (1982) case study of reporting of the Labour Party in 1980–81, which is unusual in that it compares explicitly TV with press coverage.

> Much of the television news which we analysed for this study directly paralleled coverage in the conservative press. This was so in the general direction of stories and in the assumptions that informed them. Television would simply offer a less hysterical confirmation of what people read in the papers. (Glasgow University Media Group, 1982: 92)

However, this claim appears to be based on a more systematic analysis of TV than of press content.

In short, the culturalist thesis assumes that authority within media organizations is devolved to relatively autonomous journalists. Their reporting is structured by cultural and ideological influences – whether inscribed in news routines, relayed through sources, mediated through market influences, or simply absorbed from the dominant climate of opinion – rather than by hierarchical supervision and control. This view is apparently substantiated by ethnographic research into media organizations, and supported by critical studies of broadcasting content.

Although this perspective commands support across a wide spectrum of media studies, it ought now to be subjected to more critical scrutiny, not least because there have been profound changes in the British media since the more sophisticated culturalist perspectives were first proposed in the early 1970s. This chapter will briefly argue a contrary case in which the core assumptions of culturalist analysis will be turned on their head. There are, it will be argued, important differences of perspective offered by rival media, which partly reflects differences in their ownership and control. The much-vaunted 'relative autonomy' of journalists is best understood as 'licensed autonomy': journalists are allowed to be independent only as long as their independence is exercised in a form that conforms to the requirements of their employing organizations. In general, the relationship between media and society needs to be reconceptualized in more complex ways which integrate both culturalist and materialist insights.

Divergence of media agendas

There are very few data available that compare directly representations on radio and newspapers,[4] especially in Britain, and none that convincingly substantiate the convergence hypothesis. Critical studies of TV reporting alone are not really an adequate basis on which to conclude that press and broadcasting transmit similar perspectives.

Certainly, this conclusion is not borne out by a study of media coverage of local government in London, now in progress.[5] At times, there have been striking dissimilarities in media portrayals of left-wing councils. This was particularly true of the Greater London Council (GLC) after it was captured by the Labour left under the leadership of Ken Livingstone in May 1981. This will be illustrated, first, by a brief re-analysis of data about the topics covered in media reports of the GLC during three seven-day periods in 1982, 1984 and 1985[6] and, second, by considering more generally the interpretative frameworks and reporting conventions that were used.

In the first sample period (20–26 November 1982), television profiled the GLC as working for London in a consensual way – saving Riverside Studios (Channel Four News), staging the Spirit of London Exhibition and planning the opening of the Thames Barrier (Thames News), and campaigning for the low paid (LWT's London Programme). Similarly, five out of the eight stories about the Livingstone administration on local radio portrayed it as acting consensually on behalf of the local community.

In contrast, all seven items about the GLC appearing in the national tabloid press were critical, portraying the council as either incompetent, authoritarian or morally subversive. The quality papers were situated between the polarities represented by broadcasting and the tabloids: they featured the GLC as both working for Londoners and acting in a misguided and extreme way.

A similar diversity was apparent in the second sample period, 14–20 January 1984, when the political battle over the future of the GLC was almost at its height. The GLC item that attracted most attention in the broadcasting media and the quality press was the council's formal reply to the Government's White Paper proposing its abolition, and the GLC Conservative leader's denunciation of the Government's abolition plans. This double story was reported in all four national quality dailies as well as on local radio and television, with Livingstone appearing on both Thames News and ITN News at Ten. However, it was completely ignored in all national tabloids.

This omission was not simply due to the tabloids' smaller size. On the day on which quality newspapers reported the GLC's response to the Government's White Paper, the *Daily Express*, for example, found room for three anti-GLC items. This was merely one manifestation of a basic difference of news values. Broadcasting continued to focus on the council's contribution to the local community. In contrast, the tabloids' agenda was dominated by 'loony left' excess at County Hall, with six out of eight items coming under this heading. The agenda of the quality press was again situated between the two polarities represented by the tabloids and broadcasting.[7]

The third sample period, 1–7 June 1985, was at the tail-end of the political battle over the GLC. It was clear by then that the GLC's campaign for a reprieve had failed, and attention had shifted to some kind of London-wide body. A report by leading management consultants Coopers and Lybrand, which advocated a London-wide body on grounds both of efficiency and economy, received considerable attention in all the quality national dailies and was reported by Thames TV News. It was also reported or commented upon by local radio on two consecutive days.

But, predictably, it was ignored by the popular press. The story which gained greatest tabloid prominence during the week was a report that a GLC committee was considering a proposal for London to be twinned with Managua, the capital city of Nicaragua. The Managua story was also reported by the *Daily Telegraph* and BBC TV's London Plus.

Again, different news values were being applied. The tabloid press carried fifteen items about the GLC, nine of which were about the council's left-wing extremism. This is in marked contrast to what the available evidence reveals about concurrent broadcasting news selection.[8] Seven out of the ten GLC stories on TV featured the GLC working on behalf of Londoners. A similar pattern prevailed on local radio.

As before, the quality press agenda was a negotiated version of the broadcast – tabloid antinomy. Taking the three sample periods as a whole, there were shifts in the orientation of individual titles. But these shifts were overshadowed by the striking continuity of approach of most media. Broadcasting tended to portray the GLC in terms of its contribution to the welfare of the local community: the tabloids, in terms of the threat it posed to society.

Divergence of interpretative frameworks

A more complex picture emerges, however, if a comparison is made in terms of the interpretative frameworks employed in reporting the GLC and if greater attention is given to TV current affairs programmes. These tended to be more critical in orientation than regional news programmes which accounted for the majority of TV items about the GLC. This shift of focus also serves to underline the often overlooked point that there is a considerable diversity in broadcasting output as a whole. But even when TV's internal differentiation is allowed for, a striking dissimilarity continues to emerge between TV and tabloid coverage of the GLC.

This is particularly evident in the way in which the battle over the GLC's abolition was covered. In general, the tabloid press did not debate the pros and cons of abolition: rather, it sought to establish the case for closing down the GLC. It did this both through its selection of news which highlighted the council's 'loony' policies and, explicitly, through editorials (often triggered by the latest 'outrage') which called for the council's closure.

The tabloid case for abolition was constructed principally around four arguments: Red Ken and his colleagues were undemocratic or anti-democratic; they were subverting the moral consensus; they were undermining law and order; and they were irresponsibly profligate. Some of the central themes of this campaign were succinctly restated by a retired trade-union leader in the *Daily Mail* (27 March 1986): 'The GLC has made London the laughing stock of local government', he wrote, 'by opening its doors to every no-hoper, Marxist troublemaker, political scrounger, foreign terrorist and sexual pervert who wanted a public hand-out.'

This general characterization of tabloid coverage needs to be qualified. One aspect of the GLC's abolition – the proposal to cancel the GLC elections before the GLC was abolished – was debated and criticized in some tabloid leaders. Second, the Mirror Group changed its editorial line from opposition to support for the GLC in early 1984. Third, some tabloids did not join in the denunciation of the GLC administration as Marxist enemies of democracy. But, in general, the tabloid press constructed the issue of the GLC's abolition in terms of justified retribution.

This was in marked contrast to broadcasting which debated abolition of the GLC more in terms of general principles of local government reform. The terms of this debate varied, however, between different programmes.[9]

One approach adopted in some programmes, such as Thames TV's Reporting London (6 December 1982) and LBC's Countdown to Abolition (25 January 1986) was to employ a relatively open framework. This formula was carried to its logical conclusion in a set-piece duel between the Environment Minister, Kenneth Baker, and Ken Livingstone, staged by Reporting London (26 February 1985), in which each was assigned a camera crew and technical facilities to make a ten-minute film as a prelude to a studio debate. Baker argued that the GLC was unnecessary and would not be missed: it was also expensive and its functions could be devolved to borough councils. Livingstone countered by saying that the GLC was being closed down to silence a political opponent. Its abolition would lead to loss of local democratic control and increased centralization by Whitehall.

The contrasting sets of argument occupied separate terrains: they glided past each other, and only really 'engaged' over the issue of whether abolition would lead to more centralized or decentralized local government. This highlighted the fact that both sides were competing with each other over how the GLC debate was to be framed. The Government believed that its strongest argument was that the GLC had little to do and was not needed.[10] In contrast, the GLC's leadership concluded that their best defence was to occupy the moral high ground of democracy and local determination.[11]

However, most current affairs programmes about the GLC did not follow the open-ended approach. Instead, they were organized within a tight, relatively 'closed' structure. This generally took the form of a negotiated version of the GLC's framework, which marginalized the Government's main arguments.

One form of negotiation involved playing off the GLC's case against the attack mounted on the council by the tabloid press. For example, London Weekend Television's 'The GLC Abolition' (4 November 1983) was framed in terms of two competing arguments: the 'Conservative' case that 'loony left' excess should be curbed, and the GLC case that Londoners, not central government, should determine council policy.

Tucked inside this framework was a wide-ranging debate about the best form of government for London in which the central thrust of the Government's case – that the GLC had few functions and was unnecessary – received little attention. This debate format at least entailed negotiating the GLC's framework. But in some cases little attempt was made to depart from the terrain marked out by County Hall's publicists. Thus, Channel Four's 'Week in Politics' (13 April 1984) discussed the GLC's abolition almost exclusively in terms of centralization and democracy.

A subsequent 'Week in Politics' item (21 March 1986) gave only a token nod to the Government's substantive case against the GLC. Its introductory section provided an extended description of the Tory revolt against abolition 'balanced' by a short clip of Kenneth Baker saying tersely, 'We came to the conclusion that they [metropolitan authorities including the GLC] did not have a real function'. Baker's claim was then rebutted by the central core of the programme. This reported that the Government was having difficulty winding up the GLC and had not reallocated all its functions; that serious difficulties had arisen in new arrangements for co-ordinating London-wise services; and that it may be necessary to resurrect the GLC in a new form, at some point in the future. The programme's heavily ironic commentary implied that this muddle had been caused by a political vendetta: 'Red Ken will be gone . . . Tories will be able to sleep soundly in their beds at night.' The programme ended with Baker briefly reiterating his argument that the GLC was unnecessary. But he was not given space in which to develop his argument with supporting evidence. As he spoke, the camera cut away to his interviewer, Vivian White, who looked frankly disbelieving.

Only in the last months of the council's existence did the GLC's framework lose its hold on TV. Thus, LWT transmitted a relatively loosely structured and 'open' programme (21 March 1986) around the issue of what will happen after the GLC, which enabled Government supporters to make some of the anti-GLC arguments that had been under-represented on TV. News reports of the GLC during its final days were also critical in tone and tended to be organized around opposing perspectives of the GLC as a 'loony left' authority and as a council struggling to work for Londoners until the very end.

But, in general, broadcasting coverage of the GLC's abolition had two striking features. It debated the council's abolition, unlike the tabloid press, in terms of general tenets of good administration. And it did so largely on terms favourable to a far left council and unfavourable to a Conservative government.

Divergence of reporting conventions

Brief reference should be made also to the different conventions that govern tabloid and broadcasting reporting. In general, the language used in broadcasting reports is much less adversarial and partisan than in the tabloid press; viewpoints opposed to those that are dominant are given more 'space'; the targets of tabloid attacks are given more opportunities to defend themselves; and greater care is taken to check out stories. These differences have become more pronounced as a consequence of the increasing partisanship of tabloid newspapers, and the declining commitment of some of them to accurate reporting.

This divergence of approach is well illustrated by the media's response to a controversial statement about Northern Ireland made by Ken Livingstone. When replying to a question at a meeting of the Cambridge Tory Reform Group, Livingstone sought to question the official definition of the Ulster crisis as a battle between the forces of law and order and criminals: 'If they [the IRA] were *just* criminals or psychopaths,' Livingstone declared, 'they could be crushed. But they have a motive force which they think is good . . .' He went on to argue that the Ulster crisis was a political crisis, requiring a political solution. However, Livingstone was also reported as saying that he did not condone a recent bomb attack in London.

The *Sun* (13 October 1981) published the following day a front-page news report, beginning, 'This morning the *Sun* presents the most odious man in Britain. . . . Mr Livingstone steps forward as the defender and the apologist of the criminal, murderous activities of the IRA. . . . From London's chief citizen there was not one word of condemnation or even rebuke for the monsters responsible for so much suffering.' This was contradicted later in the article by a reference to Livingstone's remark, 'Nobody supports what happened last Saturday in London,' referring to an IRA bomb attack. But the way in which the article was written swamped this internal inconsistency: Livingstone was projected as the defender and apologist of terrorism.

Unlike the *Sun* on that day, the *Daily Mail* and *Daily Express* did not convert their news reports of the meeting into an editorial. But their leaders on the subject provided none the less a strongly adversarial framework for interpreting Livingstone's views. Livingstone, according to the *Daily Mail*, is 'a man who through Marxist dogma has become an alien in his own country, blind to the IRA's bloodiest crimes when even committed on his own doorstep'. Similarly, the *Daily Express* declared: 'London has endured fire, plague and the blitz. It should not have to endure Mr Livingstone at the head of its affairs for one more day.'

Livingstone's subsequent attempts to restate his opposition to violence, and contextualize his portrayal of the IRA as not *just* criminals, received a mixed reception in the tabloids. The *Sun* (14 October) repeated its attack, while the *Daily Express* (15 October) misleadingly interpreted his remarks as a recantation: 'GLC leader Ken Livingstone last night retracted his remarks about the IRA nail bomb gang.'

In marked contrast, Livingstone was given time on both radio and TV to present his case in full. 'I at no time said that people who set off a bomb aren't criminals . . . Quite frankly, I wouldn't agree with what I was quoted as "saying"', he declared on BBC2 TV's Newsnight (14 October). On Thames TV's Reporting London (20 October), he repeated the same thing, adding that in 'every speech I have made on Ireland I condemn violence, but violence by everybody involved'. He was also given the opportunity to put his views on the IRA in context. 'As long as you actually assume they are motivated simply as a murderer or criminal would be, we are going to fail to resolve the problem . . . You have to resolve the political problem.'

This example illustrates the way in which broadcasting sometimes provides an opportunity for tabloid targets to argue back even when they are opposed to the ruling consensus. It is especially noteworthy because it related to Northern Ireland, an area where British broadcasting has abandoned its commitment to balanced reporting and has a poor record in censoring both itself and others (Schlesinger et al., 1983).

Explaining media diversity

The diversity of media representations of the GLC raises questions about the adequacy of even the most beguiling and persuasive of the culturalist interpretations of the media, the structuralist approach associated with Stuart Hall and his colleagues. This offers an explanation of media *convergence*, based on the assumption that press and broadcasting generally revolve around uniform, 'primary' definitions of events furnished by powerful institutions and groups in the context of what they call 'the control culture' (Hall et al., 1978). Although this analysis is in some ways highly illuminating, it has three shortcomings. It tends to overstate, in practice, the degree of coherence and consistency of the dominant culture; it exaggerates the congruence between 'primary definers', at least in the context of Britain in the 1980s;[12] and it pays too little attention to hierarchical controls within media organizations.

Thus, one key explanation of why the media offered divergent definitions of the GLC abolition issue is that press and broadcasting journalists were subject to different pressures within their respective organizations. Right-wing tabloid newspapers adopted a partisan, adversarial perspective of the GLC mainly because senior press executives were committed to mounting a crusade against County Hall. Indeed, Sir David English, editor of the *Daily Mail*, was so personally involved as a political protagonist that he even tried to plant through the Conservative GLC press officer, Arthur Williamson, a question to be asked in the council chamber that would embarrass the GLC administration (Hollingsworth, 1986). A *Daily Mail* reporter,

Richard Holliday, was assigned to investigate Livingstone's political background and private life. Holliday duly checked out whether Livingstone was a secret homosexual or revolutionary, and even tried to obtain an interview with Livingstone's mother by presenting himself as a market researcher conducting a local survey. Holliday, a journalist of radical sympathies, was not acting out of personal animus against Livingstone: he was merely doing what was expected of him. In marked contrast, the organizational ethos of broadcasting organizations encouraged a more passive, bipartisan approach to news gathering.

Other organizational influences also contributed to the bifurcated response of broadcasting and the tabloid press. Both BBC-TV and ITV have regional news organizations, and are committed to covering regional news; the abolition of the largest local authority in the South-east was thus a major story. The public service commitment of TV organizations to inform and explain also encouraged them to report each stage of the political battle over the GLC, and to provide an account of the arguments on both sides. Quite why the tabloids, with a national constituency, devoted so much space to the GLC is more difficult to explain. The stories they ran mostly conformed to two criteria: they were generally entertaining and they revealed the GLC in a negative light. This orientation towards partisan entertainment led to the exclusion of a wide range of GLC stories regularly covered by broadcasting.

The other major explanation of media diversity is that the Government was not able to invoke a 'control culture' or 'dominant ideology' in its attack on the GLC. There was no upsurge of popular support for political retribution against the GLC for its left-wing policies; nor did it become the received wisdom that a strategic authority for London was unnecessary. If there had been a national consensus in favour of closing down the GLC, broadcasting coverage would probably have been more closely aligned to that of the tabloid press. As it was, broadcasters responded to the build-up of public opposition to the GLC's abolition.

One key to explaining favourable broadcasting coverage of the GLC is thus to account for the GLC's success in mobilizing support. The GLC Labour administration succeeded in turning the tide partly because it built a broad counter-coalition of support extending far beyond 'the alliance of the dispossessed' and the 'rainbow coalition' with which it was popularly identified. This included a substantial number of young, middle-class people who, although predisposed to vote for the Liberal–SDP Alliance, were attracted to the GLC because of its championing of public transport and support for women's, ethnic and gay rights (Waller, 1988). The GLC also drew upon a reservoir of local patriotism, and benefited from the widespread belief that its services would be lost rather than transferred after it was abolished (Harris Research Centre, 1985).

The GLC also out-spent and outwitted the Government. It allocated at least £30 million to various forms of promotion between 1983 and 1986,[13] whereas the Government earmarked no special funds for presenting its case. The GLC, with the help of expert advice, also constructed its campaign against abolition in a way that maximized its support. By appealing to consensual values – support for the ballot box and opposition to centralization – it diverted attention away from its left-wing image and made it easier for those who were politically out of sympathy with it to rally to its defence. The GLC's propaganda was also persuasive partly because it was based on themes that people were predisposed to believe: contemporary opinion polls and research undertaken for the GLC indicated that there was growing resentment against what many people perceived to be the increasing high-handedness and authoritarianism of the Government (Curran, 1987).

The Government also misplayed a difficult hand. It needlessly alienated key sectors of elite opinion by failing to do the necessary, detailed homework before announcing its plans to abolish the GLC. It failed, as did its political allies in the press, to project clearly how it would replace the GLC. Above all, its ham-fisted scheme for cancelling the GLC elections and transferring control of the GLC to a Conservative-dominated interim body played into the GLC's hands and made its propaganda seem more convincing.

The GLC won the battle for public opinion even before its expensive advertising campaign got under way in March 1984. As early as October 1983, 54 per cent of Londoners in a MORI poll opposed the GLC's abolition, and this proportion later rose to a peak of 79 per cent. The GLC's success in winning support influenced broadcasting coverage in a variety of ways. First, it created a running 'story': the biggest back-bench revolt since the 1983 General Election, the Government forced to abandon its plans to cancel GLC elections, a series of closely contested votes in the Lords whose outcome was uncertain. This had the effect of making the GLC more newsworthy and increased the time and attention given to it.

Second, key institutions, groups and individuals with privileged access to broadcasting media were mobilized. Especially important was the support won by the GLC among Conservative rebels in the Commons and Lords (including a former prime minister), who were frequently quoted or interviewed and who played an influential role in shaping the broadcasting agenda on terms favourable to the GLC; and representatives of 'informed opinion', notably academics and quality-paper journalists, who were also frequently used and adopted a generally dismissive attitude towards the Government's proposals. Other 'primary definers' opposed to the GLC's closure included leaders of the opposition parties, the leader of the Conservative minority group on the GLC, and a variety of interest groups, of which the London arts lobby was the best organized publicist. In contrast, the Government was only able to mobilize as accredited TV sources or interviewees representatives of the Institute of Directors, loyalist Conservative MPs and some local Conservative borough leaders.

The GLC also created a climate of opinion which influenced directly broadcasters' perception of the abolition issue. A significant number of broadcasters, working in local radio and regional TV, were drawn from a young, middle-class milieu where support for the GLC was strong. This may partly explain why some of them were sympathetic to the GLC and its leadership. Public opinion polls registering mass support for the GLC also increased its standing and ensured that it was not dismissed as an unrepresentative, 'loony' authority.

However, any explanation of the success of the GLC in winning the battle of the airwaves also needs to take into account the skill with which it managed the news. The GLC had a very large press department, numbering some twenty full-time press officers, with additional support staff. They shrewdly gave priority to broadcasters, and developed what was arguably an excessively cosy relationship with reporters on local radio and regional TV.

But the GLC's press office also had certain built-in advantages. It had indirectly an enormous budget with which to 'create' news;[14] it could draw upon more knowledge and expertise about governing London than was available to the Department of the Environment; it could concentrate on fighting just one media battle; it was able to float on the goodwill created by the GLC's heavy promotion;[15] it had political masters who became willing to compromise for the sake of good publicity.[16]

Thus, what emerges from this case study is a complex picture in which organizational and 'culturalist' influences interacted to produce divergent media responses. Right-wing tabloid newspapers had a relatively 'closed' response to the unfolding pattern of events because hierarchical pressures within their organizations directed them along a committed partisan path from which they did not deviate. Their campaign against the GLC was sustained in much the same register until it closed down on 1 April 1986, almost regardless of the shift of public attitudes in favour of the GLC.[17]

In contrast, broadcasting organizations had a more 'open' response to the growth of public opposition to the GLC's abolition. Its greater orientation towards routine regional news gathering, its public service commitment to inform and explain events, its obligation to be bipartisan, its links to a wider network of sources than that used by the tabloid press and its targeting by skilled publicists, all made broadcasting more receptive to the political campaign mounted in defence of the GLC.

Licensed autonomy of journalists

Our research indicates that media coverage of the abolition of the GLC fits a more general pattern in which the ideological distance between the popular press and broadcasting varied in relation to the balance of contending political forces in society. Thus, the more politically isolated and unpopular the municipal left became during the course of the 1980s, the more the gap between TV and popular press reporting of radical councils was reduced.

This pattern of media coverage is consistent with our portrayal of broadcasting organizations as relatively 'open' and of tabloids as relatively 'closed'. But this portrayal runs foul of the academic consensus about journalistic autonomy since it assumes that journalists working for highly partisan newspapers are more responsive to internal organizational influences than they are to the external environment. However, this consensus proves, on close inspection, to be less securely anchored than it seems to be at first sight.

The key British source, Tunstall's pioneering *Journalists at Work* (1971) is based on fieldwork conducted between 1965 and 1968. This was before the new generation of interventionist proprietors, most notably Murdoch and Maxwell, had emerged as a formative force. Tunstall's conclusions may well be out of date. Tunstall's admirable study is also not without ambiguity. It focused on specialist correspondents – an elite group within national news organizations. No generalization about journalists can be inferred from such an atypical, minority group.

At the heart of Tunstall's analysis, there is also a central but little noted qualification. 'Specialists tend to feel, or claim they feel, relatively free', Tunstall acknowledged, 'because occupational norms stress that once a journalist works for a particular news organisation he should regard most of its requirements as legitimate' (Tunstall 1971: 117). This comes close to saying that journalists feel autonomous because they broadly internalize what is demanded of them.

Hetherington's follow-up study, which did not include the Murdoch tabloids and paid little attention to feature writers, is also ambivalent. Although his opening comments emphasize the 'dispassionate and open-minded approach' of independent, professionally oriented journalists, his concrete evidence partly contradicts this conclusion.

For example, he later argues that 'the *Daily Mail*'s news values are, above all, Sir David English's news values', and proceeds to record a series of incidents indicative of English's domineering and highly partisan style of editorship (Hetherington, 1986: 13 and 148 and *passim*). A similar ambiguity can be found also in a number of American studies, which wrestle with the contradiction between journalists' insistence that they are highly autonomous and evidence which suggests that they are not.[18]

The way in which 'relative autonomy' is commonly conceptualized and researched is also problematic. Schlesinger (1987b: 149) interestingly argues that the 'BBC's micro-myth of independence' mistakes tactical autonomy for real freedom because it fails to acknowledge that 'the value framework for the taking of those [supposedly autonomous] decisions has already been developed at higher levels of control'. What this rightly points to is the need to obtain a clearer understanding of the relationship between ownership and control of media organizations and the framework of values within which journalists work.

This is not easy to achieve. It is difficult to gain regular access as a participant observer to senior levels of management. Second, managerial controls are rarely exercised with continuous force. Evidence that journalists internalize the norms of their news organization without overt managerial pressure is not proof, therefore, that this has always been the case. The 'inherited' norms of an organization may have been decisively shaped by managerial intervention in the past – something that one-off ethnographic studies are unlikely to reveal.

One way round this problem is to gain access to news organizations when they are undergoing a change of editorial direction since this is the time when the possible role of management is likely to be most exposed to view. Unfortunately, this is also the time when the presence of researchers has been judged to be most intrusive. The alternative strategy is to reconstruct historically the way in which media organizations have changed. A study of the *Sunday Times* between 1979 and 1987, in progress, follows this second route. It is of particular interest here because it suggests that a change of ownership was a significant factor in the editorial evolution of the *Sunday Times* from a liberal, centre-right to a neo-Thatcherite paper.[19]

The *Sunday Times* was acquired by Rupert Murdoch in 1981. His first editor, Frank Giles, recalls the numerous occasions in which he came under pressure from the proprietor to shift the paper to the right (Giles, 1986: 203 and *passim*). Giles retired in 1983, one year before his contract expired, to make way for Andrew Neil, whose right-wing views were more in line with those of the proprietor. Senior editorial executives from the old regime were also weeded out, exposing rank-and-file journalists to new and unaccustomed management pressure in a general editorial reorientation of the paper. This pressure was at times overt and abrasive, according to most journalists who have been interviewed. Their testimony is further borne out by the high turn-over of staff. The editorial establishment of the *Sunday Times* in 1981 amounted to some 170 journalists. Between February 1981 and March 1986, more than a hundred journalists left the paper. The majority of these left because they did not like working under the new regime or because they were squeezed out.

What the *Sunday Times* experience highlights is the revocable and conditional nature of journalistic autonomy: it is a freedom exercised on terms determined ultimately by employers. However, the extent of influence generated directly and indirectly by owners varies greatly from one news organization to another, and perhaps from one period to another. But always present, in some form or other, are the influences exerted by the cultural patterns of society, the repertoire of images and meanings readily available to journalists, and the wider context of ideological contest to which they are exposed. These influences are mediated through the structures and values of news organizations. However, it is the way in which these structures and values are shaped by internal processes of control within news organizations which require more critical attention. In short, what is needed is a new synthesis combining political economy and culturalist insights.

Notes

1 For purposes of exposition, this review concentrates principally on the relevant British literature.

2 One consequence of the increased emphasis on entertainment in national tabloid newspapers is that their audiences are now much less socially and politically homogeneous than they were. For example, only 41 per cent of readers of the *Sun*, an ardently pro-Conservative newspaper, voted Conservative in the 1987 General Election (Harrop, 1988).

3 The editors of the two daily papers with the largest circulation in Britain were both educated at public schools, attended by some 7 per cent of their peers. Although they are not typical, a large number of national newspaper journalists live in the London suburbs and have very little experience in common with many of their readers.

4 Studies that compare British press and television content include Hartmann (1975), Butler and Kavanagh (1984 and 1988) and Hetherington (1985).

5 This is being carried out by myself and colleagues at Goldsmiths' College. It will be published as Curran et al. (forthcoming).

6   This analysis is based on two sources of data: a summary of broadcasting items referring to the GLC undertaken by Peter Ray and his associates as a commercial service for the GLC, and cuttings of all articles in national newspapers mentioning the GLC collated on a daily basis in the GLC press office. The national radio channels and the local radio station, Capital Radio, have been excluded on the grounds that they were not systematically monitored.

7   Of the thirty-six articles about the GLC appearing in the quality press, eight had as their main theme the GLC's contribution to the welfare of the local community, balanced by seven items featuring 'loony/lethal left' excess. But the majority of items were concerned with the general arguments for or against abolition (fourteen) or took the form of routine reports (seven).

8   The analysis of broadcasting is confined to the last four days of the sample period since recording during the first three days was incomplete.

9   My thanks to Jane Fountain for securing some of these television transcripts when she was on placement from Middlesex Polytechnic.

10   Interview with Lord Jenkin of Roding (Patrick Jenkin, Secretary of State for the Environment, 1983–85).

11   Interviews with former senior GLC officials and a senior executive in the GLC's advertising agency, Boase Massimi Pollitt. For a selective view, see Livingstone (1987).

12   This point is well argued by Philip Schlesinger in another chapter in this book, to which this chapter owes a great deal.

13   This estimate is derived from an interview with Tony Wilson, the former head of the GLC's public relations. A more precise figure is impossible to obtain, since the GLC deliberately obscured the extent of its promotional expenditure by the way in which it presented its accounts.

14   The GLC, with a budget of over £800 million, spent money to make news. For example, the Cooper and Lybrand report which, as we have seen, attracted much positive media attention, was commissioned by the GLC. The sheer organizational scale of the GLC also made it easy to generate stories since it was involved in so many different things.

15   A survey of twenty-four senior press and broadcasting journalists by MORI in June 1986 indicated that the GLC's skilled advertising campaign had heightened media interest in the GLC, and caused some journalists to pay more attention to the issue of democracy versus central control.

16   Thus, in 1981, the GLC leadership boycotted the wedding of Prince Charles and Lady Diana Spencer. Four years later, it persuaded the Queen to open the Thames Barrier and then claimed that she supported the GLC.

17   The central themes of the tabloid attack on the GLC remained essentially unchanged. The only significant modification was that the personal invective directed against Ken Livingstone was toned down.

18   For example, Gans (1979: 101) writes, 'delegation of power also takes place because the news organisation consists of professionals who insist on individual autonomy', but then observes that corporate executives sometimes 'suggest, select and veto news stories whenever they choose'.

19   My thanks to Brendan Wall for his help in carrying out interviews with *Sunday Times* journalists.

PART THREE

RETHINKING CONCEPTS AND METHODS

Traditions, Technologies and Audiences

8

Communication Research Past, Present and Future: American Roots and European Branches

Denis McQuail

It is widely thought that communication research is an American invention, one subsequently imported by other nations, which adapted its style and methods to their own native circumstances. As far as most of Western Europe is concerned, this is a defensible view, at least for the immediate post-war years, when the American model was very influential in the founding or revival of media research (Tunstall, 1977). However, this chapter argues that more recent developments call for a different assessment. We can observe a relatively strong new growth, which is developing in ways which deviate from the original model or roots. It now makes some sense to speak of a distinctively European school, or version, of communication research, however vague may be the outlines or hybrid the species.

This view will be advanced by a descriptive argument based on a personal assessment of what is happening in Europe. It also involves an important assumption: that communication research is bound to reflect the pressures and influences from the surrounding culture and society, which, in this case, means those arising from the conditons of contemporary Europe. It is instructive, nevertheless, to take account of earlier American experience of an emerging school of communication research, which is the only case available for comparison. The aim is less to compare than to find some guidance in the task of identifying the main kinds of external factor which we should consider as relevant influences.

Adopting these assumptions, we can start with a sketch of the core structure of American communication research as it appeared towards the end of its own key formative period, from 1930 to 1960. The emphasis will be on themes and issues, the agenda and guiding assumptions of research, rather than on theory and method, which *ought* to have a more universal character. This will also be the emphasis in outlining the diversity of European research concerns addressed later in this chapter, for reasons to which we can return. The main sources for this sketch are to be found in the many reflections on the origins of communication research in the United States which have been published from time to time (good recent examples are Rogers, 1986 and Delia, 1987).

The thematic structure of communication research in the United States in its formative period

From a considerable distance in time and space, it is possible to suggest that the issues and directions of communication research in the United States were shaped by key features of contemporary historical experience. The main social factors were the Depression and New Deal, the reaffirmation of the American form of democracy between the wars (in the face of anti-democratic trends elsewhere) and the perennial matter of assimilating successive waves of immigrants. In international politics, the United States was coming to terms with being a world power as well as a rich nation. The most relevant industrial and economic influences were the development of new industries of film and broadcasting, based on new technologies and business arrangements, with major implications for existing mass media and media functions. These were all potent factors, the effects of which can be traced in the new field of communication research, which was itself based on new techniques of sample survey and experiment. Here we can only try to summarize the outcome of contemporary circumstances in terms of a few thematic headings, under which significant themes and biases of research are located, as shown in Table 1. The entries are only *examples* of prominent lines of research of the period. The presentation adopts an approximate division according to whether the research indicated is more theoretical and descriptive or more empirical and applied.

The first of three main themes of early American research, 'social change', was generally viewed in a positive light, as very much part of the 'American way' and closely intertwined with processes of communication, especially with the effects of the mass media.

Table 1   *Early US communication research: thematic agenda (exemplified)*

	Type of research activity	
	Theoretical/descriptive	Empirical/applied
Social change	Modernization; Mass society & mass culture	Diffusion of innovation; Mass leisure/audience behaviour; Persuasion; Advertising
Democracy US style	Civic culture; Free and responsible press; Public opinion	Election campaigns; Prejudice; Personal influence
Order	Socialization & social control; Local integration; Cultural assimilation	Mass behaviour; Individual crime, violence; Pro-social effects

Research was seen as helping to clarify these processes and enabling mass communication to work more efficiently. The salient aspects of change which influenced communication research were: the transition from rural to urban living; the modernization of farming; and the growth of mass leisure and mass consumption. The dark side of massive social change was recognized, and is accounted for, in this sketch, partly by pessimistic views of modern mass society and partly under the third main theme heading, that of 'order'.

Democratic processes were also very much identified with communication and with the mass media in particular. Contemporary ideas about democracy in America placed much emphasis on participation in civic life, on having opinions and information and voting in elections. It was also a generally progressive creed, or presented as such against the outer darkness of fascism and communism.

The relevant American concept of 'order' appears in retrospect as one in which consensus and patriotism were highly valued, as was individual conformity. Class and ethnicity were not favoured as bases for identity, preference being given ot locality, family or community. The assimilation of new immigrants, prompted by diaspora and war, was one reason for this. Communication was assigned a normative task – to combat disorder and promote consensus – and this is reflected in research priorities of the period. The identification of mass culture as a 'problem' reflects both a strain to reassert elite values and also the imported theories of Frankfurt School emigrés, who reacted against media commercialism.

More generally, early American communication research, in its academic version, was dominated from the start by rationalistic, utilitarian, fairly liberal and ameliorative tendencies (the dominant climate for much of the period). Despite an internationalist thrust during and after the Second World War, research remained predominantly ethnocentric in character, applying home-grown values to cross-cultural problems (for example, Lerner, 1958). On the whole, communication research, when not helping to serve media industries, was assigned a role in advancing progress and reform, as seen through the eyes of the established middle class.

This view is highly subjective and approximate and its categories cut across more conventional ways of classifying communication research. Its main purpose has been to offer some historical perspective and guidance in the task of identifying the *kind* of influence from society which might now be affecting the agenda of research in Europe in the late 1980s and the 1990s.

The social and geo-political roots of communication research in Europe

Following the line of argument that the study of communication will be forged according to the main features of its environment in society and in response to communication practice (whether as supportive or critical), it is now in order to say what is distinctive (and relevant) about European circumstances. The generalizations made are bound to be very imprecise, given the internal differentiation of Europe, but most involve some degree of contrast with the situation in the United States. The main features, dealt with in turn in the following paragraphs, are:

1 the great importance attached to place;
2 the residual statism and paternalism of government;
3 some political and economic peculiarities, especially the coexistence of communalism, egalitarianism, socialism, conflict and commerce;
4 recurring discontinuity and reconstruction;
5 distinctive European media institutions.

The emphasis on place refers especially to nationalism, regionalism and local city or community identification. Modern European history has to be described in terms of significant locations, which have their own settled populations, institutions, cultures and sense

of identity. There are many such places, and the range of communication networks, as well as the content they carry, their forms and
purposes have been shaped by facts of location. Unlike the situation
in the United States, many different sub-national and regional
cultures have survived in surprisingly good shape, even if in forms
adapted to modern ways of life and to modern media, especially
where supported by a distinctive language. A qualitative diversity
as well as multiplicity of 'significant places' has thus to be recognized.
An important corollary to this diversity is the expectation that
communication media will serve and be loyal to their own local
place (for example, Hagerstrand, 1986; Gifreu, 1986).

An important political tradition of continental Europe in the
period, overlapping with the age of mass media and mass democracy,
was represented by the role of a centralized state bureaucracy which
would take care of essential national or imperial interests, especially
in matters of social order and international relations. Such regimes
are now largely dismantled, but they have left a mixed heritage for
politics, for the practitioners of communication, and thus for
research. The key features of this heritage are: a penchant for
integrated planning; an interest in sponsoring campaigns and propaganda for 'approved' ends; a residual claim to access to, or
supervision of, the media for overriding national or public interests;
a somewhat paternalistic approach to the working of public communication.

The autocratic state is not the only model inherited by modern
Europe. Equally important were forms of politics typical of city
states, republics and the early liberal bourgeois governments. The
heritage for communication has been a concern for liberty of
expression and a conception of the public good which embraces
aspects of communication as an essential service to society. European
history, when not the story of places, is one of conflicting ideas and
movements, especially in religion and politics, not to mention
nations fighting over territory. Modern communication media have
inherited an expectation that they will engage in debate, and
represent opposed points of view, within the framework of loyalty
to nation, region or local place.

Prominent within the spectrum of political ideas and influential
on communication have been the several varieties of socialism. The
most powerful core idea of socialism is that of equality, and, for
communication this has meant, especially, an emphasis on universal
provision, the reduction of barriers to equal participation as senders
and receivers and a resistance to commercialization and, especially,
to commercial monopoly.

This aversion notwithstanding, modern Europe is founded on

capitalistic manufacture and trading and, beneath the many forms of politics and culture, business and money are major preoccupations and shapers of communication and of priorities for communication research. It is commercial aims that are currently largely responsible for the transformation of European communication by technology and for the current technocratic direction of some communication research.

Europe has been much disrupted by war and revolution during the first mass-media century and is accustomed to the reshaping of media institutions after severe dislocation. This has sometimes worked in favour of innovation and the importation of institutional models; sometimes it has helped to reinforce tradition. It does at least mean that the unthinkable has from time to time actually happened in collective memory, despite an outward European façade of stability and complacency.

The last and most recent geo-political characteristic of Europe is the fact of movement towards integration, as exemplified by the EC, affecting, albeit slowly, almost every area of social, political and economic life. So far, the direct results for communication have been less significant than most of the 'older' geo-political circumstances described already, but they are on the way. The internationalization of European communication is not yet really a Europeanization, but the issue of 'transnationalization' within Europe is very salient and becoming more so, as is the preoccupation with the meaning of a European cultural identity (Sepstrup, 1989). This matter is taken up later.

If this helps to describe the soil and climate of Europe, it also leads on to questions about what kind of media flora, or distinctive media institutions, have been produced. The answer is that there are large differences between national societies, especially in respect of print media. The main dimensions of variation between and, in some cases, within countries relate to: the strength of the reading habit and the literate culture; the degree and kind of regional differentiation of media; the degree to which media are structured along social class lines; the degree of political partisanship of media.

The broadcast media, while rarely, if anywhere, any longer full public monopolies, are mostly controlled by public bodies and operate under regulatory regimes which are often restrictive. Public control is designed to secure diversity, equality, cultural quality and order in varying proportions. The most important dimension of differentiation of broadcasting within Europe is according to the degree of commercialization of the broadcasting system (McQuail and Siune, 1986). A generally unifying characteristic of European media systems is the rather warm welcome which has been given to new communication technologies, often with government sponsorship, for economic and industrial reasons. This has certainly had consequences for communication research.

The fragmentation of European communication research: the main national schools in outline

Although the aim is to give an integrated overview, it would be misleading not to acknowledge the divided and uneven nature of communication research in Europe. So far, research results published in book or article form are somewhat fragmentary, and the quality of work in terms of design and method has been mixed and often derivative. The harvest, in short, has been insufficient and variable in quality. Among the explanations, chronic under-funding and retarded institutionalization of higher education and research in communication certainly deserve prominence.

More fundamental, however, is the compartmentalization of research in Europe into a number of separate and not always compatible or co-operating schools, generally inside national frontiers. The resources for research are spread very thinly on the ground in Europe and the conditions for cumulation of theory and research findings have not been good. Even so, these separate 'schools' or traditions have their own special qualities and offer some promise for the future, by the very fact of their diversity and separate past development.

It is very obvious that the roots of communication research are planted in older disciplines and traditions of enquiry, which are often to be found in national variants. The diversity can be described and accounted for in more than one way. In the absence of a clearly defined discipline of communication, the work in the field can be found in almost any of the social sciences or humanities, as well as in relation to professional training. The generation of researchers now trying to establish their field are unlikely to share a common intellectual background, even within the same society. Equally to the point, research has also been fragmented by sharp differences of theoretical perspectives, as Rosengren (1983) has pointed out. Especially relevant are the divisions which separate Marxist-critical from functionalist-pluralist approaches and those dividing those who emphasize culture (the media-centric) from those who stress material and structural factors (society-centric).

There are other possible variants of style and ideology which show up in European research. It does not help very much to proceed by this manner of differentiation, given the broad similarity across Europe of the main relevant, social scientific disciplines, although one can recognize a major fault line approximately following the line of the Rhine and the Danube. There is nothing especially European about the map of research interests that would emerge, except perhaps the greater incidence (than in the United States or Soviet Union, for example) of neo-Marxist-critical thought and the greater tendency to define research issues in cultural terms.

An alternative way of accounting for the divisions of communication research in Europe is according to national or regional 'schools', each with its own typical features. The main European traditions of communication research which seem to be emerging from their varied scientific origins can be sketched as follows.

The study of communication in *Britain* reached a plateau in the 1970s and now shows signs of stagnation, if not decline. Existing university research centres are, for instance, being run down or vandalized. British communication research has its main roots in a combination of literary and cultural studies on the one hand and social problem-diagnosing on the other. The domination of broadcasting by one large cultural bureaucracy (the BBC) has been more negative than positive in its effect on communication research and the newspaper press has been consistently negative *towards* research. Otherwise, North America has readily supplied missing parts to the research apparatus in Britain.

In *Germany*, communication research, while far from unified, does at least rest on a long, native, scholarly tradition of press study and has been much influenced by the period of post-war reconstruction of media. It is characterized by high productivity of empirical data, often following models (re-)imported from the United States and by a sensitivity to historical political-juridical questions. It also possesses a strong tradition of critical scholarship although this does not seem to have borne as much empirical fruit as its British equivalent. The relation of research to the practice of mass media is generally closer than is the case in Britain, despite tensions, partly because communication education provides one route into media-related professions.

French communication research has also tended to be self-sufficient and somewhat idiosyncratic, seeming to be dominated either by home-grown varieties of cultural theory (often Marxist and/or semiological in inspiration) or (now especially) by media-technocratic interests (Flichy, 1980; Mattelart, 1983). Both of these tendencies have held back the inroads of Anglo-American research models and methods, but have also restricted the amount of research on media organizations or the social and political effects of mass media. Despite relatively low and only selective institutional support, research has been fruitful in some directions, especially in matters to do with local communication and the application of new media (the technocratic drive). France has perhaps been more distinctive in influencing the *style* rather than the substance or methods of communication research in Europe. But of the several countries of Europe, it may well possess more of the conditions for self-rejuvenation.

Communication research in *Italy* (Mancini, 1986; Grandi, 1983; Richieri, 1988) is somewhat eclectic, partly because of its low degree of institutionalization, which is only recently starting to be remedied. After its early normative phase, it has shown alternative attraction either towards French theory or to Anglo-American empiricism. In Italy, the influence of a large cultural bureaucracy, Radiotelevisione Italiana (RAI), as patron of research has been beneficial, even vital, providing both funds and facilities for research and an interest in results and their dissemination.

The *Spanish* case is too early to assess, given the relatively recent experience of economic and political progress, although productivity seems to have been quite high (Pares, 1988) though often of discursive, philosophical books rather than the results of empirical enquiry. The signs are of a potential split (observable more widely in Europe) between an established tradition of textual analysis, influenced by Mediterranean Marxist theory (and semiology) and a technocratic tendency, for which France is likely to provide the model. The ties to Latin America, reinvigorated in the post-Franco era, are another important element in the Spanish case, providing access to another vigorous research tradition and a large market for research results.

Although there are other, smaller, countries in Europe where research is active and diverse (especially Holland, Belgium and Austria), only one other possible 'school' of research needs to be identified – that of the Nordic countries. It has some claim to be considered the most productive and best-institutionalized scholarly tradition of communication research in Europe, as well as the most professional (consult, for instance, the *Nordicom Review* for evidence on this point). This position has been achieved initially by plundering the rest of Europe and North America on a familiar Scandinavian pattern, then forging a research elite characterized by a high degree of professionalism, pragmatism, ingenuity, empiricism and policy-orientation. The small countries (in population) which comprise the whole Nordic world benefit from several features which seem quite characteristic of smaller European nations: they can less afford to waste resources or to disagree on priorities, especially in matters of cultural or economic survival; they can be culturally nationalistic without losing ideological virtue; and relations between research and media institutions are generally more co-operative.

Towards 1992 and all that

One more ingredient which needs to be added to the mixture is the notion of a more integrated Europe, as introduced above. Although the core and driving force is the economic union of the European Community, there are broader tendencies at work. The dynamic towards a more united Europe is an extra geo-political factor which is adding some impetus and direction to a process of institutionalization of communication research which has been independently under way. The reasons for thinking so are as follows.

The 'new Europe' is itself a major communication event, being consciously forged within European politics, or imposed on disinterested citizens, depending on point of view. It is a concept which attracts interest and certainly mobilizes a good deal of communicative activity, especially under the new emblem of '1992'. It is not entirely fanciful to draw a parallel with the 'invention' of America in images, symbols, and stories of the early popular mass media, a symbolic process which still goes on. While the images and ideology of Europe may often be looked at with some scepticism, it is hard for Europeans to escape completely from some side-effects, especially from messages which increasingly identify a European identity and common interest, based on shared space and time. Even less escapable are practical effects on media institutions and audience experience.

The wider Europe being proposed also offers some antidote to the fragmentation and divisions noted above. There are more possibilities for comparative research, for becoming aware of shared communication problems, for exchanging ideas and talent. Smaller countries are less isolated, larger countries less inclined to be satisfied with a self-sufficiency which can be limiting and counterproductive. It is less easy for amateurism in research to survive unnoticed when the stage is larger and the audience bigger. Taken as a whole, Europe also offers a very rich set of objects for communication research and enquiry within a relatively small space – very diverse communication institutions and cultural forms, once national boundaries are transcended. Broader patterns can be perceived, helping to account for what might otherwise pass for local oddities.

It is, further, arguable that several of the themes which are embedded in the discussion about Europe are closely linked to problems which are likely to be central to communication research in general. These especially have to do with economic and social change in a competitive international environment, cultural identity, and the achievement of some of the social promises which have been made to the citizens of Europe. In the summary version of a structure for the concerns of communication research which is given below, one can certainly see more than a hint of the issues which are raised in relation to political development of a more integrated Europe. It is hard, for this reason, to describe the ongoing research without echoing some of the terms which are heard in various versions of official pro-European propaganda (Europrop). A new dimension to concerns of research is being added by developments in Central and Eastern Europe which are likely greatly to increase intercommunication between 'First' and 'Second' Worlds and alter definitions of international communication issues.

Media change as an additional factor

Of the current 'realities' of context in a more integrated Europe, two in particular deserve to be emphasized. One of these is the development of many new technologies of distribution which are changing the whole politics and economics of public communication as now organized. Along with this has emerged into public consciousness the idea of an 'information society', in the sense that information activities and concerns are increasingly salient in almost all aspects of daily life and in society. Unlike the 'mass society' which was the main over-arching concept when American communication science was forged, the information society has a much more positive image, however much it is suspected by some of being more an ideological and manipulative concept than an unmixed real life blessing (Brants, 1989).

Related to this are changes in policies and structures for handling the informational developments. Superficially, this might be interpreted as a, possibly temporary, love affair with the free market and the desire to shift economic burdens from the public to the private sphere. But, more fundamentally, it involves both a rethinking of the nature and scope of the public interest and how best to secure it and also a falling back on the market as a tried recipe for managing and allocating the threatened abundance of communication goods and services, in both telecommunications and broadcasting. The required investment decisions at a time of rapid innovation and obsolescence make the market an attractive solution. There are also strong external pressures towards finding European policy solutions (McQuail and Siune, 1986). The global environment is reducing the scope for independent national policy, and major multi-national capitalist interests are scouting the media territory and actively staking their claims.

The agenda for European communication research

In setting out to sketch the structure of European communication research issues (see Table 2), the early American model, as described above, cannot be expected to serve as a framework. Europe is as different from the United States of forty years ago as is the America of today. Even so, the thematic structure which presents itself now is not so very different, even if the specific agenda items and their varying priorities are different. The similarity of structure might conceivably stem from the enduring strength of American influence, but is more likely to derive from a continuity in the fundamental processes of communication in society.

The term 'social change' might still serve as a heading, but it is now so trite and vague as to mean very little. In its place, we can choose 'innovation and efficiency' to capture the current preoccupation with both new media technology and the management and application of information as a societal resource. In the early American model of salient features of communication, there was more emphasis on human than on technological processes and, possibly, more awareness of the human problems associated with change.

Clearly 'democracy American style' will not do as a relevant theme for Europe, despite the continuing fascination in Europe with American-style politicking. More fundamentally, democracy in Europe still has a stronger weighting towards economic equality and balancing of power between classes and groups, while citizenship is a more collective phenomenon than the set of rational, individualistic, tendencies deployed in the earlier American concept. The political party has also traditionally been more important than the individual voter as a focus of attention, and this remains a European bias, despite the weakening of party ties.

The 'order' theme can better be rendered in terms of the idea of 'identity' – the identity of nations, linguistic and cultural minorities and European identity in the world or within a wider conception of the unity of European nations. The notion of 'solidarity' has also retained a respectable and more prominent place in conceptions of order in European politics and society, paralleling the idea of equality as a political goal. Lastly, identity includes a preoccupation with culture(s), which is more common in the European than in the American context. Order has more positive connotations in the present-day agenda of European research than it seems to have had in the American founding school. This may only reflect a pragmatic tendency at that time to formulate research in terms of 'social problems' in order to gain funding for research.

These characteristic themes can now be identified more specifically as issues for communication research in contemporary Europe. They are summarily presented in Table 2.

European research, under the banner of 'efficiency and innovation', here assigned to it, is being increasingly guided by an awareness of the social and economic significance of new information technologies. The self-interest of national governments and European-level agencies lends its material weight to this trend. Several countries as well as the European Commission have established research programmes specifically to explore the impact and potential of new communication technologies. Researchers are being asked to look at problems of effective communication in commercial as well as public service contexts. Theoretical developments tend towards a consideration of the 'information society' and of information as a new societal resource. A more general 'communication science' is being sought which can encompass the 'old' mass media, the new technologies, and some basic processes of human communication in society.

The concern with communication 'equity' leads to a focus on the maintenance of universal communication provision under conditions of change and of the increased scope for market forces. Attention to the survival of public broadcasting in a multi-channel environment is illustrative of this concern. But researchers still care about access, participation and minority rights to communicate. The problem of media concentration remains on the agenda of critical researchers, with the added element of a European 'multi-nationalism', to complicate the older model of American media imperialism. There is a renewed attention to imbalances in global information flows, which apply beyond the sphere of news and television programme exchange. Discussion of the emerging 'information society' dwells on the growing gaps in access to the new technologies and the new sources of information.

In the matter of 'communication and identity', there is renewed curiosity about the meaning of different national cultures in relation to some concept of a pan-European culture, about which there is some uncertainty. There are more pragmatic concerns about the effects of 'commercialization' in European culture, and also of 'Americanization'. Equally practical is the question of the healthy survival of small national cultures and languages and those of regions and ethnic minorities within larger nation states. Research burgeons into the ways in which cultural offerings from television and other new media are being interpreted and incorporated into existing cultures and frameworks of meaning. These entries all help to group and summarize many of the communication research activities which are to be observed in the growing schools and centres of research in a number of European countries and provide an indication of the agenda for research referred to above, even if they give little clue as to theory and method in communication research.

To make the description clearer and an assessment of progress more definite, it is useful to make another kind of distinction according to the type of research or intellectual activity which is involved. Three categories can be separated out:

1   a process of describing and reflecting on what is currently happening in communications, often in the form of critical accounts of media institutions and policies, formulation of theory, with historical and philosophical rather than social scientific–empirical modes of enquiry;
2   'middle range' social research, guided by established theory and methods of the 'dominant paradigm' of communication research,

Table 2   *European communication research: thematic agenda (exemplified)*

	Type of research activity		
	Theory	Middle-range empirical	Applied
Efficiency/ innovation	Direction and determination of media-technological change; Information science and theory development	Effects of communication change on work and social life	(Pan-European) media use; Advertising/ marketing, media planning
Equality	Consequence of media policy change; Information society; Gender and media	Information gaps; Minority access; Bias/diversity news research	Information needs; Public information campaigns
Identity	Meaning of trans-nationalization; Media culture	Reception and cultural diversity analysis; Response to trans-border flow; cultural production	Propaganda for Europe (Europrop); International communication (North–South; East–West)

or by newer modes of social-cultural analysis. This type of research activity is likely to produce specific findings about mass communication uses, content and effects, to test or establish limited propositions belonging to the corpus of academic science;
3 applied communication research, for public or commercial purposes, designed to guide or evaluate planned communication activities and the development of communication.

The way in which a research agenda is shaping up can now be further illustrated by cross-classifying this three-fold division by the main themes and by giving examples of research topics. It is obviously impracticable to enter all main kinds of research, but the illustrations are chosen to reflect the author's view of what are the most significant kinds of research theme at present.

Conclusion

This discussion has deliberately avoided some familiar lines of comment about the differences between European and American research, in particular those comparisons which emphasize the European tendency to be, compared to the American versions, all of the following: more theoretical; more 'society' than 'media'-centred; more critical; more oriented to texts than to behaviour (for example, Blumler, 1978, 1980b). There is some truth in these points, despite an element of stereotype and caricature, and they are each reflected in the substance of the agenda just outlined. The main change in European research during the last ten years has been a shift towards technocratic and applied kinds of research and a change in balance from cultural to more cognitive (information-related) concerns.

However, the main aim here has not been to show how far European research has grown away from its American roots, or what its current style might be, but rather to say something of its current substantive concerns and possible directions. There is no reason to expect more consensus on research priorities or on theoretical formulations than in the past, given the diversity already described. On the other hand, there is reason to expect some more accommodation and collaboration on methods, certainly if the academic study of communication is to continue its path of institutional development.

It has already been suggested that the harvest of research is still somewhat limited, and this is especially so in the 'middle-range' empirical area identified above. It is also the area which is most essential to the growth of an institutionalized branch of knowledge. But the signs are fairly encouraging for more fruit, even if the now middle-aged (second) generation of communication researchers in Europe may find the product either flavourless or not at all to their taste. Despite the increasing consensus about the definition and boundaries of a more autonomous field of study of communication, there are a good many other sources of strain, which relate to fundamental matters and which keep reappearing, or being resurrected, after being pronounced dead. One has to do with methods: the variable acceptance or prominence of 'quantitative' methods and the associated systematic measurement of behaviour and of 'information'.

This is much more than a dispute about method, since it involves a difference of view about communication and about what is important in communication. Within Europe itself, the difference between 'scientific' and 'cultural' approaches (Rosengren, 1983), which has often been said to differentiate Europe from America, is still marked and may become sharper rather than otherwise, as communication or information 'science' gains ground against the study of 'media' or 'mass communication' and as the technocratic tendencies noted above gain ground, for political-economic reasons.

Second, the differences of view about *whose* interest is to be served by communication research will remain and may also reappear in other forms. The dimming, latterly, of the social critical spirit and the assertion of 'businesslike' discourse and practice, which is being widely adopted by, or imposed on, the university and research community, is an undeniable feature of the times. To a certain extent it is just a change of orthodoxy, and the stream of idological conflict and of critical theory will not simply dry up. It takes time to find new forms and protagonists and may temporarily flow underground. The experience rather than the theory of commercialization may well concentrate the mind and oblige researchers to take sides.

Finally, there is a source of tension which is as familiar in the United States as it is in Europe: the uneasy relationship between communication research and communication practice. There is a continual friction between researchers advancing theoretical models of how communication does, or might, take place and the 'doers', who still see communication largely as a series of creative, unplannable and unpredictable happenings. There is no immediate bridge-building operation in prospect to help close this divide, although the rapid growth of higher educational programmes of study, which many future communicators are likely to be following, may help to reduce the level of misunderstanding that still prevails.

This closing litany of persistent problems in the field is not meant to be read as a pessimistic end-note. The problematic character of the field of communication research is also a sign of vitality and an promise of discoveries still to be made and fruit still to be harvested by European toilers in the vineyard of research.

9

Electronic Media and the Redefining
of Time and Space

Marjorie Ferguson

> Collapsing time and distance, TV created instant history and
> hurled it at light-speed into our homes and memories.[1]

This chapter explores the impact of electronic media on our
perceptions of, and responses to, changing temporal and spatial
horizons. It examines how our lexicon of time–space meanings is
changing in response to modernity and to the growing internationalism
of knowledge, entertainment, economic and social networks linked
by new technologies of public communication.

Despite the significance of time–space imperatives for social and
economic organization and as an aspect of the post-1960s transformation of media systems, this issue has received comparatively little
academic attention when compared with the research and rhetoric
devoted to, for example, the economic consequences of satellite,
digital and fibre optic communications.[2]

The persistence of a 'techno-orthodoxy' which early acquired the
status of Holy Writ in many policy, industrial and scholarly circles
is one reason for this. At its simplest, the techno-orthodoxist world-
view proclaims that the swiftness and pervasiveness of satellite,
digital and fibre optic communication has effectively reduced time–
space differences to insignificance. In contrast, I conclude the
reverse to be the case, and will argue that two decades of rapid
technological change in global communications have made temporal
and spatial concerns more paramount and more problematic than
previously.

The 'techno-orthodoxy' I am contesting derives from the early
claims about the positive effects of new communication and information technologies. This school of optimism predicted significant
economic and social benefits as a result of technological 'revolution'.
Despite the failure of prophecy and the non-arrival of many of the
predicted advantages, the tenacity of belief in the diminution of
time–space constraints is typified in the quotation that begins this
chapter, and evinced in the literature and official reports.[3]

There is, however, a problem in arguing against the 'techno-orthodoxy'. There is insufficient research and historical detail relating to the cognitive or social consequences of the new media to permit us to answer questions about *how* they help to shift our everyday understanding of time and space, or *which* media forms influence the way people think about or experience duration and distance. If, indeed, we are constructing new models of spatial and temporal understanding and organization, we first need to discover if these new models are market-efficient and personally dysfunctional.

In the absence of ready answers to such questions, what is clear is that the new media are acting and interacting in ways which require us to think anew about these categories in everyday work and personal life. Equally clearly, the restructuring of economic and cultural institutions across national and regional boundaries, as is happening today, has time–space consequences which occur in more than overt ways. They also occur in covert ways about which we as yet know little.

Apart from an insufficiency of qualitative evidence, there are paradoxes involved in turning the techno-orthodoxy on its head. The first concerns studies of the media production process which clearly demonstrate how electronic technology has magnified, not reduced, time–space priorities. The second paradox concerns the media timing and spacing strategies of, for example, political information managers. Their packaging of personalities and policies for 20-second television 'sound bites' reaffirms the high value placed historically on exercising political or economic control over temporal and spatial matters.

More generally, the determinist assumption that communication technology almost unilaterally possesses the power to render time–space differences insignificant can be denied by an abundance of historical, anthropological and psycho-social evidence, irrespective of any technology. Just as they have differential access to new or old communication media, so do different cultures, social groups and institutional sources of power perceive, categorize and prioritize temporal and spatial boundaries differently. Two classic examples of cultural variation in this respect are provided by the cattle clock time of the Nuer (Evans-Pritchard, 1973), and the gender-loaded spatial arrangements of the Berber household (Bourdieu, 1973).

Changing time–space relations: calendars, clocks and communications

The extent to which any electronic medium, from the early telegraph to state-of-the-art satellites, can shape or shift time–space perceptions and priorities is open to historical, sociological, ethnographic and political-economic investigation. Control over the production and reception systems of mass communication represents more than the power to define and redefine experience through printed or programme content. Command over media institutions also serves to legitimize and validate wider systems of authority in society. Repetition plays a part in this, and the links between time, space and recurrence is significant for social development (Giddens, 1979: 204), a point germane to the political and cultural significance of time–space dominion and governance through the ages.

The meso-American civilization of fifteenth-century central Mexico illustrates how authority over the temporal symbolic structure was linked to political control over socio-cultural space. The mathematical precision and elaborate animal symbolism important to time measurement in these cultures involved reading a solar calendar of 360 plus 5 'ominous' days against a 260-day calendar of 13 day weeks, thereby investing a privileged class with the power to define experience by interpreting the present and forecasting the future (Léon-Portilla, 1982).

Another example of the link between power and dominion over temporality concerns that earlier, and slower, metamorphosis of the European social order from cock-crow time to clock-strike time. The development and diffusion of clock technology between 1300 and 1700 had significant economic and social consequences, not least for the disciplined work rhythms of capitalist production. Time became 'currency', and control over its resources became the power to stretch the length of the working day when workers were forbidden to own clocks (Thompson, 1967: 82; see also Cipolla, 1967).

Similarly, the history of the first electronic medium in the nineteenth century, the telegraph, indicates how innovation in communication technology extended economic (and political) dominion over time and space. Bit by bit, this enhanced communication environment allowed firms with small advantages to lever them into much larger advantages, extending businesses from local to regional, then regional to national and from national to new international markets (Du Boff, 1983).

Apart from its impact on market structures and practices, the telegraph made a profound impression on common-sense thinking about time and space. As the telegraph reduced the significance of space for trade and communication, it also, as Carey (1988) makes clear, transformed time to 'a new region of experience, uncertainty, speculation, and exploration', which led to 'changes in the nature of language, of ordinary knowledge, of the very structures of awareness' (Carey, 1988: 219, 202).

What is evident is that each generation of electronic communication, from the telegraph to the computer, has offered from its inception an expansion of meanings, as well as facilities, to a diversity of commercial constituencies and 'publics' from the robber baron clients of the nineteenth-century telegraph to the soft porn cable subscribers of the late twentieth century.

As new modes of transmission and reception diffuse, among other things, novel definitions of duration, location or distance and these become commonplace, they become routinized within the organizational structures of public and private life. A recent study of time-use changes in the Soviet Union and United States, between the mid-1960s and the mid-1980s, indicates processes of social transformation linked to increased usage of media and other new technologies across nation-state and cultural frontiers. In the two radically different socio-political systems, these led to broadly similar behaviour patterns: for instance, more time spent watching television and less time doing housework (Robinson et al., 1989: 136).

New models, new dynamics of time–space significance?
Clearly changes in the public use and private consumption of new communication systems and services have implications for how we comprehend time–space relations and priorities. Despite the technological ease with which electronic media seemingly render time transparent through instantaneity or culture opaque through quasi-universality, such mediations do not necessarily provide new sets of categorical certainties or universal meanings about duration and distance.

What seems more probable is that increased internationalism in all forms of communication overlays both the current, local ideas about time and space, and the earlier, sensory-based epistemologies where what was directly experienced (seen, heard, touched, tasted or smelled) defined the world with alternative definitions and meanings. This layering of the new upon the old, the novel upon the customary, conveys a temporal elasticity and locational indeterminacy which is, I suggest, more problematic for organizations and individuals than is generally conceded.

If this is the case, the new media are not providing a boundless media-land of common understandings. Rather, formerly finite absolutes take on a notably relativist character where the temporal consequences may include a trans-historical eliding of past, present and future which replaces old certainties with new ambiguities.[4] As notions of distance and duration acquire mutliple meanings it seems probable that new time–space 'zones' are created. These can be denoted as a suspended, limbo-ish view of 'time-without-time', and a de-contextualized sense of 'space-without-space' to connote their kaleidoscopic frames of temporal and spatial reference.[5]

Clearly, all processes of social definition and redefinition are complicated. Any changes in our structure of awareness relating to time and space owe as much to our place in history and the social structure as to any particular media technology or market entre-preneurs. Understandings of time and space, old or new, develop at different rates and take different forms within all traditional, developing, industrial, service or 'information' societies. With elec-tronic communications media, however, local definitions more readily interact with the larger communication system that comprises the totality of culture (or cultures – nationally, regionally, inter-nationally) and can best be explored in that context.

How might such a cultural dynamic operate? The role of the household television set, as an increasingly universal medium, is suggestive. To the extent that imported television programmes penetrate local meaning systems, do they perhaps mediate an audio-visual version of the 'uncertainty principle' as to the where and when of everyday life? By offering alternative temporal and spatial connotations and contexts, 'foreign' television content may not so much homogenize diverse cultures as reinforce the de-stabilizing and future-oriented characteristics associated with modernity. In this way, imported programming may contribute to the generalized anxiety and 'futurity' orientation noted, for example, by Berger (1979). It may also intensify the contradictions between our welath of scientific knowledge and incapacity to control our individual or global environments acknowledged by Giddens (1987).

The foregoing discussion and the remainder of this chapter explores the relationship between modernity, public communi-cation, new technologies and time–space redefinition. Several of the more conceptual and speculative questions surveyed here derive from the sociology of knowledge and social anthropology literature, whereas the more purely economic, political and social issues they raise are pursued empirically. The former concern questions of methodological clarification; the latter concern questions of agency, as to which sets of actors are helping to demarcate time–space boundaries through policy, regulation, ownership and professional or interpersonal practices.

Frequently both lines of enquiry are difficult to separate. Both involve wider issues concerning relations between the symbolic and political orders, and how mass communications as a system of cultural production influences and is influenced by changing spatial and temporal horizons. A start can be made, however, by examining the evidence of increased time–space significance in international television and telecommunications, and by re-examining the work of theorists such as Durkheim and Mauss (1967), Durkheim (1976), Innis (1950, 1951, 1952, 1954), Lasswell (1941, 1948, 1954), McLuhan (1964) and McLuhan and Fiore, (1967).

Electronic media: new world orders of temporal and contextual indeterminacy?

> The trading opportunity is in Tokyo, the corporate treasurer is in his kitchen, in Connecticut, at 8.30 in the evening. The trader who alerted him . . . [is] . . . in New York. At Citicorp's foreign exchange night desk.[6]

As the text of this advertisement makes clear, when the techno-orthodoxy meets global trading ideology we have answers, in part, as to which sets of actors, located in which structural strata, exert power over public communications networks, nationally and internationally. The participatory chances and choices are not evenly distributed, however, between nations and groups. When it comes to the bending of culture-bound temporal orders or national-state spatial borders by increases in international telephone traffic, financial network trading, satellite and cable broadcasting, consumer electronic application or corresponding changes in household behaviour, some are more equal than others.

For telecommunications
There is persuasive evidence of the capacity of telecommunications to redefine temporal and spatial significance with the exponential growth of commercial and domestic international telephone traffic. The 1980s witnessed a world-wide user explosion of an early electronic medium, the telephone, due among other factors to the impact of improved fibre optic and satellite technologies, the de-regulation of common carriers, reductions in tariffs and the growth in world markets and tourism.

For example, between 1975 and 1987 the revenues of international telephone common carriers in the United States increased from $589.6 million to $2.4 billion; the volume of calls originating or terminating in the United States rose from 42.6 to 625 million messages over the same period (Federal Communications Commission, 1988: 1). Two cases typify increased traffic and time–space significance in developed and developing economies. Between 1982 and 1987: the number of calls between the United Kingdom and the United States more than doubled, from 21.5 to 58.2 million;

similarly, calls between Jamaica and the United States trebled during the same period, from 2.5 to 6.7 million (FCC, 1988: Table 13).

For financial networks

A second area where the redefinition of time–space meanings has proved significant is in the market-places of the international financial trading system. The 'Black Monday' stock-market crash of October 1987 illustrated the quantitative effects of electronic information networks and the relativizing of time–space differences to the activities of economic institutions. As this drama of falling share prices unfolded around the world, it starkly showed how national economies locked into the international division of labour were rendered equal. Whatever their respective starting positions in the economic pecking order, all the players were confronting the same electronic domino effect in the new world commercial order as a panic of electronic share-selling took its toll.

The dynamics of this situation highlight the paradoxes and contradictions of communication and economic inter-dependency. On the one hand, this phenomenon did manifest the collapsing of time and shrinking of space proclaimed as axiomatic by the techno-orthodoxy. On the other, it showed how clock time and distance remain critical in the split-second situations of financial risk management, and how such processes are made more hazardous because of the speed, ubiquity and connectedness of sophisticated information systems.

For television

The third area where time–space considerations are magnified is international television, with the spread of 'live' global coverage. The rapid expansion of cable, microwave and satellite technologies over the last quarter-century has helped to restructure broadcasting ownership and institutions, with a corresponding measure of innovation in programme content and scheduling. In the highly competitive, de-regulated market economies of national and international broadcasting, new genres of audio-visual cultural production have developed and have circled the globe. The new formats which emerged in the 1980s include MTV rock-around-the-clock videos and the repackaging of television news as entertainment, whereby we amuse ourselves if not to death, to inform (Postman, 1986).

There are two further aspects to the expansion of television coverage. One concerns broadcasting's 'colonization' of time with the expansion of radio and television programming to fill the night as well as the day, in part as response to the increasing wakefulness of urban populations (Melbin, 1978). The second concerns the 'colonization' of global television space by such means as the growth of transnational media ownership and international co-production. Cable News Network's (CNN) 24-hour service typifies both the international and round-the-clock aspects of the colonization of time and space by the broadcasting industry. CNN markets its particular brand of non-stop cultural diffusion from whatever times and whichever places into homes and hotel rooms in seventy countries around the world.

In some respects the story of broadcasting re-enacts the earlier saga of the telegraph: the enhanced information provision of colour over black-and-white television or radio, and the moving from local to regional, national and international markets. These developments have facilitated the emergence of another programme genre, the global totemic festivals of the Olympic Games, Live Aid concerts and British royal family rites of passage which are ritually celebrated by satellite.[7]

For work organization
The spread of electronic media consumer goods appears to give individuals greater autonomy and control over time and space but actually functions to place them more at the mercy of employers, institutions or significant others. Compact computers on the plane, facsimile machines in the home and cellular car phones in traffic jams demonstrate the extent to which temporal and spatial constraints have become more relative than absolute as a result of portable, personal communication systems. These consumption patterns, largely confined to the affluent, also represent a further case and refinement of the self-serving society thesis which contends that we are buying more goods and fewer services (Gershuny and Miles, 1986).

An example of how consumer electronics are magnifying time–space imperatives in workday life is the impact of the 'lap-top' computer on the professional journalist's role. The romantic myth of the far-flung foreign correspondent in the Evelyn Waugh *Scoop!* tradition is no more when the Nicaraguan hotel provides our man in Managua with a modem to access Lord Copper's office, and British Telecom provides Lord Copper with a Fax number to thunder at the journalist from afar.

For household behaviour
The growth of entertainment, information and communication interdependence is not divorced from social and cultural change at the domestic level. Growing numbers of households around the

world have experiential knowledge of the implications of new zones of 'time-without-time' and 'space-without-space' for everyday social organization and family life.

Among the interpersonal skills honed and routinized by this decade's new generation of telecommunications has been learning how to adjust our perceptual clocks to spatially far away, but communicative near, times and places. This commonplace behaviour will acquire added significance in the future with video via the telephone line,[8] when facial and body language will overlay that of the spoken word. Among the everyday technical skills demanded by self-serving electronic media in the home is the mastery of the estimated 187.32 million VCRs around the world on the part of householders intent on shifting the time, space and place of film and television viewing (*Screen Digest*, June 1989).

Systems of classification and the social construction of time and space

All known societies use forms of time allocation – sequential, durational, horological, seasonal, astrological, lunar, sereal – and forms of distance calculation – cubits, chains, leagues, kilometres, light years, microns, parsecs, and so on – as organizing principles of social life. When we turn to the social science literature for insights into institutional, cognitive and behavioural changes such as those explored above, we find that among classical social theorists, Durkheim (Durkheim and Mauss, 1967; Durkheim, 1976) has most influenced our thinking about social classificatory systems such as those of time and space. He treated them as social constructs within the body of his work on collective representations.

The world has moved on since Durkheim's day. Writing almost a century ago he could not foresee the development of a global division of labour or market economy linked by electronic communication. Moreover, primary definitions of time and space are no longer merely culture-specific constructs as Durkheim contended, but are exposed to accidental or imposed change processes by tourism or conquest as well as by economy or technology. Any determinisms deriving from the latter would imply that new meanings associated with, for example, global market growth function more as pre-ordained Kantian categories than as Durkheimian ones bubbling up through the cultural residues of a particular social system.

In an era of transnational markets in consumer, information and cultural goods, aspects of Durkheim's thesis are still valid if we reposition them on the larger context of the world stage. In this connection, the notion of 'world time' (Giddens, 1984: 245) can be usefully expanded to encompass 'world time–space' in order to infer the interconnection between the growth of the capitalist world market and shifting temporal and spatial horizons. This requires us to 'scale up' our frames of reference and relocate them in a larger cultural context of what constitutes the 'society' of men from which categories of meaning are being socially (and economy) derived.

Several scholarly critiques of the modernity process have noted the impact of institutional change, technology and bureaucracy on how we see and experience the world (see, for example, Gellner, 1964; Giddens, 1984). The consequences cited by Berger (1979) as symptomatic include the dilemmas of 'abstraction' and 'futurity'. The former concerns the anomie or alienation associated with the spread of the market economy, the mass media and the technologizing of society; the latter concerns a shift in our temporal structure: at the levels of biography (how we conceive our life in terms of a career), everyday life (the dominance of clock-watching), and society (institutional forward-planning) (Berger, 1979: 103–5). If it is clear that electronic media contribute to these transformations, what is not clear is how they are doing this and within which social and cognitive dimensions.

Harold Innis and Harold Lasswell: the historical and the a-historical approaches to time–space relations

When we turn to the history of communications scholarship for insights into how new communication networks may be redefining time–space priorities and perceptions, we find a considerable legacy. Deep in the vaults of received wisdom lie several concepts worthy of reincarnation, one or two worthy of canonization, and not a few overdue for permanent interment. The search for concepts and methods can profit from a return to the work of two early giants in the field, Harold Innis and Harold Lasswell. From both we can learn as much, perhaps, about what not to do as what to do.

The Innisian inheritance
Few communication scholars would dispute the importance of the contribution of Canadian economic historian Harold Innis (1950, 1951, 1952, 1954) to understanding relations between communications technology and political dominion extended over time and space. His work blazed a few trails which still provide routes for later explorers of shifting time–space horizons in the electronic media universe.

His ideas are still 'not merely things to read but things to think with' (Carey, 1981: 73). And his concern with politico-economic control over 'monopolies of knowledge', allied to the time duration or spatial distance 'bias' of durable and non-durable communications media, still provides compass points for surveying the global empires of satellite and digitalized information and communication.[9]

Innis's compilation of eclectic historical detail gave his thesis of public communication 'bias' a panoramic back-drop drawn from the administrative systems of ancient Egypt, Babylonia, imperial Rome and China to those of Reformation England, Holland and Germany. This broad canvas demonstrated for Innis that 'culture is concerned with the capacity of the individual to appraise problems in terms of space and time' (Innis, 1951: 85).

Writing in the context of a post-Hiroshima, McCarthyite culture, Innis's preoccupation with the survival of Western civilization as he knew it expressed itself in his political economy of communications. His introduction to *Empire and Communications* (1950: 7) stresses: 'Large scale political organizations such as empires must be considered from the standpoint of the two dimensions, and persist by overcoming the bias of media which over-emphasize either dimension' (1950: 7). Innis returned repeatedly to the theme of changing communication media and political administration over time and space without developing his initial insights into a coherent theoretical framework on the one hand, or embracing economic, cultural or technological determinism on the other (see, for example, Carey, 1981; Kroker, 1984; Parker, 1985; Theall, 1986; Wernick, 1986).

The Innisian critique focused on his political concern that print-media monopolies of knowledge invoked control over space and neglected the problems of time monopoly, where 'Time has been cut into pieces the length of a day's newspaper' (Innis, 1954: 94).[10] Although he welcomed radio broadcasting as a return to a more oral, participatory public communication, Innis could not intuit how later electronic media would redefine time–space boundaries or create opportunities for more universal monopolies of knowledge.[11]

However, Innis also cautions against over-simplifying the relationship between technology, economy and power, reminding us that 'disequilibrium created by the character of technological changes in communication strikes at the heart of the economic systems' (Innis, 1952: 108), a caution apposite to the proven sensitivity of markets to the information services of global electronic publishers such as Reuters. Retrospective prophecy also emerges from his claim that the Western concept of linear time has 'a capacity for infinite extension to the past and future and a limited capacity for adaptation' (ibid.). If 'time-without-time' is no longer single culture specific, then distinctions between linear and non-linear time may also have changed, despite the former's limited capacity for adaptation.

Innis, then, acknowledged the material force of technology, the epistemological significance of culture and the political imperium of economy without succumbing to any of these potential determinisms. He has left us a legacy of important but imperfectly inscribed signposts for future research. First, he reminds us that a historical comparative perspective is critical to understanding global information and communication networks. Second, his aversion to quantitative methods and statistics as the last refuge of rationality offers encouragement for those more inclined to speculation or qualitative debate about media and the public world.

Among scholars who have trodden the paths Innis surveyed, a direct beneficiary was his fellow member of the 'Toronto School of Communication', Marshall McLuhan. Although McLuhan acknowledged his debt, scholarly opinion has largely concluded that the self-proclaimed disciple, in Cooper's (1981: 153) words, '"did something" to Innis – popularized, over-simplified, developed, improved, misunderstood, clarified, immortalized, bastardized or resurrected him'.

In contrast to Innis's comparative approach, McLuhan attributed direct causal, not to say cosmic, effects to the impact of television and computer technology on individuals. An early proselytizer of the techno-orthodoxy that electronic media erase time–space differences, McLuhan (1964; McLuhan and Fiore, 1967) heralded a new audio-visual age of global *Gemeinschaft*, and set an agenda of acceptance that television had made this a *fait accompli*:

> Electric circuitry has overthrown the regime of 'time' and 'space' and pours upon us instantly and continuously the concerns of all other men. . . . Ours is a brand new world of allatonceness. 'Time' has ceased, 'space' has vanished. We now live in a global village . . . a simultaneous happening. (McLuhan and Fiore, 1967: 16, 63)

As with other McLuhanesque pronouncements, this vision of a universal New Jerusalem contains elements of prophecy subsequently fulfilled. It also displays his disregard for Innis's distinction between the consequences of time- and space-biased communication, and a sociological *naïveté* which neglects the roles both of political and economic institutions and the social actors with interests in applying such technologies.

The Lasswellian inheritance

In contrast to the magpie collecting of historical nuggets of Innis, the theorizing of Lasswell the political scientist is dramatically a-historical. This absent category requires that any re-evaluation of

Lasswell's work must begin with what I call his 'sin of omission'. It has long struck me as curious that the most invoked sacred text, the Lasswellian dictum of the communication process, is blind to the temporal and historical/contextual aspects of the message. There is no '*when*' in 'who says what in which channel to whom with what effect?' (Lasswell, 1964: 37), just as there is no '*where*'. Nor for that matter is there any recognition of the explanatory significance of 'why' a particular message comes to be the way it is.

Given the ritual invocation and sacerdotal status accorded his telegraphic prescription, the omission of the key ingredients of time and space in Lasswell's research recipe for the communication process merits further critical reflection.[12] First, the inherent limitations of Lasswell's 'organizing formula' are unsurprising given its implicit functionalist perspective. Second, and equally problematic, the formula was anthropomorphic in intent: Lasswell sought to show how a radio station or newspaper could be likened to a person communicating a flow of messages (Katz and Lazarsfeld, 1955: 1).

This image and heuristic may have fitted the biological analogy and dominant tradition of American sociology in the late 1940s and 1950s. But it ignores how social actors and media institutions interact within the context of a specific historical moment and a particular communications power structure in the production of a given message.

This omission on Lasswell's part is all the more remarkable given his personal concern with the political issues of his day, and the role of public opinion and propaganda in the democratic process in particular, In the 1940s this led him to favour democracy-serving public-relations experts intent upon the invention of ideas that will 'achieve results' based on a keen awareness of the 'swiftly moving events of the time' (Lasswell, 1941: 71); while as a cold warrior in the 1950s he censured Soviet manipulation of public opinion as 'the management of mass communications for power purposes' (Lasswell, 1954: 537–8).[13]

The sophistication and reach of 'propaganda' and 'public opinion' in the satellite age exceeds that of Lasswell's proto-television era, and suggests a long-overdue recasting of his formula. If it is still to be invoked, its use involves a re-commitment on the part of communication scholars to embrace as axiomatic a contextual framing for their enterprise. The framework of when and where must be added to those of person, organization, medium, content or process if we are to understand why the message takes the form it does, at whose behest and with what consequences.

Methodologically, it is evident that a-historical or de-contextualized enquiry into media messages and processes is insufficient both at the level of meaning and of explanation. For example, the bureaucratic structures and creative processes of media organizations must be included within Lasswell's 'what' when studying television production (Cantor, 1980: 14). Moreover, the consequences of mass communication are contingent on their location in time and place, and a-historicity avoided, if we are to refrain from making direct causal connection between media messages and a given set of 'effects' (McQuail, 1978: 19).

The Lasswellian inheritance then proffers more false trails than signposts to mapping the new communication universe. By omitting where and when from his communication formula, he left us a significant negative legacy. Based upon an a-historical mediography, it lends itself to the attribution of direct effects on the part of mass-mediated communications.

The fruits of this tradition are still with us. They are particularly evident in studies of television's alleged 'effects'. The causal connections made range from more general debates about cultural imperialism, television programme imports and national identity (see, for example, Schlesinger 1987a; Tracey, 1985) to more specific attributions – for instance, the arguments about the link between television content and violence in society (see, for example, Gunter, 1987).

Denying the techno-orthodoxy 1: Media professionals and the art and craft of timing and placing

The paradox noted above between the techno-orthodoxist view that electronic media have reduced time–space imperatives, and the primacy given to message timing and placing by professional journalists and political-media actors is well documented. Empirical studies of the media production process clarify the plasticity of 'time', the historicity of 'the times' and the priority of 'timing' in structuring work rhythms, deadlines and news content (Epstein, 1974; Schlesinger, 1987b; Schudson, 1986; Scannell, 1988; Tuchman, 1978).

Several studies document the extent to which the television news-assembly process, with its frenetic knitting together of image-text-voice, is time and space obsessed. Advertisers and would-be news-makers also mark these rhythms in plotting their capture of prime-time news frames and audiences. The televising of international sport demonstrates this, just as it falsifies the techno-orthodoxy that electronic media have reduced time–space imperatives. Both the 1984 Los Angeles and 1988 Seoul Olympiads exhibited the redefining of sporting contests to fit the commercial time slots of advertising-supported television, with events staged to maximize multi-national audiences when television for profit operates on the global scale.

As such, the coverage of the Olympic Games in the 1980s represents ideal-typical cases of the television news 'stop-watch culture' identified by Schlesinger (1987b) as a work culture embedded in the larger clock-watching routines of industrialized societies and the market conditions of television production. The regularity of radio and television programme scheduling, on the other hand, lends itself to a Durkheimian interpretation where the ends of social membership are served by collective representations in the symbolic system. Thus, broadcast programmes of seasonal and festive events reproduce 'calendrical time', an ordering of experience which helps sustain the daily routines of audiences (Scannell, 1988).[14]

The time imperatives of television professionals are more than matched by graduates of the Front Page school of journalism. Their practices in creating what might be called 'time within time' include the layering and reconstruction of past, present and future in the story through such stratagems as 'depths of the past on page one' and 'the continuous present' (Schudson, 1986: 89). Here Lasswell's 'who says what in which channel to whom with what effect' can be compared with the equally formulaic 'five Ws and the H' – the who, what, when, where, why and how defined as mandatory by print journalists and sacred to their professional mythology (Carey, 1986: 147–9).

If American newspapermen do not suffer from Lasswell's sin of omission, none the less their professional world-view raises an interesting methodological issue. Whose approach to constructing (or de-constructing) social context or message content is likely to produce the more sociologically valid explanation? Is it the Lasswell-following, a-historical communications scholar who down-plays the 'where' and 'when' in de-constructing the 'what' or 'why' of message content and reception? Or is it the journeyman journalist who specifies time and context but often eschews the 'why' of interpretative analysis? The fact that these are empirical, rather than philosophical, questions does not render them more readily answerable.

Such combination and re-combination of meaning is not the outcome of manipulation on the part of monolithic media institutions; nor is it a solo performance executed on a one-way street of uni-directional influence. Communication content is the outcome of a framing process negotiated between institutions, individuals, groups and events; and the ensuing dialogue of media exposure and closure is one where temporal, spatial and cultural contexts are defined and redefined by all the interested parties.[15]

Denying the techno-orthodoxy 2: the iron law of imagery and public relations as public policy

The time–space imperatives of electronic media also have implications for the growing commodification of the political process. Just as social theorists and historians have analysed the commodification of time and space in capitalist production (Giddens, 1981; Thompson, 1967), and media scholars the significance of historical context and the world market for the commodification of culture (Garnham, 1983, 1986), so here I want to examine the media packaging practices of political power-holders supremely cognizant of the critical importance of time, space and place in framing and targeting their messages.

This marketing, or 'commodifying', of the political process represents more than the selling of politicians and policies. It also represents the power to define experience by elevating presentational form over substantive content in political discourse, and the making of impression management strategies mandatory to the governmental process itself. This 'propaganda model' (Herman, 1986) of the power elite of the political control-communications media and its processes can usefully be put in a historical perspective.

Once again, Innis (1951) provides precedents to illustrate that control over temporal affairs has long been a correlate of power-holding. The self-serving ends of manipulative time–space management is not the invention of twentieth-century public relations gurus, nor a new breed of government propagandists. It is at least as old as the Romans. In a variety of ingenious ways, the Roman bureaucracy exercised control over temporal and imperial affairs, using changes in tax cycles, festival days and calendar divisions better to serve political or administrative ends (Innis, 1951: 68–70).

In more recent times, media scholars and critics have noted the negative consequences for public communication of increased information management in the public sphere. The two most frequently cited contributing factors are the ubiquity of television locally, nationally and internationally on the one hand, and concentration of corporate media ownership on the other. There seems little doubt that in a landscape littered with media 'pseudo-events' there has been a debasement of public communication. The line is a fine one between propaganda and a pseudo-event. They share a common ancestry of manipulative intent but differ in their approach: 'a pseudo-event is an ambiguous truth, propaganda is an appealing falsehood' (Boorstin, 1961: 34). Almost thirty years later, it could be argued that in an age of 'sound bite' and 'photo opportunity' mass communication, the reverse is the case.

Conceived as the power to influence public opinion, influence over media presentation is crucial to governments seeking to enlist support for their economic, defence, social or foreign policy aims. It follows that the escalation and routinization of message management in the public sphere poses a deceptively simple question. Do messages so conceived and constituted inform and empower the electorate in democractic socio-political systems to exercise influence over public policy? Chomsky (1987), for example, emphatically contends that they do not; and that the prerequisite of full, unbiased information is overwhelmingly absent from much of the content and intent of present-day public communication.

Similar conflicts also arise as a consequence of structural concentration in the cultural industries, in this case between factual accuracy and corporate self-interest. In the American case, it is contended that this has had the result where 'modern technology and American economics have quietly created a new kind of central authority over information' (Bagdikian, 1987: xix).

The iron law of imagery
What is evident is that those who seek to 'manage' the general flow of information in the public sphere strive hardest to manage the flow of information about themselves. In doing this they obey what I call the 'iron law of imagery', performing their power-seeker roles on an increasingly visible media stage. This pursuit of favourable publicity is based upon beliefs in media power, not confined to certain communication scholars, that media images and messages produce direct effects. It appears that far from the early Silver Bullet theory of media messages having died a dishonourable death, it is very much alive and well.

Resurrected as the strategic rationale of those who seek the national and international news spotlight, all media become fair game for what is at best a ritualized courtship and at worst a collusory 'dealing' between news-makers and journalists for time and space on talk radio, television slots or newspaper headlines. What this suggests is that the most popular drama now being played upon the stage of public communication is a Goffmanesque (1959) extravaganza. In this performance the image is all-powerful, and the pursuit of issues or 'objective facts' diminished or disregarded in deference to the absolute power of the (preferably) television *Gestalt*. Thus 'the presentation of self in everyday media life' prevails as the dominant form of political discourse with a concomitant distortion of the structures, processes and contents of public communication.

Public relations as public policy
The growth of political advertising and government media management is often linked with the immediacy advantages of broadcasting.
Such was the perceived power of this technology that its mastery did
not for long remain the monopoly of American presidents such as
Roosevelt with radio or Kennedy with television. Imitators were
soon everywhere, and British prime ministers, for example, from
Harold Macmillan onward, have attempted to ape their American
role models. This tradition of the cultural migration of political
styles continues.

If Nixon was the first President to apply mass-marketing techniques
to national elections, the Reagan administration successfully changed
his rules of the political game. Timing and placing was critical to
the Reagan team's news management, and their selling of policy
and personality combined political with media strategies: forward
planning, control of information flow, setting the issue agenda,
restricting access to the President, staying on the attack, speaking
the same message and repeating it (Hertsgaard, 1988: 34). These
lessons were not lost on British politicians. By her third electoral
engagement in 1987, such was Mrs Thatcher's wholehearted embrace
of the advertising and public relations industries that she had two
sets of competing information managers at work, sometimes counter-
productively (Tyler, 1987).[16]

The media–centric approach to public communication, deployed
by government as advertisements or concealments for itself, is most
clearly evident in wartime. Rallying cries of 'the national interest'
reverberate throughout history,and predate the age of print let
alone electronic mass communication as a legitimating rationale for
information control.

An example of official news management as an attempt to define
experience among other things in relation to time, space and
television technology, was the conduct of the British Government
during the 1982 Falklands War, as this has been documented by the
Glasgow University Media Group (1985) and Harris (1983). The
latter contends the 'managed' time scales for television film during
the Falklands conflict meant the average delay for television film
shown on British screens was seventeen days, just three days less
than it took *The Times* to publish news of the Charge of the Light
Brigade in the Crimean War (Harris, 1983: 56).

This case of official 'monopolies of knowledge' in the 1980s as
control over time–space relations illustrates the essential paradox
of electronically mediated definitions of duration and distance. The
high news value placed on television's immediacy, and its frustration

by the political value placed on damming its free flow, stress how time does matter very precisely. Temporal and spatial horizons are rendered both meaningless and more meaningful by such blocking of the technological means for instantaneity.

Towards the further exploration of renewed time–space significance

In this chapter I have tried to argue that, contrary to the techno-orthodoxy that new communication technologies have reduced time–space significances, the reverse is the case. Not only is there evidence of this in the knowledge networks of international markets and social networks of everyday life but also in the timing and placing priorities of the media production process and the information strategies of politico-media power elites.

In the context of a modernity characterized by the growth of economic and communication interdependence, I have suggested that satellite, digital and fibre optic communication are supplying new definitions of, and imperatives for, time and space. Moreover, these are not erasing the old everyday understandings of distance and duration but overlaying them with new definitions of the situation. These new notations of when and where, I have proposed, are providing plural or alternative meanings denoted as 'time-without-time' and 'space-without-space'.

Despite the evidence of increased time–space awareness in social and economic organization, in the broadcasting and telecommunications industries, in media and political institutions and in everyday life, we know little about how processes of media redefinition operate – just as we know little about the cognitive and behavioural, as compared with the economic, consequences of electronic media across a diversity of politico-cultural and psycho-social contexts. The argument that time–space significances are being magnified in differing institutional and interpersonal contexts reinforces an earlier contention; namely, that new communication technologies play an enabling role, providing a 'transformational logic' which contributes to the wider social, cultural and economic change processes in society (Ferguson, 1986: 53).

Clearly, any changes in our thinking or modifications to our behaviour which are associated with new modes of communication and reception result from social and cultural conditions as well as mechanical or market ones. The extent to which electronic media may be instrumental in producing new models of temporal and spatial organization which are market-efficient but personally dysfunctional requires further research. Investigation of this order, which addresses a complexity of institutional and individual responses to the changing modes and meanings of public discourse, calls for work that is historical and developmental as well as psychosocial and political–economic in its scope.

There are few well-marked trails or Baedekers to guide explorers across the wider horizons of the new media universe. Only comparative, qualitative research into *how* electronic communications magnify time–space imperatives, and *which* forms produce which kinds of intended and unintended consequences, will permit more fruitful analysis of the changing temporal and spatial horizons of public and private communication. To this end we may usefully recall a 400-year-old nostrum: 'He that will not apply new remedies must expect new evils; for time is the greatest innovator' (Francis Bacon, 'Of Innovations', *Essays*, 24, 1597).

Notes

This chapter has benefited greatly from the helpful critiques of an early version by John Carrier and Denis McQuail, and of a later version by Edward L. Fink.

1 Special issue of *People* magazine commemorating fifty years of American television, Summer, 1989.

2 The work of human geographers and social-psychologists provide notable exceptions to the economic-technology bias. See, for example, T. Carlstein et al., (1978), and J. McGrath (ed.) (1988).

3 Promulgated by prophets such as McLuhan (1964), popularized by futurologists like Toffler (1971) and Naisbitt (1982), and echoed in academic work such as Rice (1984), and Williams (1983), the techno-orthodoxy is also writ large in official reports of the past two decades; for example, *Instant World* (Information Canada, 1971), and *Making a Business of Information* (ITAP, 1983).

4 Boorstin (1975) deploys the notion of 'the extended contemporary' to denote the temporal ambiguity communicated by American television content.

5 See Meyrowitz (1985) for an interesting examination of the role of electronic media in altering perceptions of place as location and 'place' in the social structure.

6 Text of a Citicorp advertisement (*The Economist*, May 1989).

7 Exploring the transformations involved in the televising of public occasions such as these, Dayan and Katz (1987: 174) ask: 'is the broadcast a representation of a ceremony or is the ceremony nothing more than a live prop for the media event?'

8 Codec technology, Discrete Cosine Transform (DCT).

9 For Innis a presupposition of democratic life was the existence of a public sphere in the classic oral tradition and that print technology altered public discourse by making it more privatized as well as spatially biased (Carey, 1981: 86).

10 I am indebted to the University of Toronto librarian who provided this article when it could not be located in any British library.

11 When the Innisian model is applied to durable media such as film, records and video its insufficiencies are evident: it fails to take into account aspects such as information storage and collective memory (Wernick, 1986).

12 These omissions have not gone entirely unremarked. Braddock (1958) enlarged the cryptic formula to include 'what circumstance?' and 'what purpose?'

13   This definition of propaganda goals is more inclusive than exclusive, and differs little in its ends from those pursued by today's practitioners of 'information management' and 'economies of the truth'.

14   What Scannell appears to overlook is the Northern Euro-centric, public-service broadcasting ethos which produced these formerly unchanging rhythms of broadcast time as perpetuated, for example, by the BBC.

15   Analysing a negotiated relationship of this type, Gitlin (1980: 223) noted that 'one of the most striking effects of the whole media system on the texture of modern life lies in its reconstruction of the experience of time', but did not develop the idea further.

16   The Saatchi and Saatchi agency *de jure* were running the campaign from Tory Central Office, whereas *de facto* the Prime Minister's personal favourite, political packaging expert Tim Bell, was in frequent, secret conclave (Tyler, 1987).

10

Television and Everyday Life: Towards an Anthropology of the Television Audience

Roger Silverstone

No consideration of public communication can reasonably ignore the audience: the readers, viewers, consumers of the content of the mass media. Indeed, the history of mass communication research has been continuously sustained and informed by concerns with its effects on audiences – on their moral, political and economic lives. That history has been an uneven one. It has been dominated by a concern with effects, effectiveness and power, but judgements on each of these, and of the relative weight to be attached to the overall capacity of the media to influence its audiences in significant ways, has, as countless observers have noted, produced little convincing evidence of the media's potency one way or the other. The problems are substantial. The media operate in an already complex world. Audiences live in a complex world. Both are rapidly changing. The belief that the media can affect an audience in some direct or measurable ways has passed, despite commonsensical views to the contrary.

Nevertheless, the audience remains a problem for media research, as indeed it must. It has become once again a primary focus of much that is compelling in media studies, a potentially crucial pivot for the understanding of a whole range of social and cultural processes that bear on the central questions of public communication. These questions, I want to suggest, are essentially questions of culture. As our world becomes an increasingly mass-mediated world, as the number of communication technologies and services continues to expand, as the power of both producers and consumers grows (the power of producers to impose a transnational culture through media content, the power of consumers actively to select and interact with their own media content), an understanding of the dynamic work of audiences, as they manage the contradictions between the specificities of their own lives and the imposed generalities of an increasingly homogenized mass culture, becomes essential.

In this chapter I would like to offer an approach to some of the questions posed for the study of the television audience, not so much in the hope of providing conclusive answers as marking out a territory for future exploration. I will argue for a broadly anthropological conceptualization of the audience and for a methodological approach, or a set of approaches, which sets the audience for television in a context of the world of everyday life: the daily experiences of home, technologies and neighbourhood, and of the public and private mythologies and rituals which define the basic patterns of our cultural experience.

The embedded audience

Previous studies of the television audience (and the film and radio audience before it) have tended to concern themselves with issues which have to do with the extent 'to which an audience is a social group, the degree and kinds of activity which audiences can and do engage in, the forces which contribute to the formation of audiences and the extent to which media "manipulate" their audiences or are, in turn, responsive to them' (McQuail, 1987: 215). Audiences have been constituted as aggregates with similar characteristics, as masses, as public or social groups, as markets. There has been a major effort, for both academic and commercial reasons, to produce typologies. There has been, equally, a major effort, principally through the work of those pursuing 'uses and gratifications' research, to come to grips with the social and social-psychological dimensions of mass-media use. More recently audience studies have taken two other turns: the first, as a result of a preoccupation with media as texts and with texts to be deconstructed, in which the audience is presumed to be textually inscribed and as such conceived to be without empirical substance; and the second, which is directed towards an understanding of the social dynamics of audience activity and the specific social and cultural complexity of the audience precisely as an empirical phenomenon (cf. Morley, 1987: 28).

Hitherto, what seems substantially absent is a conceptualization of the television audience as a social and cultural object within the complex reality of everyday life. Such a conceptualization would encourage a view of the audience as embedded both in the macro-environment of political economy and in the micro-world of domestic and daily existence. What it also encourages, of course, is a view of the audience as heterogeneous, and as diffuse: audiences are both potential and actual; audiences are audiences for only some of the time; audiences are both active and passive, both discriminated against and discriminating. Audiences' relationships to television are mediated by what Peter Dahlgren calls their 'social ecology' (1985: 242) and what I am referring to as their embedding.

I need to provide some substance to this notion, which I shall do under three broad heads: the plurality of the television audience; the audience in space and time; the active and the passive audience.

The plurality of the television audience
The plurality of the audience consists not just in its inevitable differentiation by familiar sociological category, though gender and ethnicity, class and subculture have all been the object of study as mediatory factors in reception and negotiation with television content. It also consists in the plurality of the social and the individual, a plurality which in turn involves both a sociology and a psychology, and in their interrelationship, an understanding of the dynamics of the processes of mediation. The isolation of the audience from social context which much psychological work insists upon, and the collectivization of the audience which much sociological work insists upon, both distort the complex realities of an audience's identity and culture. And equally it must be recognized, as Martin Allor (1987) and Ien Ang (in press) in their ways recognize, that the audience is not a discrete phenomenon. An audience is both ephemeral and partial, both by virtue of its enthusiasms and its attention, as well as by virtue of its fragmentation and dispersion.

In a similar way television must also be understood as plural, not only in the phenomenological sense that television is different things to different people, but also in the material sense that television is increasingly able to offer a greater choice of programmes and services. More and more, television is becoming part of a combinatory of communication and information (mediating) technologies, requiring further choices and many further possibilities of use. As Denis McQuail argues, the greater availability of content is likely to involve changes 'in the relation between receivers and senders', changes in turn which will require greater attention to a view of audience behaviour as 'individual acts of purchase or consumption, or acts of consultation' (McQuail, 1987: 312).[1] What remains so far unclear, of course, is how far this potential for individuation and for the fragmentation of the audience will be realized, especially when it is set against an equally plausible cultural resistance by audiences committed in their various ways to national or regional identities as they are presently articulated through broadcast media.

The audience in space and time
There are very few studies of audience attitudes or behaviour which take into account the spatial and temporal dynamics of the work of, for want of a better word at this point, what I will call 'audiencing' (cf. Wolf et al., 1982). Those recent studies which do (for example,

Ang, 1985; Katz and Liebes, 1985), indeed identify the complexities and contradictions associated with active viewing in important ways, but they have not yet been able to contextualize their respondents, the Dutch fans of *Dallas* (Ang, 1985) on the one hand and the Israeli immigrants (Katz and Liebes, 1985) on the other, either in relation to the flow and fragmentation of television as a whole, or to the sociology of their domestic lives. Although each study makes a significant contribution to our understanding of the dynamics of the social processes of television reception, this understanding is still curiously limited.

Even in those studies which purport to be studying the audience sociologically, there is often an empty space where the audience should be (Belson, 1978). This empty space is the space of description, the simple matter of fact attention to the daily processes of life around the television set or prompted in some way by it (cf. Bausinger, 1984). This research presumes that there is a sufficient descriptive base of audience behaviour upon which to build elaborate models of effects and processes. But it seems fair to say that we have little knowledge of the settings and the dynamics of an audience's relationship to the medium, though the work of James Lull (1980a, 1980b) in particular, has prompted increasing attention to them (cf. Lindlof, 1988; Collett and Lamb, 1986).

The audience is present geographically and contextually within the private space of the home and within the public space of leisure and work, neighbourhood and nation. As many commentators have noted (for example, Hobson, 1982) television provides the material for much of our daily gossip, but equally our relationship to it is mediated by the quality of our informational, social and technical networks (Douglas and Isherwood, 1978). And, as Katz and Lazarsfeld (1955) noted all those years ago, an understanding of the use we make of the media must be contextualized by an understanding of the social world through which the media pass.[2]

The audience is present also in time. Its activity and passivity (of which more shortly) is the product of a number of different histories and futures, all of which converge on the here and now of daily routines: the histories and futures of individuals, communities, technologies, markets and schedules (Paterson, 1980), the histories and futures of fantasy and reality. If an audience's histories are to some extent objective constructs, able to be shared, perhaps incorporated in family myths (Byng-Hall, 1982), then an audience's futures are subjective constructs, expressed through ambitions, dreams or anxieties, but none the less significant for all that. Both are inflected and refracted by particular culture and individual experience; both, of course, are informed by a society's ideologies and utopias. They are both public and private, marketed and consumed (Miller, 1987). To understand, once again, the quality of 'audiencing', we must focus on the temporal qualities of everyday life, their narratives and their sequences, their short and their long *durées* and of the role of the mass media in defining and sustaining them (Scannell, 1988).

The active and the passive audience
The passivity of the audience is a significant theme in three versions of media research. The first is in effects studies, where the dominant concerns have been with the role of television in influencing pro-social or unsocial behaviour and on the vulnerability of the audience, particularly the child audience, to the stimuli provided by the medium (Comstock et al., 1978). The second is within the broad Marxist tradition which insists, *pace The German Ideology*, on the audience's dependence on, and vulnerability to, the play of ideological forces. The third occurs in the predominantly text-based analyses advanced in the 1970s in the journal *Screen* where the audience was assumed to be inscribed in the texts of film and television and to have no significant empirical reality beyond those texts.

The move away from the first strand of research towards a perception of the audience as active came with uses and gratifications research in the 1950s and 1960s. This was essentially grounded in a social psychology of individual needs and left open the question of cultural or social mediation. The move away from the second and third strands (Willeman, 1978; Neale, 1977; Morley, 1980; among others) is still in train. It consists in theoretical and empirical efforts to identify both the mechanisms and the spaces for the operative work of 'real' subjects, socially and historically located and engaging in some form of dialogue with the texts that the mass media provide. I say 'some form of dialogue' because I believe it is still an open question as to what is involved here, and the problems of assessing the dynamics of, for example, such social factors as class position or gender, cultural factors such as values or beliefs, geographical factors, individual interests and needs and the indeterminacies of texts and technologies remain formidable. They are, however, the substantive ones for present and future research. The recent work of Katz and Liebes (1985), Hodge and Tripp (1986), Morley (1986) and Corner and Richardson (1986), among others, provide a number of starting-points for the development of a theory and practice of the active audience, the audience as producer.

There is a danger, however, in pursuing the active audience too far. In some recent work (especially Fiske, 1987), the audience is granted an imperial sway over the products of mass culture, relatively unconstrained by text, ideology or social structure. This romanticism confuses the difference between power over a text and power over an agenda; or what Michel de Certeau (1984) would identify as the difference between tactical and strategic power. It is a confusion generated in an unexamined elision of the individual and the structural.

Towards a framework for the analysis of the television audience

In this, the second half of the chapter, I intend to explore a number of possible avenues for the pursuit of the television audience, and to argue for a naturalistic methodology – a critical ethnography – as the appropriate way to proceed. There are three elements to the argument. The first is the status of television as technology. The second concerns the nature of mass and mass-mediated consumption. The third focuses on the principles of rhetoric as a way of approaching the relationship between medium and content (technology and text) and its receivers. I will conclude by considering the methodological consequences of perceiving the audience through the various lenses I have offered, in the hope of defining an approach to the study of the television audience which takes into account the rapidly changing context of its embedding.

Television as technology
Television is a technology, a machine, and as such it is as much socially shaped as socially shaping (MacKenzie and Wacjman, 1985; Williams, 1974). Inscribed in its design and creation (and crucially, also in its marketing) is a model of the viewer, the audience, the household (Boddy, 1985; Spigel, 1986; Keen, 1987). Its inscription as a social object and its ability, in turn to inscribe its audience (its users) is a feature it shares with all technologies. In this sense television as technology can be compared to a text, which embodies intentions (however contradictory) and rhetorical claims for attention in the same way that all inscriptions do. Television as technology creates a space for the user, a space of operation and the creation of meaning, a space of possibility and indeterminacy. What distinguishes television (and other information and communication technologies) from non-communicating domestic appliances, though by no absolute divide, is its double articulation: it is both meaningful in itself and it is the transmitter of meanings.[3]

Television, then, has been constructed as domestic, for the family and the household., As such it takes and holds its place alongside other technologies; it takes its place and necessarily alters the technological environment of the household. And as Lynn Spigel has pointed out, this domestic occupation was neither straightforward nor uncontested (Spigel, 1986). Television is, relatively speaking, an open technology; its double articulation creates an enormous space (as compared, for example, to a washing machine or an iron, but in a similar way to other mediating and informing technologies) for variations in use – hence, among other things, the problem of meaning, the problem of the audience. Television is potentially meaningful and therefore open to the constructive work of the consumer-viewer both in terms of how it is used, or placed, in the household – in what rooms, where, associated with what other furniture or machines, the subject of what kinds of discourses inside and outside the home – and in terms of how the meanings it makes available through the content of its programmes are in turn worked with by the individuals and household groups who receive them.

So, even though I have major reservations about the notion of television as text (with the implication that the audience must be understood as reader), I want now to suggest an extension of the metaphor in relation to television as technology. However the relationship between television and its audience comes finally to be understood, it will need to take into account two kinds of mutually interdependent 'textualities': that of the content and that of the technology – the textuality both of message and of medium. Audiences, as I argue below, consume both, and the processes of consumption, while quite specific in relation to each, are nevertheless of a piece.

However, there is a further context to be taken into account, of course, and that is the social one. Technologies and meanings appear in a social environment – initially, but not solely, the household (the household itself is further contextualized by the wider political-economic environment). The status of television as technology and as the transmitter of meanings is in turn vulnerable to the exigencies, the social structuring, the conflicts and the rituals of domestic daily life. Television is a shared and gendered medium (Morley, 1986); so is video (Gray, 1987); it is also an age-related one.

It is in these senses, therefore, that I want to suggest that the technological aspects of television must intrude into our understanding of its relationship to its audience, especially if by 'audience' we assume some kind of listener and viewer rather than reader. Two things follow from this. The first is a perception of the place of television as embedded in a dialectic of domestic technology and culture; and the second is a requirement to get to grips with the dynamics of that dialectic as it works itself out in specific settings.

The dynamics are multiple and increasingly problematic, for not only do they involve changes in families and households, but, and crucially, they involve major technological changes, involving convergence of video and telecommunication technologies and a potentially explosive increase in the range of goods and services available to the domestic consumer (Miles, 1988). These are questions to which I shall return, but they are also very much the preoocupation of those who have concerned themselves recently with the nature of consumption in contemporary society (Morley and Silverstone, 1988). The quality of the domestic use of television, and of the particular characteristics of 'audiencing', is a function of the negotiation of consumer choices within the market.

Television and consumption
The purchase of a television set or a cable subscription or a video cassette or even a satellite dish (or their rental) buys the purchaser into complex economy of meanings, a cultural economy. The subsequent use of these technologies, their incorporation into the daily lives of their users, as technologies and as carriers of meanings, transforms their status as commodities into objects of consumption. This transformative work is active, and powerful. The shift from production through marketing to consumption is dynamic. The goods bought, the meanings appropriated and transformed, are embedded in a social web of distinctions and claims for identity and status (Bourdieu, 1986). If we are to make sense of the ways in which television is and might be used, then we need to understand better than we appear to do now the nature and consequences of the choices that are daily made in the public and private acts of consumption.

There is not a great deal to go on. John Fiske (1987), towards the end of his discussion of television culture, addresses these problems directly, arguing for a distinction between the financial and cultural economies, and ascribing consumer power principally to those involved in the latter. It is in the selection and 'reading' of films or programmes that consumers exert their power, and the producers of such commodities cannot ever be certain of success, hence the production of what Nicholas Garnham (1987) calls 'repertoires of products'. Of course viewers and listeners have significant freedoms to reconstruct and redefine the meanings generated in their favourite (or least favourite) programmes, but Fiske's assumption that this is sufficient to distinguish the cultural from the economic is wide of the mark. Goods too, are meaningful, and the meanings we attach to them circulate just as do those associated with the consumption of programmes. The consumption of meaningful technologies and the consumption of technologically transmitted meanings are not, one assumes, identical (meanings are not finite, for example), but I would like to suggest that they differ only relatively, not absolutely. And I would like to suggest that it is in what they share (as well as in what distinguishes them) that the key to their significance in contemporary society might be found. If we are interested in the quality of television culture and in the pivotal role of the audience in articulating this culture, then we have to understand the relationship between goods and meanings in a more dialectical way.

Consumption, of course, has as one of its bases utility, and as one of its foundations human need, but neither utility nor need exhaust it. Consumption, following Mary Douglas and Baron Isherwood (1979), Marshall Sahlins (1976) and Daniel Miller (1987), is a general process of the construction of meaning; it is 'concerned with the internalization of culture in everyday life' (Miller, 1987: 212), the result of 'a positive recontextualization' of the alienating possibilities of the commodity (Miller, 1987: 175).

Daniel Miller's (1987) argument, beginning with a discussion of Hegel, Marx and Simmel, develops and deepens two anthropological approaches to the problem of consumption; the first that of Douglas and Isherwood (1979), and the second that of Pierre Bourdieu (1986). From the critical juxtaposition of these two views Miller offers an analysis of consumption which attempts to place it within both a subjective and an objective frame, and to characterize goods, correlatively, as both symbolic and material. The key to understanding consumption is the interactive possibilities in play. The social differentiation of objects through consumption need not (indeed, in a world of mass consumption will not) simply be an expression of social divisions or the power of the producer to define how a product will be used, nor indeed will it be necessarily defined or determined by the intrinsic properties of the object in itself. Miller, like Michel de Certeau (1984; cf. Silverstone, 1989) draws attention to the possibilities for the transformative work of consumption, but equally to the limits of that work in particular circumstances:

> All . . . objects . . . are the direct product of commercial concerns and industrial processes. Taken together, they appear to imply that in certain circumstances segments of the population are able to appropriate such industrial objects and utilize them in the creation of their own image. In other cases, people are forced to live in and through objects which are created through the images held of them by a different and dominant section of the population. The possibilities of recontextualization may vary for any given object according to its historical power, or for one particular individual according to his or her changing social environment. (Miller, 1987: 175)

And not just material objects. There is a precise parallel here with the arguments offered by Stuart Hall in what has now become a classic paper (Hall, 1980). In discussing the (always analytic) distinction between denotative and connotative levels of television's signification he draws attention to its polysemy, a polysemy which 'must not be confused with pluralism' and to the existence of 'a dominant cultural order though it is neither univocal nor uncontested' (p. 134).

I have dwelt on Miller's argument because I think that it provides an important route not only into an understanding of the nature of consumption, but also into the nature of the television audience. We are already aware of the audience's capacity to work creatively with the meanings generated by their involvement with the medium. We also know how important the communication of those meanings is for the creation and maintenance of the group and of individual identities within it. Miller's argument allows us to recognize the same processes at work in all acts of consumption, and it seems to suggest that we can now look at the audience as multiply embedded in a consumer culture in which technologies and messages are juxtaposed, both implicated in the creation of meaning, and in what Michel de Certeau calls the 'perambulatory rhetorics' (de Certeau, 1984: 100ff.) of everyday life. Consumption, from this point of view, is a rhetorical activity.

The rhetorics of technologies, 'texts' and consumption
Rhetoric (like myth) is usually identified as pejorative: the phrase 'mere rhetoric' signifies that a particular communication is distorting and aimed to deceive. Television is often charged with such deception. I wish to use the notion of rhetoric in three different but compatible senses. The first is the traditional and perhaps most familiar sense: rhetoric as persuasion (Burke, 1955). The second is rhetoric as argument (Billig, 1987) and the third is what Richard McKeon (1987) describes as architectonic: 'an art of structuring all principles and products of knowing, doing and making' (p. 2). These notions of rhetoric offer, I would like to suggest, a major route into the study of contemporary culture. To apply them both to 'texts' and technology, and to the processes of their appropriation through consumption, involves the consideration not just of persuasion and appeal, but also of the mutual involvement by producer and consumer, addresser and addressee, in the structuring of experience.

The point about identifying this process of communication and consumption, therefore, in terms of rhetoric is first of all to see it as a bid or a claim for attention and action, more or less open to resistance or negotiation; second, to see that the relative success or otherwise of a rhetorical appeal depends significantly on an a priori sharing of interests between the addresser and addressee; and third, it is to bring to the fore a requirement to focus on, and analyse, the mechanisms, the strategies and tactics, of rhetorical address and response, and to identify the creativity and invention that is possible in both. By implication, what follows is the possibility of a methodology which insists on an examination of the processes of communication as situated, motivated, textual, interactive, politically asymmetrical and skilful. The goal is to understand not just the generality of rhetorical appeal which articulates consumption, but also the specific rhetorics of different texts, technologies and arguments as they bid for attention and action. At issue, therefore, is the need to produce a semiological and a sociological analysis which generates a view of the audience both as the focus of these various rhetorical appeals and more or less imaginatively responsive to them within the domestic rhetorics of their own lives and culture. There is a great deal to be said about all of these dimensions of rhetorical analysis. I can only hope, in this chapter, to sketch out a few of them.

Situation The first requirement of any rhetorical claim is a shared experience or culture. Rhetoric operates within a taken for granted world, the world of the 'commonplace'. The 'commonplace' is both, within rhetoric, a statement of something entirely familiar and understood and the basis for creativity, a spur to novelty and invention. The commonplace is the place of memory and invention. The 'texts' of television are entirely understood, predictable, shared and familiar, almost inert, yet they can spark an audience into creative work, to new thoughts, into a recontextualization of meanings, indeed into the new commonplaces of daily life.[4] Technologies are marketed through the commonplaces of advertising, the basis for a continuous invention of image and idea; and indeed advertising, as many writers have noted (Barthes, McLuhan and others), is the source of many of the commonplaces of everyday life. The domestic technologies themselves are built to fit into common places, as gadgetty or user-friendly, and then appropriated more or less inventively in households where they become part of domestic consumer rhetoric, a private or sub-cultural textuality of style and status (de Certeau, 1984; Hebdige, 1979).

A shared situation is therefore a precondition for effective rhetorical address, but effective rhetorical address also creates, even within the 'as-if' culture of mass communication, a shared situation. The 15 or 17 million people who regularly have their sets tuned to 'Eastenders' or 'Neighbours' are an audience who, for that time, become a community engaged in some measure with a community. The programmes' rhetoric of character and narrative provides the stuff, the commonplaces, for the sustenance of community in the talk at work, in the canteen or in the school playground. The purchase of a new television set or domestic technology is articulated into a consuming rhetoric in a similar way, as it provides the basis often, not just of individual display, but also as the effective entry into 'insider talk', the rhetoric of a bid for membership into a particular sub-culture or group.

The schedule is another dimension of this, as far as broadcast television is concerned (Paterson, 1980): a bid for mass regulation through the management of texts and time, though vulnerable increasingly to the effects of new communication technologies which release the viewers from its grip. The art of scheduling is, however, a rhetorical art in a strict sense. It is dependent on the effective management of commonplaces and common times to create and hold an audience.

Textuality   Television audiences occupy a site of overlapping, competing and sometimes overdetermining textualities: the 'primary texts' of television; the 'secondary texts' of their embedding in the ephemera of newspaper and magazine discussions; the 'texts' of consumption, of advertising and marketing; the 'texts' of the technologies, of the goods consumed; and the 'texts' of their audience's own reworking, their own perambulations and displays, their identities, their histories and their geographies. These textualities are predominantly of a secondary oral kind: framed and to some extent dependent on literary and literacy skills, they nevertheless do not necessarily require them. They are persistent, ubiquitous, insistent, yet ephemeral and fragmentary.

The 'rhetoricization' of these textualities is simply to invite a concern with both a universalization and particularization of the strategies and tactics of public and private meaning creation: to focus attention on the dynamic processes of communication through the analysis of specific acts and contexts. The history of rhetoric itself, which is a history of just such analysis (Todorov, 1977), is entirely instructive in this regard, for its offers a whole world of work on the analysis of the coincidence of meaning and action.

I want to suggest that it is precisely in the formal and dynamic relationship between 'text' and audience that rhetorical theory can prove instructive. This ought to be the case at a general level – that is, in the identification of those processes: homology (Ricoeur, 1984; and see Silverstone, 1987), identification (Burke, 1955), amplification and suppression (Group μ, 1981), which can be seen to define the quality of the links between 'texts' and the discourses of everyday life. It ought also to be the case at a specific level where the particularities of individuals', households' and groups' responses to the figures and tropes of images, sounds and narratives of technologies and 'texts' (either programmes or flows) can be assessed and understood. Here what is involved is the identification and analysis of narrative and rhetorical structures in such a way as to demonstrate their effectiveness and their reincorporation in the activities of audiences: the identification of the tropes, metaphors, ironies and commonplaces that stud our public 'texts' and our private discourses (Lakoff and Johnson, 1980); and the analysis of different levels of meaning – image, sound, voice, music, titles – unevenly present and unevenly significant in (for the present argument at least) the television 'text' (Silverstone, 1981, 1984, 1986; cf. Mercer, 1986; Masterman, 1988).

Motivation and resistance   Both Michel de Certeau (1984) and Claude Lévi-Strauss (1966) identify the rhetorical work of daily life as motivated, but motivated in the spaces and cracks (de Certeau) or with the flotsam and jetsam (Lévi-Strauss) of contemporary culture. Their concepts of 'la perruque' and 'bricolage' focus on the creative possibilities for individual and collective rhetorical work which become available within hegemonic culture, without any prejudgement about the likelihood of major transformations of that culture: 'Here order is *tricked* by an art' (de Certeau, 1984; 26). The world of everyday life is constituted by these tricks and turns, the figures of conversation and of daily ritual and display, which are meaningful not only for themselves (and within 'popular' discourse), but also as visible transformations and recontextualizations of the dominant in contemporary culture. This play of power, and the clash of intentions and motivations which mark it, defines the limits and possibilities of pleasurable participation in daily life: the successes and failures in the construction and assertion of individual, domestic and collective identities.

I am suggesting that we ought to be interested in these relationships between public and private 'texts', in the parallel and competing rhetorics (and mythologies) of the relatively powerful and the relatively powerless; in the cultural stratification of everyday life. And in this stratified world we need to establish how much room there is for doing what and by whom, in the transformations of fashion into style, commodities into objects, and broadcasts into action and gossip. It is in these transformations that we can gain a measure of the strengths and weaknesses of contemporary culture and of its asymmetries. And it is this formulation rather than the classic 'who says what in which channel to whom and with what effect' (Lasswell, 1948) which should now orient our research into the television audience.

The audience and the consumer are, for all their activity and creativity, still at the end of a process of production, even though in many circumstances (Miller, 1987; Fiske, 1987) their activities work back to redefine the product and challenge the producer. It is tempting to romanticize audience freedoms, significant though they may increasingly be as mass communication fragments and becomes increasingly demand-led. It is also tempting to make a fetish of the idea of consumer choice, of programmes and software as much as of the technologies that we must continued to consume. Choices are constantly being made, perhaps increasingly narrow ones as cable and satellite offer the possibility of much more focused consumption. But the questions of what those choices might mean, and how they work their way into the lives of those who make them, separating those lives from others perhaps just down the street, and linking them perhaps with others who share everything but locality; these questions remain.

Towards an anthropology of the television audience

Television as 'text' and television as technology are united by their construction, their recontextualization, within the practices of our daily lives – behind and beyond the closed doors of our houses – in our display of goods and cultural competences, both in private and in public. If we are to make sense of the significance of these activities, which after all, are the primary ones for any understanding of the dynamics of the pervasiveness and power of the mass media in contemporary culture, then we have to take seriously the varied and detailed ways in which they are undertaken. This is the basis for the case for an anthropology of the television audience, and for a commitment to ethnography as an empirical method.[5]

The starting-point for any such study is the household or the family, for it is here that the primary involvement with television is created, and where the primary articulation of meanings is undertaken. The household or family, itself embedded in a wider social and cultural environment, provides through its patterns of daily interaction, through its own internal system of relationships, and its own culture of legitimation and identity formation, a laboratory for the naturalistic investigation of the consumption and production of meaning (Anderson, 1988).

The empirical questions raised are many and various. Significantly, they revolve around three sets of issues. First, *description*: we need to know about the different patterns of consumption in different families and households in different areas at different stages of their life cycles. We can hardly hope to ask more sophisticated questions of the processes of consumption and reception, or provide more enlightened suggestions for policy, until we have some knowledge of the what and the how and the who of audience involvement with their television in the context defined by their involvements with other technologies and other things and people.

Such a requirement in turn suggests another: an ethnographic approach to family and household use of television. Observation and detailed and specific interviewing, at least as a first step, must ground any attempt to understand the embedded practices of the audience in the domestic setting. In short, we need to provide substance to the notion of the embedded audience by a consideration of the particular patterns of family and household life. This is a problem of the place of the household or family in the wider context of society, culture and technology – a problem which suggests the need for an integration of ethnography and political economy (Marcus and Fischer, 1986: 85) – but it is also a problem of the dynamics of the household and the family itself as the specificity of social and cultural and technology relations are negotiated within its own domestic space and time.

Second, *dynamics*: we need to understand the differences between the active and the passive viewer and to define these terms (or reject them entirely) within a context of the differential practices of different individuals, and in relation to different family and household 'techno-cultures' (Giner, 1985). We ought to be in a position to distinguish both within families and households and comparatively between families and households the various kinds of relationships that audiences generate with television and other communication and information technologies, beginning, for example, with the distinction between primary and secondary viewing or between referentiality and poeticality (Katz and Liebes, 1985). We also need to know who is involved and in what kinds of ways with television and to identify gender-, age- and class-based differences where they occur and where they seem to be significant.

The argument that new technologies based on the computer and telephone are interactive in a way that the older ones based on the television and the video are not, needs to be tested against such assessments as I have suggested in relation to the activities surrounding the television set. We also, finally, need a sense of changing patterns of use, particularly in so far as technological developments are offering a more complex and varied communication culture to the domestic consumer, who in turn is being offered more choices and more encouragement to make them. 'More choice' is itself a problematic notion in this context.

Third, *consequences*: there is a whole series of questions to be asked about the consequences, both for individuals within the household or family and for the household and in particular for the family as a whole, of their involvement with television. These are important questions, of course, having major implications for policies, not just for the future of television but also for the future of the family.

The key issues, I would suggest, revolve around questions of isolation and integration. What are the consequences of differential involvement with television for individual and family identity and social and cultural involvement? How does the differential pattern of use and consumption affect the boundary around the household? This question itself fragments into a number of separate but necessarily interrelated further questions: questions to do with the separation of the public and the private; the existence or absence of different networks (social, technical or informational) along which different family or household members might find routes to the community; the links between home and school, home and work, home and leisure opportunities, and the question of to what extent they are affected by the household's use of television and an increasingly wide range of television-based services.

It has also been suggested that the incorporation of television (and of television-based technologies and services) into the household is likely not to be without consequence also for the daily lives of family members, for their material and moral identities. The use of television and video can integrate or separate not just the family as a whole from its neighbours or wider society, but can integrate or separate the individuals within the family, as age and gender groups form and re-form around particular activities that centre on the use of the screen or screens in the family home (Lull, 1980a and b; Morley, 1986). Here the questions have to do with the placing of the television in the micro-geography of the home (cf. Palmer, 1986: ch. 4), its articulation with other information and communication technologies, its role in defining age and gender identities, its significance as an ameliorator or prompter of conflict.

In making such sweeping suggestions and in framing them, as I have done here within the triangle of technology, consumption and rhetoric, I am not for one moment suggesting that research has to start from scratch. There is a wealth of literature and work already undertaken to draw upon, and I have referred to some of it. The key challenge lies in our ability to construct the audience as both a social and a semiological (a cultural) phenomenon, and in our ability to recognize the relationship between viewers and the television set as one powerfully mediated by the determinacies and indeterminacies of everyday life – by the audience's daily involvement with its daily medium. This is certainly not a new idea, but it is one which we have barely begun to take seriously.

Notes

This chapter arises out of work currently in progress under an ESRC (PICT) project into the household and communication and information technologies. It has benefited from the enormously helpful comments of David Morley, Sonia Livingstone, Virginia Valentine and Marjorie Ferguson.

1 McQuail's reference to the individual, of course, begs the question of the significance of 'individual' choice for an understanding of the specific and differential character of television's audiences. In this case the individual, important from a psychological point of view, only becomes important as a member of a collectivity, contributing by his or her actions and choices to a pattern of consumption – thus becoming an audience defined by the coincidence of shared enthusiasms: the coincidence of a shared life-style.

2 The present argument implies an openness to research within earlier paradigms, where concepts of social network (Bott, 1955), two-step flow, opinion leaders and much that followed the work of Katz and Lazarsfeld become once again relevant. What makes it so is the present empirical concern with the coincidence of social and psychological processes of media consumption. Thoughts of a convergence between theorizing on cultural studies and the earlier social psychology may be premature, but the direction of movement is clear.

3 The notion of television and other mass media as being 'doubly articulated' is derived from models of language, especially from the work of André Martinet (1969), though the parallel is not an exact one. The intention is to identify the double and interdependent character of the meaningfulness of the mass media: the first articulation is the 'meaning' of the technology as an object of consumption, and the second is the 'meaning' that communicating and informing technologies carry. In other words, there is meaning in the texts of both hardware and software.

4 Billig, 1987: 199. 'On the one hand these [common] places of argument were common because they represented the useful platitudes, whose indexed places were frequently visited by orators. These common-places were the stock phrases of oratorical productions, to be used time and time again. On the other hand, the commonness of the common-places related to the fact that these bits of folk wisdom were commonly shared by members of the audience, and also by the speaker. Thus, the common-places were assumed to be both commonly used by orators and commonly held by their audiences.'

5 This is not quite as straightforward as it might seem, for ethnography as a method of empirical investigation is currently the subject of considerable interest and interrogation. It is not possible, within the scope of the present chapter, to pursue this issue, fascinating as it is (cf. Marcus and Fischer, 1986).

References

Adams, V. (1986) *The Media and the Falklands Campaign*. London: Macmillan.

Allor, M. (1987) 'Relocating the Site of the Audience: Reconstructive Theory and the Social Subject', mimeo, 1987.

Anderson, J.A. (1988) 'Commentary on Qualitative Research and Mediated Communication in the Family', in Thomas R. Lindlof, (ed.), *Natural Audiences*. Beverly Hills: Sage.

Ang, I. (1985) *Watching Dallas: Soap Opera and the Melodramatic Imagination*. London: Methuen.

Ang, I. (in press) 'Wanted: Audiences – on the Politics of Empirical Audience Studies', in E. Seiter et al. (eds), *Remote Control*. London: Routledge.

Archer, M.S. (1988) *Culture and Agency: The Place of Culture in Social Theory*. Cambridge: Cambridge University Press.

Arterton, F. (1987) *Teledemocracy: Can Technology Protect Democracy?* Beverly Hills: Sage.

Aspinall, A. (1973) *Politics and the Press c.1780–1850*. Brighton: Harvester.

Asquith, I. (1975) 'Advertising and the Press in the late Eighteenth and Early Nineteenth Centuries: James Perry and the Morning Chronicle 1790–1821', *Historical Journal*, 18 (4).

Bagdikian, B.H. (1985) 'The US Media: Supermarket or Assembly Line?' *Journal of Communication*, 35 (3): 97–109.

Bagdikian, B.H. (1987) *The Media Monopoly*. 2nd edition. Boston: Beacon Press. First published 1983.

Baudrillard, J. (1983) *In the Shadow of the Silent Majorities*. New York: Semiotext.

Bausinger, H. (1984) 'Media, Technology and Daily Life', *Media, Culture and Society*, 6 (4): 343–51.

Belson, W.A. (1978) *Television Violence and the Adolescent Boy*. Farnborough: Saxon House.

Berger, P.L. (1979) *Facing Up to Modernity*. Harmondsworth: Penguin Education.

Billig, M. (1987) *Arguing and Thinking: A Rhetorical Approach to Social Psychology*. Cambridge: Cambridge University Press.

Birmingham Centre for Contemporary Cultural Studies Media Group (1976) 'The Unity of Current Affairs', *Working Papers in Cultural Studies*, 9.

Blumler, J.G. (1978) 'Purposes of Mass Communications Research: A Transatlantic Perspective', *Journalism Quarterly*, 55: 219–30.

Blumler, J.G. (1980a) 'Political Communication: Democratic Theory and Broadcast Practice', inaugural lecture, Leeds University.

Blumler, J.G. (1980b) 'Mass Communication Research in Europe: Some Origins and Prospects', *Media, Culture and Society*, 2: 59–82.

Blumler, J.G. (ed.) (1983) *Communicating to Voters: The Role of Television in the First European Parliamentary Elections*. Beverly Hills, CA: Sage.

Blumler, J.G. (1987) 'Paradigm Lost', pp. 65–6 in M. Gurevitch and M. Levy (eds), *Mass Communication Review Yearbook*, vol. 6. Beverly Hills, CA: Sage.

Blumler, J.G. (1989) 'Pressure Groups and the Mass Media', in E. Barnouw (ed.),

International Encyclopedia of Communications. New York: Oxford University Press.

Blumler, J.G. and Gurevitch, M. (1975) 'Towards a Comparative Framework for Political Communication Research', pp. 165–93 in Steven H. Chaffee (ed.), *Political Communication: Issues and Strategies for Research.* Beverly Hills, CA: Sage.

Blumler, J.G. and Gurevitch, M. (1977) 'Linkages between the Mass Media and Politics: A Model for the Analysis of Political Communication Systems', pp. 270–90 in J. Curran, M. Gurevitch and J. Woollacott (eds), *Mass Communication and Society.* London: Edward Arnold.

Blumler, J.G. and Gurevitch, M. (1986a) 'The Election Agenda-Setting Roles of Television Journalists: Comparative Observation at the BBC and NBC', paper presented at the 36th Annual Conference of the International Communication Association, Chicago, IL.

Blumler, J.G. and Gurevitch, M. (1986b) 'Journalists' Orientations to Political Institutions: The Case of Parliamentary Broadcasting', in P. Golding, G. Murdock and P. Schlesinger (eds), *Communicating Politics: Mass Communications and the Political Process.* Leicester: Leicester University Press/New York: Holmes and Meier.

Blumler, J.G., Gurevitch, M. and Katz, E. (1985) 'Reaching Out: A Future for Gratifications Research', pp. 255–73 in K.E. Rosengren, L.A. Wenner and P. Palmgreen, (eds), *Media Gratifications Research: Current Perspectives.* Beverly Hills, CA: Sage.

Blumler, J.G., Gurevitch, M. and Nossiter, T.J. (forthcoming) 'The Earnest vs. the Determined: Election Newsmaking at the BBC, 1987', in I. Crewe and M. Harrop (eds), *Political Communications: The General Election Campaign of 1987.* Cambridge: Cambridge University Press.

Boddy, W. (1985) 'The Shining Centre of the Home': Ontologies of Television in the "Golden Age"', pp. 125–34 in P. Drummond and R. Paterson (eds), *Television in Transition.* London: British Film Institute.

Boorstin, D.J. (1975) 'The Enlarged Contemporary', The Sixth Reith Lecture, *Listener,* 11 Dec.: 786–8.

Boorstin, D.J. (1961) *The Image or What Happened to the American Dream.* London: Weidenfeld & Nicolson.

Bott, E. (1955) *Family and Social Network.* London: Tavistock.

Bourdieu, P. (1971) 'Intellectual Field and Creative Project', pp. 161–88 in M.F.D. Young (ed.), *Knowledge and Control: New Directions for the Sociology of Education.* London: Collier-Macmillan.

Bourdieu, P. (1973) 'The Berber House', pp. 98–110 in M. Douglas (ed.), *Rules and Meanings.* Harmondsworth: Penguin Education. First published 1971.

Bourdieu, P. (1975) 'The Specificity of the Scientific Field and the Social Conditions of the Progress of Reason', *Social Science Information,* 14 (6): 19–47.

Bourdieu, P. (1977) *Outline of a Theory of Practice.* Cambridge: Cambridge University Press.

Bourdieu, P. (1986) *Distinction: A Social Critique of the Judgement of Taste.* London: Routledge & Kegan Paul.

Boyce, G. (1978) 'The Fourth Estate: A Reappraisal', in G. Boyce, J. Curran and P. Wingate (eds), *Newspaper History.* London: Constable.

Braddock, R. (1958) 'An Extension of the "Lasswell Formula"', *Journal of Communication,* 8 (2): 88–93.

Brants, K. (1989) 'The Information Revolution as a Social Construction', *European Journal of Communication*, 4 (1).

Brown, A. (1988) *Restructure of Australian Commercial Television*, paper presented to the Oz Media '89 National Conference, Brisbane, 24 Sept.

Brown, L. (1985) *Victorian News and Newspapers*. Oxford: Oxford University Press.

Burke, K. (1955) *A Rhetoric of Motives*. New York: George Brazillier.

Burns, T. (1977) *The BBC: Public Institution and Private World*. London: Macmillan.

Butler, D. and Kavanagh, D. (1984) *The British General Election of 1983*. London: Macmillan.

Butler, D. and Kavanagh, D. (1988) *The British General Election of 1987*. London: Macmillan.

Byng-Hall, J. (1982) 'Family Legends: Their Significance for the Family Therapist', pp. 213–28 in A. Bentovim, G. Gorrell Barnes and A. Cooklin (eds), *Family Therapy: Complementary Frameworks of Theory and Practice*. London: Academic Press.

Cantor, M. (1980) *Prime-Time Television: Content and Control*. Beverly Hills, CA: Sage.

Carey, J.W. (1981) 'Culture, Geography and Communications: The Work of Harold Innis in an American Context', pp. 73–91 in W. Melody, L. Salter and P. Heyer (eds), *Culture, Communication and Dependency: The Tradition of H.A. Innis*. Norwood, NJ: Ablex Publishing Corp.

Carey, J.W. (1986) 'The Dark Continent of American Journalism', pp. 146–96 in R.K. Manoff and M. Schudson (eds), *Reading the News*. New York: Pantheon Books.

Carey, J.W. (1988) 'Technology and Ideology: The Case of the Telegraph', in J.W. Carey, *Communication as Culture – Essays on Media and Society*. Winchester, MA: Unwin & Hyman Inc.

Carlstein, T., Parkes, D. and Thrift, N. (eds) (1978) *Human Activity and Time Geography, Timing Space and Spacing Time*, vol 2. New York: Wiley.

Cave, M. and Melody, W.H. (1989) 'Models of Broadcast Regulation: The UK and North American Experience', pp. 224–43 in C. Veljanovski (ed.), *Freedom in Broadcasting*. London: Institute of Economic Affairs.

Chibnall, S. (1977) *Law-and-order News: An Analysis of Crime Reporting in the British Press*. London: Tavistock.

Chomsky, N. (1987) *On Power and Ideology: the Managua Lectures*. Boston, MA: South End Press.

Christie, I. (1970) *Myth and Reality in Late Eighteenth Century British Politics*. London: Macmillan.

Cipolla, C.M. (1967) *Clocks and Culture 1300–1700*. London: Collins.

Cobb, R.W. and Elder, C.D. (1981) 'Communication and Public Policy', pp. 391–416 in D.D. Nimmo and K.R. Sanders (eds), *Handbook of Political Communication*. Beverly Hills, CA: Sage.

Cockerell, M., Hennessy, P. and Walker, D. (1984) *Sources Close to the Prime Minister: Inside the Hidden World of the News Manipulators*. London: Macmillan.

Collett, P. and Lamb, R. (1986) *Watching Families Watching TV: A Report to the Independent Broadcasting Authority*. London: IBA.

Collins, R., Garnham, N. and Locksley, G. (1988) *The Economics of Television*. London: Sage.

Commission of the European Communities (1984) *Television without Frontiers*. Brussels: EEC.

Comstock, G., Chaffee, S., Katzman, N., McCombs, M. and Roberts, D. (1978) *Television and Human Behavior*. New York: Columbia University Press.

Connell, I. (1980) 'Television News and the Social Contract', in S. Hall, D. Hobson, A. Lowe and P. Willis (eds), *Culture, Media, Language*. London: Hutchinson.

Cooper, T. (1981) 'McLuhan and Innis: The Canadian Theme of Boundless Exploration', *Journal of Communication*, Summer: 153–61.

Corner, J. and Richardson, K. (1986) 'Documentary Meanings and the Discourse of Interpretation', pp. 141–60 in J. Corner (ed.), *Documentary and the Mass Media*. London: Edward Arnold.

Crandall, R.W. (1978) 'Regulation of Television Broadcasting: How Costly is the Public Interest?', *Regulation*, Jan./Feb.

Crewe, I. (1983) 'The Electorate: Partisan Dealignment Ten Years On', *West European Politics*, 6 (2): 183–215.

Crewe, I. (1987) 'A New Class of Politics', *Guardian* 15 June, p. 9.

Crouch, C. (1983) 'New Thinking on Pluralism', *Political Quarterly*, 54 (4): 363–74.

Curran, C. (1979) *A Seamless Robe: Broadcasting – Philosophy and Practice?* London: Collins.

Curran, J. (1977) 'Capitalism and Control of the Press, 1800–1975', in J. Curran, M. Gurevitch and J. Woollacott (eds), *Mass Communication and Society*. London: Edward Arnold.

Curran, J. (1978) 'The Press as an Agency of Social Control: An Historical Perspective', in G. Boyce, J. Curran and J. Woollacott (eds), *Newspaper History*. London; Constable

Curran, J. (1979) 'Press Freedom as a Property Right: The Crisis of Press Legitimacy', *Media, Culture and Society*, 1 (1).

Curran, J. (1980) 'Advertising as a Patronage System', in H. Christian (ed.), *The Sociology of Journalism and the Press*. Sociological Review Monograph 29. Keele: University of Keele.

Curran, J. (1986) 'The Impact of Advertising on the British Mass Media', in R. Collins, J. Curran, N. Garnham, P. Scannell, P. Schlesinger and C. Sparks (eds), *Media, Culture and Society*. London: Sage.

Curran, J. (1987) 'The Boomerang Effect: The Press and the Battle for London, 1981–6', in J. Curran, A. Smith and P. Wingate (eds), *Impacta and Influences*. London: Methuen.

Curran, J. and Seaton, J. (1988) *Power without Responsibility: The Press and Broadcasting in Britain*. 3rd edition, London: Routledge.

Curran, J., Gurevitch, M. and Woollacott, J. (eds) (1977) *Mass Communication and Society*. London: Edward Arnold.

Curran, J., Gurevitch, M. and Woollacott, J. (1982) 'The Study of the Media: Theoretical Approaches', pp. 11–29 in M. Gurevitch, T. Bennett, J. Curran, and J. Woollacott (eds), *Culture, Society and the Media*. London: Methuen.

Curran, J., Martell, L., Petley, J. and Wood, B. (forthcoming) *Loony Tunes: Media and the Decline of Local Democracy*. London: Routledge.

Curtis, L. (1984) *Ireland: The Propaganda War*. London: Pluto Press.

Dahlgren, P. (1985) 'The Modes of Reception: For a Hermeneutic of TV News', pp. 235–49 in P. Drummond and R. Paterson (eds), *Television in Transition*. London: British Film Institute.

Dayan, D. and Katz, E. (1987) 'Performing media events', pp. 174–97 in J. Curran, A. Smith, and P. Wingate (eds), *Impacts and Influences, Essays on Media Power in the Twentieth Century*. London: Methuen.

de Certeau, M. (1984) *The Practice of Everyday Life*. Berkeley, CA, University of California Press.

Delia, J.G. (1987) 'Communication Research: A History', in C. Berger and S. Chaffee (eds), *Handbook of Communication Science*. Newbury Park: Sage Inc.

Dervin, B. (1980) 'Communication Gaps and Inequalities: Moving towards a Reconceptualisation', in B. Dervin and M.J. Voigt (eds), *Progress in Communication Sciences*, vol. II. Norwood, NJ: Ablex.

Douglas, M. and Isherwood, B. (1979) *The World of Goods: Towards an Anthropology of Consumption*. Harmondsworth: Penguin.

Du Boff, R.B. (1983) 'The Telegraph and the Structure of Markets in the United States, 1845–1890', *Research in Economic History*, 8: 253–77.

Dunleavy, P. and Husbands, C. (1985) *British Democracy at the Crossroads*. London: Allen & Unwin.

Durkheim, E. (1976) *The Elementary Forms of the Religious Life*. London: George Allen & Unwin. First published 1915.

Durkheim, E. and Mauss, M. (1967) *Primitive Classification*, translated and introduction by R. Needham. Chicago: Phoenix Books. First published 1963.

Economist, The (1988) 'Pocket Vetoes: Licence to Kill', 19 Nov., p. 50.

Elliott, P. and Schlesinger, P. (1980) 'Eurocommunism: Their World or Ours?', pp. 37–73 in D. Childs (ed.), *The Changing Face of Western Communism*. London: Croom Helm.

Employment Gazette (1987) *Patterns of Household Spending in 1986*, Dec.

Epstein, E.J. (1974) *News from Nowhere: Television and the News*. New York: Vintage Books. First published 1973.

Ericson, R.V., Baranek, P.M. and Chan, J.B.L. (1987) *Visualizing Deviance: A Study of News Organization*. Milton Keynes: Open University Press.

Ericson, R.V., Baranek, P.M. and Chan, J.B.L. (1989) *Negotiating Control: A Study of News Sources*. Milton Keynes: Open University Press.

Etzioni-Halevi, E. (1987) *National Broadcasting under Siege*. London: Macmillan.

Evans-Pritchard, E.E. (1973) 'Time is not a Continuum', pp. 75–81 in M. Douglas (ed.), *Rules and Meanings*. Harmondsworth: Penguin Education. First published 1940.

Federal Communications Commission (FCC) (1988) *Trends in the International Telecommunications Industry: 1975–1988*. Washington, DC: FCC Industry Analysis Division, Common Carrier Bureau.

Ferguson, M. (1985) *Forever Feminine: Women's Magazines and the Cult of Feminity*. London: Gower.

Ferguson, M. (ed.) (1986) *New Communication Technologies and the Public Interest: Comparative Perspectives on Policy and Research*. London: Sage.

Fiddick, P. (1988) 'Risk-risk at the Top-top', *The Guardian*, 15 Feb., p. 21.

Fiske, J. (1987) *Television Culture*. London: Methuen.

Flichy, P. (1980) 'Current Approaches to Mass Communication Research in France', *Media, Culture and Society*, 2: 367–76.

Franklin, B. (1988) 'Central Government Information versus Local Government Propaganda', University of Leeds, mimeo.

Friedman, A. (1988a) 'Putting Himself in the Picture', *Financial Times*, 1 Aug., p. 32.

Friedman, A. (1988b) *Agnelli and the Network of Italian Power*. London: Harrap.

Gandy, O. (1980) 'Information in Health: Subsidised News', *Media, Culture and Society*, 2: 103–15.

Gandy, O. (1982) *Beyond Agenda-Setting*. Norwood, NJ: Ablex.

Gandy, O.H., Jr. (1987) 'A Research Agenda for the Information Age', pp. 30–5 in M. Gurevitch and M.R. Levy (eds), *Mass Communication Review Yearbook*, vol. 6. Beverly Hills, CA, and London: Sage.

Gans, H.J., (1979) *Deciding What's News: A Study of CBS Evening News, NBC Nightly News, Newsweek and Time*. New York: Pantheon Books/London: Constable.

Garnham, N. (1983) 'Towards a Theory of Cultural Materialism', *Journal of Communication*, 33 (3) (Summer): 314–29.

Garnham, N. (1986) 'The Media and the Public Sphere', pp. 37–53 in P. Golding, G. Murdock and P. Schlesinger (eds), *Communicating Politics: Mass Communications and the Political Process*. Leicester: Leicester University Press/New York: Holmes and Meier.

Garnham, N. (1987) 'Concepts of Culture: Public Policy and the Cultural Industries', *Cultural Studies*, 1: 23–37.

Gaziano, C. (1983) 'The Knowledge Gap: An Analytical Review of Media Effects?' *Communication Research*, 10 (4): 447–86.

Gellner, E. (1964) *Thought and Change*. London: Weidenfeld & Nicolson.

Gellner, E. (1987) *Culture, Identity and Politics*. Cambridge: Cambridge University Press.

Gerbner, G. (1986) 'Television Imagery and the New Populism', paper given at IAMCR Conference, New Delhi.

Gerbner, G., Cross, L., Signorelli, N., Morgan, M. and Jackson-Beck, M. (1979) 'The Demonstration of Power: Violence Profile No. 10', *Journal of Communication*, 29 (1): 177–96.

Gershuny, J. (1983) *Social Innovation and the Division of Labour*. Oxford: Oxford University Press.

Gershuny, J. and Miles, I. (1986) 'The Social Economics of Information Technology', in M. Ferguson (ed.), *New Communication Technologies and the Public Interest*. London: Sage.

Giddens, A. (1979) *Central Problems in Social Theory*. London: Macmillan.

Giddens, A. (1981) *A Contemporary Critique of Historical Materialism*, vol. I, *Power, Property and the State*. London: Macmillan.

Giddens, A. (1984) *The Constitution of Society: Outline of the Theory of Structuration*. Cambridge: Polity Press.

Giddens, A. (1985) *A Contemporary Critique of Historical Materialism*, vol. II, *The National State and Violence*. Cambridge: Polity Press.

Giddens, A. (1987) 'Living in the Interregnum: in Conversation with A. Giddens (and Others)', pp. 102–19 in B. Bourne, U. Eichler and D. Herman (eds), *Voices: Modernity and its Discontents*. Nottingham: Spokesman.

Gifreu, J. (1986) 'From Communication Policy to Reconstruction of Cultural Identity: Prospects for Catalonia', *European Journal of Communication*, 1 (4).

Giles, F. (1986) *Sundry Times*. London: John Murray.

Giner, S. (1985) *Communio, Domini, Innovacio: per una Teoria de la Cultura*. Barcelona: Editorial Laia.

Gitlin, T. (1980) *The Whole World is Watching: Mass Media in the Making and Unmaking of the New Left*. Berkeley, CA: University of California Press.

Glasgow University Media Group (1976) *Bad News*. London: Routledge & Kegan Paul.

Glasgow University Media Group (1980) *More Bad News*. London: Routledge & Kegan Paul.

Glasgow University Media Group (1982) *Really Bad News*. London: Writers and Readers.

Glasgow University Media Group (1985) *War and Peace News*. Milton Keynes: Open University Press.

Goffman, E. (1959) *The Presentation of Self in Everyday Life*. New York: Doubleday.

Golding, P. (1986a) 'Power in the information society', pp. 73–84 in G. Muskens and C. Hamelink (eds), *Global Networks and European Communities – Applied Social and Comparative Approaches*. Tilburg: IVA.

Golding, P. (1986b) *Excluding the Poor*. London: Child Poverty Action Group.

Golding, P. and Elliott, P. (1979) *Making the News*. Harlow, Essex: Longman.

Golding, P. and Middleton, S. (1982) *Images of Welfare: Press and Public Attitudes to Poverty*. Oxford: Martin Robertson.

Golding, P. and Murdock, G. (1986) 'Unequal Information: Access and Exclusion in the New Communications Market Place', in M. Ferguson (ed.), *New Communications Technologies and the Public Interest*. London: Sage.

Goldsmiths' Media Research Group (1987) *Media Coverage of London Councils: Interim Report*. London: Goldsmiths' College.

Gouldner, A.W. (1976) *The Dialectic of Ideology and Technology: The Original Grammar and Future of Ideology*. London: Macmillan.

Grandi, R. (1983) 'The Limitations of the Sociological Approach: Alternatives from Italian Communication Research', *Journal of Communication*, 33 (3): 53–8.

Gray, A. (1987) 'Behind Closed Doors: Women and Video Recorders in the Home', pp. 38–54 in H. Baehr and G. Dyer (eds), *Boxed In: Women in Television*. London: Routledge & Kegan Paul.

Group μ (1981) *A General Rhetoric*. Baltimore, MD: Johns Hopkins University Press.

Gunter, B. (1987) *Television and Violence*. London: John Libbey/Independent Broadcasting Authority.

Gurevitch, M., Bennett, T., Curran, J. and Woollacott, J. (eds) (1982) *Culture, Society and the Media*. London: Methuen.

Gusfield, J. (1981) *The Culture of Public Problems*. Chicago: University of Chicago Press.

Habermas, J. (1979) *Communication and the Evolution of Society*. Boston: Beacon Press.

Hagerstrand, T. (1986) 'Decentralization and Radio Broadcasting: On the "Possibility Space" of a Communication Technology', *European Journal of Communication*, 1 (1).

Hall, S. (1980) 'Coding and Encoding in the Television Discourse', pp. 128–38 in S. Hall, D. Hobson, A. Lowe and P. Willis, (eds), *Culture, Media, Language*. London: Hutchinson.

Hall, S. (1986) 'Media Power and Class Power', pp. 5–14 in J. Curran, J. Ecclestone, G. Oakley and A. Richardson (eds), *Bending Reality: The State of the Media*. London: Pluto Press.

Hall, S., Critcher, C., Jefferson, T., Clarke, J. and Roberts, B. (1978) *Policing the Crisis: Mugging, the State and Law and Order*. London: Macmillan.

Hamil, S. and O'Neill, G. (1986) 'Structural Changes in British Society: The Implications for Future Consumer Markets', *Journal of the Market Research Society*, 28 (4): 313–23.

Handley, N. (1988) 'Multiple Choices in the Single Market', *Marketing Week*, 25 Nov., pp. 73–7.

Harris, R. (1983) *Gotcha! The Media, the Government and the Falklands Crisis*. London: Faber & Faber.

Harris Research Centre (1985) *London Attitude Survey*. Richmond: HRC.

Harrison, B. (1982) 'Press and Pressure Group in Modern Britain', in J. Shattock and M. Wolff (eds), *The Victorian Press: Samplings and Soundings*. Leicester: University of Leicester Press.

Harrop, M. (1987) 'Voters', pp. 45–63 in J. Seaton and B. Pimlott (eds), *The Media in British Politics*. Aldershot: Avebury.

Harrop, M. (1988) 'The Press', in D. Butler and D. Kavanagh, *The British General Election of 1987*. London: Macmillan.

Hartmann, P. (1975) 'Industrial Relations in the News Media', *Industrial Relations Journal*, 4 (6).

Hartmann, P. and Husband, C. (1973) *Racism and the Mass Media*. London: Davis Poynter.

Hebdige, D. (1979) *Subculture: The Meaning of Style*. London: Methuen.

Herman, E.S. (1986) 'Gatekeeper versus Propaganda Models: A Critical American Perspective', pp. 171–95 in P. Golding, G. Murdock and P. Schlesinger (eds), *Communicating Politics, Mass Communication and the Political Process*. Leicester: Leicester University Press.

Herman, E.S. and Chomsky, N. (1988) *Manufacturing Consent: The Political Economy of the Mass Media*. New York: Pantheon Books.

Hertsgaard, M. (1988) *On Bended Knee: The Press and the Reagan Presidency*. New York: Farrar, Strauss, Giroux.

Hess, S. (1984) *The Government/Press Connection*. Washington DC: Brookings Institution.

Hetherington, A. (1985) *News, Newspapers and Television*. London: Macmillan.

Hillyard, P. and Percy-Smith, J. (1988) *The Coercive State*. London: Fontana/Collins.

Himmelweit, H.T., Humphreys, D., Jaeger, M. and Katz, M. (1985) *How Voters Decide*. Milton Keynes: Open University Press.

Hirsch, F. (1977) *Social Limits to Growth*. London: Routledge & Kegan Paul.

Hirst, P.Q. (1987) 'Retrieving Pluralism', pp. 154–74 in W. Outhwaite and M. Mulkay (eds), *Social Theory and Social Criticism*. Oxford: Blackwell.

Hobson, D. (1982) *Crossroads: The Drama of a Soap Opera*. London: Methuen.

Hodge, R. and Tripp, D. (1986) *Children and Television*. Cambridge: Polity Press.

Holland, P. (1983) 'The Page Three Girl Speaks to Women, Too', *Screen*, 3 (24).

Hollander, R. (1985) *Video Democracy*. Mount Airy, MD: Lomond.

Hollingsworth, M. (1986) *The Press and Political Dissent*. London: Pluto.

Home Office (1988) *Broadcasting in the Nineties: Competition, Choice and Quality – The Government's Plans for Broadcasting Legislation*, Cm 517. London: HMSO.

Hooper, A. (1982) *The Media and the Military*. Aldershot: Gower.

Hyman, H. and Sheatsley, P. (1947) 'Some Reasons Why Information Campaigns Fail', *Public Opinion Quarterly*, 11: 412–23.

Independent Broadcasting Authority (1988) *Independent Television in the 1990s: A Policy Statement by the IBA*. London: IBA.

Information Canada (1971) *Instant World: A Report on Telecommunications in Canada*. Ottawa: Information Canada.

Information Technology Advisory Panel (ITAP) (1983) *Making a Business of Information*. London: HMSO.

Innis, H.A. (1950) *Empire and Communications*. Oxford: Oxford University Press.

Innis, H.A. (1951) *The Bias of Communication*. Toronto: University of Toronto Press.

Innis, H.A. (1952) *Changing Concepts of Time*. Toronto: University of Toronto Press.

Innis, H.A. (1954) 'Concept of Monopoly and Civilization', *Explorations*, 3 (Aug.): 89–95. Toronto: University of Toronto Press.

International Telecommunications Union (ITU) (1989) *The Changing Telecommunications Environment: Policy Considerations for the Members of the ITU*. Geneva: ITU.

Jeffery, T. and McClelland, K. (1986) 'A World Fit to Live in: The *Daily Mail* and the Middle Classes 1918–39', in J. Curran, A. Smith and P. Wingate (eds), *Impacts and Influences*. London: Methuen.

Jensen, K.B. (1988) 'News as Social Resource: A Qualitative Empirical Study of the Reception of Danish Television News', *European Journal of Communication*, 3 (3): 275–301.

Katz, E. and Lazarsfeld, P.F. (1955) *Personal Influence: The Part Played by People in the Flow of Mass Communications*. New York: Free Press.

Katz, E. and Liebes, T. (1985) 'Mutual Aid in the Decoding of Dallas: Preliminary Notes from a Cross-Cultural Study', pp. 187–98 in P. Drummond and R. Paterson (eds), *Television in Transition*. London: British Film Institute.

Keen, B. (1987) ' "Play it Again, Sony": The Double Life of Home Video Technology', *Science as Culture*, 1: 7–42.

Kellner, D. (1987) 'Baudrillard, Semiurgy, and Death?' *Theory, Culture and Society*, 4 (1): 125–46.

Koss, S. (1981, 1984) *The Rise and Fall of the Political Press in Britain*, vols 1 and 2. London: Hamish Hamilton.

Kroker, A. (1984) *Technology and the Canadian Mind: Onnis/McLuhan/Grant*. Montreal: New World Perspectives.

Kuan-Hsing Chen (1987) 'The Masses and the Media: Baudrillard's Implosive Postmodernism', *Theory, Culture and Society*, 4 (1): 71–88.

Lakoff, G. and Johnson, M. (1980) *Metaphors We Live By*. Chicago: Chicago University Press.

Lang, G. and Lang, K. (1983) *The Battle for Public Opinion: The President, the Press, and the Polls during Watergate*. New York: Columbia University Press.

Lash, S. and Urry, J. (1987) *The End of Organised Capitalism*. Cambridge: Polity Press.

Lasswell, H.D. (1941) *Democracy through Public Opinion*. Menasha, WI: George Banta.

Lasswell, H.D. (1948) 'The Structure and Function of Communication in Society', pp. 31–51 in N. Bryson (ed.), *The Communication of Ideas*. New York: Harper/ Cooper Square Publishers Inc. (1964).

Lasswell, H.D. (1954) 'The Strategy of Soviet Propaganda', in W. Schramm (ed.), *The Process and Effects of Mass Communication*. Urbana, IL: University of Illinois Press.

Layder, D. (1985) *Structure, Interaction and Social Theory*. London: Routledge & Kegan Paul.

Lee, A.J. (1976) *The Origins of the Popular Press, 1855–1914*. London: Croom Helm.

Léon-Portilla, M. (1982) 'Three Forms of Thought in Ancient Mexico', pp. 9–24 in F.A. Hanson (ed.), *Studies in Symbolism and Cultural Communication*. Lawrence, KS: University of Kansas.

Lerner, D. (1958) *The Passing of Traditional Society*. New York: Free Press.

Lévi-Strauss, C. (1966) *The Savage Mind*. London: Weidenfeld & Nicolson.

Levy, M.R. (1981) 'Disdaining the News', *Journalism Quarterly*, 58 (3): 24–31.

Lindlof, T.R. (ed.) (1988) *Natural Audiences*. Beverly Hills, CA: Sage.

Livingstone, K. (1987) *If Voting Changed Anything, They'd Abolish It*. London: Collins.

Lockwood, D. (1960) 'The "New Working Class"'. *European Journal of Sociology*, 1 (2).

Lowenthal, L. (1961) *Literature, Popular Culture, and Society*. Englewood Cliffs, NJ: Prentice Hall.

Lull, J. (1980a) 'The Social Uses of Television', *Human Communication Research*, 6 (3): 197–209.

Lull, J. (1980b) 'Family Communication Patterns and the Social Uses of Television', *Communication Research*, 7 (3): 319–34.

McCormack, T. (1983), 'The Political Culture of the Press of Canada', *Canadian Journal of Political Science*, 26 (3): 451–72.

McGrath, J.E. (ed.) (1988) *The Social Psychology of Time*. Beverly Hills: Sage.

MacKenzie, D. and Wajcman, J. (eds) (1985) *The Social Shaping of Technology: How the Refrigerator Got its Hum*. Milton Keynes: Open University Press.

McKeon, R. (1987) *Rhetoric: Essays in Invention and Discovery* Woodbridge, CT: Ox Bow Press.

McLeod, J.M. and Blumler, J.G. (1987) 'The Macrosocial Level of Communication Science', pp. 271–322 in C.R. Berger and S.H. Chaffee (eds), *Handbook of Communication Science*. Newbury Park, CA: Sage.

McLuhan, M. (1964) *Understanding Media: The Extensions of Man*. New York: McGraw Hill.

McLuhan, M. and Fiore, Q. (1967) *The Medium is the Massage: An Inventory of Effects*. New York: Bantam Books.

McQuail, D. (1978) 'The Historicity of a Science of Mass Media', text of an Inaugural Lecture, University of Amsterdam, 6 Nov.

McQuail, D. (1987) *Mass Communication Theory: An Introduction*, 2nd edition. London: Sage.

McQuail, D. and Siune, K. (1986) *New Media Politics*. London: Sage.

Mancini, P. (1986) 'Italian Studies on Mass Communication', *European Journal of Communication*, 1 (1): 97–116.

Marcus, G.E. and Fischer, M.M.J. (1986) *Anthropology as Cultural Critique: An Experimental Moment in the Human Sciences*. Chicago: Chicago University Press.

Marketing Week (1988) 'Toshiba Forced to Turn Down Music', 15 July, p. 18.

Marshall, T.H. (1963) *Sociology at the Crossroads*. London: Heinemann.

Martinet, A. (1969) *Elements of General Linguistics*. London: Faber & Faber.

Masterman, L. (1988) *Teaching the Media*. London: Comedia.

Mattelart, A. (1983) 'Technology, Culture and Communication: Research and Policy Priorities', *Journal of Communication*, 33 (3): 59–73.

Mattelart, A., Delacourt, X. and Mattelart, M. (1984) *International Image Markets*. London: Comedia.

Mazzoleni, G. (1987) 'Media Logic and Party Logic in Campaign Coverage: The

Italian General Election of 1983', *European Journal of Communication*, 2 (1): 81–103.

Melbin, M. (1978) 'Night as Frontier', *American Sociological Review*, 43 (1): 3–22.

Melody, W.H. (1973) 'The Role of Advocacy in Public Policy Planning', pp. 165–81 in G. Gerbner, L. Gross and W. Melody (eds), *Communications Technology and Social Policy*. New York: Wiley.

Melody, W.H. (1976) 'Mass Media: The Economics of Access to the Marketplace of Ideas', pp. 216–36 in O. Aronoff (ed.), *Business and the Media*. Santa Monica, CA: Goodyear.

Melody, W.H. (1986) 'Telecommunication: Policy Directions for the Technology and Information Services', pp. 77–106 in *Oxford Surveys in Information Technology*, vol 3. Oxford: Oxford University Press.

Melody, W.H. (1987a) 'The Canadian Broadcasting Corporation's Contribution to Canadian Culture' *The Royal Society of Arts Journal*, 125: 286–97.

Melody, W.H. (1987b) 'Examining the Implications of Changing Information and Communication Structures: The UK PICT', *Prometheus*, 5 (2) (Dec.): 221–36.

Melody, W.H. (1988) 'Pan European Television: Commercial and Cultural Implications of European Satellites', pp. 267–81 in R. Paterson and P. Drummond (eds), *Television and its Audience: International Research Perspectives*. London: British Film Institute.

Melody, W.H. (1989a) 'The Changing Role of Public Policy in the Information Economy', *Papers in Science, Technology and Public Policy*. London: Imperial College and Science Policy Research Unit, University of Sussex.

Melody, W.H. (1989b) 'Policy Issues in the Evolution of ISDN', pp. 53–60 in J. Arnbak (ed.), *ISDN in Europe: Innovative Services or Innovative Technology?* Amsterdam: Elsevier Science Publishers.

Melody, W.H. (1989c) 'Efficiency and Social Policy in Telecommunication: Lessons from the US Experience', *Journal of Economic Issues*, 23 (3) (Sept.).

Melody, W.H. and Mansell, R. (1986) *Information and Communication Technologies: Social Science Research and Training*, vols 1 and 2. London: Economic and Social Research Council.

Mercer, C. (1986) 'That's Entertainment: The Resilience of Popular Forms', pp. 177–95 in T. Bennett, C. Mercer and J. Woollacott (eds), *Popular Culture and Social Relations*. Milton Keynes: Open University Press.

Meyrowitz, J. (1985) *No Sense of Place; The Impact of Electronic Media on Social Behavior*. New York: Oxford University Press.

Michael, J. (ed.) (1974) *Working on the System: A Comprehensive Manual for Citizen Access for Federal Agencies*. New York: Basic Books.

Michael, J. (1988) *The Regulation of Broadcasting by European Institutions: Convention or Chaos?* London: Economic and Social Research Council.

Miles, I. (1988) *Home Informatics: Information Technology and the Transformation of Everyday Life*. London: Frances Pinter.

Miller, D. (1987) *Material Culture and Mass Consumption*. Oxford: Basil Blackwell.

Mintz, B. and Schwartz, M. (1985) *The Power Structure of American Business*. Chicago: University of Chicago Press.

Molotch, H. and Lester, M. (1974) 'News as Purposive Behavior: On the Strategic Use of Routine Events, Accidents and Scandals', *American Sociological Review*, 39 (Feb.): 101–12.

Morley, D. (1980) *The Nationwide Audience: Structure and Decoding*. London: British Film Institute.

Morley, D. (1986) *Family Television*. London: Comedia.

Morley, D. (1987) 'Changing Paradigms in Audience Studies', paper presented at the symposium 'Rethinking the Audience', University of Tübingen.

Morley, D. and Silverstone, R. (1988) 'Domestic Communication: Technologies and Meanings', paper presented to the International Television Studies Conference, London, 1988.

Morrison, D. and Tumber, H. (1988) *Journalists at War: The Dynamics of News Reporting during the Falklands War*. London: Sage.

Murdock, G. (1982) 'Large Corporations and the Control of the Communication Industries' pp. 118–50 in M. Gurevitch, T. Bennett, J. Curran and J. Woollacott (eds), *Culture, Society and the Media*. London: Methuen.

Murdock, G. (1984) 'Reporting the Riots: Images and Impact', in J. Benyon (ed.), *Scarman and After*. Oxford: Pergamon.

Murdock, G. and Golding, P. (1977) 'Capitalism, Communication and Class Relations', in J. Curran, M. Gurevitch and J. Woollacott (eds), *Mass Communication and Society*. London: Edward Arnold.

Murphy, D. (1976) *The Silent Watchdog: The Press in Local Politics*. London: Constable.

Naisbitt, J. (1982) *Megatrends: Ten New Trends Transforming the World*. New York: Warner Books.

Neale, S. (1977) 'Propaganda', *Screen*, 18 (3): 9–40.

Newcomb, H. and Hirsch, P. (1984) 'Television as a Cultural Forum: Implications for Research', in W.D. Rowland, Jr and B. Watkins (eds), *Interpreting Television: Current Research Perspectives*. Beverly Hills, CA: Sage.

Nimmo, D. (1970) *The Political Persuaders: The Techniques of Modern Election Campaigns*. Englewood Cliffs, NJ: Prentice-Hall.

Noll, R.G., Peck, M.J. and McGowan, J.J. (1973), *Economic Aspects of Television Regulation*. Washington, DC: Brookings Institution.

Owen, B.M. (1975) *Economics and Freedom of Expression*. Lexington, MA: D.C. Heath.

Owen, B.M., Beebe, J.H. and Manning, W.G., Jr. (1974) *Television Economics*. Lexington, MA: D.C. Heath.

Padioleau, J.G. (1982) *L'Etat au Concret*. Paris: Presses Universitaires de France.

Palmer, P. (1986) *The Lively Audience: A Study of Children around the TV Set*. London: George Allen & Unwin.

Pares i Maicas, M. (1988) *Spanish Bibliography on Mass Communication*. Barcelona: Autonomous University of Barcelona, Bellaterra.

Parker, I. (1985) 'Harold Innis, Staples, Communications and the Economics of Capacity, Overhead Costs, Rigidity and Bias', in D. Cameron (ed.), *Explorations in Canadian Economic History: Essays in Honour of Irene M. Spry*. Ottawa: University of Toronto Press.

Paterson, R. (1980) 'Planning the Family: The Art of the TV Schedule', *Screen Education*, 35: 79–85.

Peacock Report (1986) *Report of the Committee on Financing the BBC*. Cmnd 9824, London: HMSO.

Pearson, J. (1987) *The Ultimate Family: The Making of the Royal House of Windsor*. London: Grafton Books.

Ploman, E.W. (ed.) (1982) *International Law Governing Communications and Information: A Collection of Basic Documents*. London: Frances Pinter.

Postman, N. (1986) *Amusing Ourselves to Death: Public Discourse in an Age of Show Business*. New York: Viking.

Rice, R.E. (1984) *The New Media – Communication, Research and Technology*. Beverly Hills, CA: Sage.

Richieri, G. (1988) 'Mass Communication Research in Italy through Crisis and Ferment', *Studies in Broadcasting*, 24: 101–24.

Ricoeur, P. (1984) *Time and Narrative*, vol 1. Chicago and London: University of Chicago Press.

Robinson, J.P., Andreyenkov, V.G. and Patrushev, V.D. (1989) *The Rhythm of Everyday Life, How Soviet and American Citizens Use Time*. Boulder, CO: Westview Press.

Roche, M. (1987) 'Citizenship, Social Theory, and Social Change', *Theory and Society*, 16: 363–99.

Rogers, E.M. (1986) *Communication Technology*. New York: Free Press.

Rosengren, K.E. (1983) 'Communication Research: One Paradigm or Four?' *Journal of Communication*, 33 (3): 185–207.

Ross, E.A. (1910) 'The Suppression of Important News', *Atlantic Monthly*, 105: 303–11.

Royal Commission on the Press 1947–9 Report (1949). London: HMSO.

Sahlins, M. (1976) *Culture and Practical Reason*. Chicago: University of Chicago Press.

Sauerberg, S. (1986) 'Democracy and Information Gaps', paper given at IAMCR Conference, New Delhi.

Scannell, P. (1988) 'Radio Times: The Temporal Arrangements of Broadcasting in the Modern World', pp. 15–31 in P. Drummond and R. Paterson (eds), *Television and its Audience: International Research Perspectives*. London: British Film Institute.

Schlesinger, P. (1977) 'Newsmen and their Time-Machine', *British Journal of Sociology*, 28 (3): 336·50.

Schlesinger, P. (1987a) 'On National Identity: Some Conceptions and Misconceptions Criticized', *Social Science Information*, 26 (2): 219–64.

Schlesinger, P. (1987b) *Putting 'Reality' Together: BBC News*. London: Methuen. First published 1978.

Schlesinger, P. and Lumley, B. (1985) 'Two Debates on Political Violence and the Mass Media: The Organisation of Intellectual Fields in Britain and Italy', in T.A. van Dijk (ed.), *Discourse and Communication: New Approaches to the Analysis of Mass Media Discourse and Communication*. Berlin: De Gruyter.

Schlesinger, P., Murdock, G. and Elliott, P. (1983) *Televising 'Terrorism': Political Violence in Political Culture*. London: Comedia.

Schudson, M. (1986) 'Deadlines, Datelines and History', in R.K. Manoff and M. Schudson (eds), *Reading the News*. New York: Pantheon Books.

Scott, J. (1986) *Capitalist Property and Financial Power: A Comparative Study of Britain, the United States and Japan*. Brighton: Wheatsheaf.

Septstrup, P. (1989) 'Research into International Television Flows', *European Journal of Communication*, 4 (4).

Seymour-Ure, C. (1968) *The Press, Politics and the Public*. London: Methuen.

Seymour-Ure, C. (1987), 'Leaders', pp. 3–24 in J. Seaton and B. Pimlott (eds), *The Media in British Politics*. Aldershot: Avebury.

Sigal, L.V. (1973) *Reporters and Officials: The Organization and Politics of News-making*. London: D.C. Heath.

Sigal, L.V. (1986) 'Who? Sources Make the News', in R.K. Manoff and M. Schudson (eds), *Reading the News*. New York: Pantheon Books.

Silverstone, R. (1981) *The Message of Television: Myth and Narrative in Contemporary Culture*. London: Heinemann Educational Books.

Silverstone, R. (1984) 'Narrative Strategies in Television Science: A Case Study', *Media, Culture and Society*, 6 (4): 377–410.

Silverstone, R. (1986) 'The Agonistic Narratives of Television Science', pp. 81–106 in J. Corner (ed.), *Documentary and the Mass Media*. London: Edward Arnold.

Silverstone, R. (1989) 'Let us then Return to the Murmuring of Everyday Practices: A Note on Michel de Certeau, Television and Everyday Life', *Theory, Culture and Society*, 6 (1): 77–94.

Smith, A. (1976) *The Shadow in the Cave*. London: Quartet.

Smith, A.C.H. (1975) *Paper Voices*. London: Chatto & Windus.

Spigel, L. (1986) 'Ambiguity and Hesitation: Discourses on Television and the Housewife in Women's Home Magazines 1948–55', paper presented to the International Television Studies Conference, London.

Summerfield, S. (1979) *Banner Headlines*. Shoreham: Scan Books.

Theall, D. (1986) 'McLuhan, Telematics and the Toronto School of Communication', *Canadian Journal of Political and Social Theory*, 10 (1–2): 79–88.

Thompson, E.P. (1967) 'Time, Work–Discipline, and Industrial Capitalism', *Past and Present*, 38: 56–97.

Tichenor, P., Donohue, G.A. and Olien, C.N. (1970) 'Mass Media Flow and Differential Growth in Knowledge', *Public Opinion Quarterly*, 34: 159–70.

Tichenor, P.J., Donohue, G.A. and Olien, C.N. (1980) *Community Conflict and the Press*. Beverly Hills, CA: Sage.

Todorov, T. (1977) *Theories of the Symbol*. Oxford: Basil Blackwell.

Toffler, A. (1971) *Future Shock*. New York: Bantam Books.

Tracey, M. (1977) *The Production of Political Television*. London: Routledge & Kegan Paul.

Tracey, M. (1985) 'The Poisoned Chalice: International Television and the Idea of Dominance', *Daedalus* (Winter): 17–56.

Tuchman, G. (1978) *Making News*. New York: Free Press.

Tunstall, J. (1970) *The Westminster Lobby Correspondents: A Sociological Study of National Political Journalism*. London: Routledge & Kegan Paul.

Tunstall, J. (1971) *Journalists at Work: Specialist Correspondents, their News Organizations, News Sources and Competitor-colleagues*. London: Constable.

Tunstall, J. (1977) *The Media are American*. London: Constable.

Tunstall, J. (1983) *The Media in Britain*. London: Constable.

Turow, J. (1989) *Playing Doctor: Television, Storytelling, and Medical Power*. New York: Oxford University Press.

Tyler, R. (1987) *Campaign! The Selling of the Prime Minister*. London: Grafton Books.

Veljanovski, C. (1987) *Selling the State: Privatisation in Britain*. London: Weidenfeld & Nicolson.

Villafañé, J., Bustamante, E. and Prado, E. (1987) *Fabricar Noticias: las Rutinas Productivas en Radio y Televisión*. Barcelona: Editorial Mitre.

Waller, R. (1988) *Moulding Political Opinion*. Beckenham: Croom Helm.

Weaver, D. (1987) 'Thoughts on an Agenda for Mass Communication Research', pp. 60–4 in M. Gurevitch and M.R. Levy (eds), *Mass Communication Review Yearbook*, vol. 6. Beverly Hills, CA: Sage.

Weaver, D. and Wilhoit, C. (1986) *The American Journalist*. Bloomington: University of Indiana Press.

Wedell, G. (1983) 'The End of Media Nationalism in Europe', *Intermedia*, 2 (4/5).

Wernick, A. (1986) 'The Post-Innisian Significance of Innis', *Canadian Journal of Political and Social Theory*, 10 (1–2): 128–50.

Westergaard, J. (1977) 'Power, Class and the Media', pp. 95–115 in J. Curran, M. Gurevitch and J. Woollacott (eds), *Mass Communication and Society*. London: Edward Arnold.

Whale, J. (1977) *The Politics of the Media*. London: Fontana.

Wilcox, D.F. (1900) 'The American Newspaper: A Study of Political and Social Science', *Annals of the American Academy of Political and Social Science*, 16 (July): 56–92.

Willeman, P. (1978) 'Notes on Subjectivity: On Reading Edward Brannigan's *Subjectivity under Siege*', *Screen*, 19 (1): 41–69.

Williams, F. (1983) *The Communications Revolution*. Revised edition. New York: Mentor Books.

Williams, R. (1974) *Television, Technology and Cultural Form*. London: Fontana.

Wober, M. and Gunter, B. (1988) *Television and Social Control*. London: Gower.

Wolf, M.A., Meyer, T.P. and White, C. (1982) 'A Rules-based Study of Television's Role in the Construction of Reality', *Journal of Broadcasting*, 26 (4): 813–29.

Zald, M.N. and McCarthy, J.C. (1980) 'Social Movement Industries: Competition and Cooperation among Movement Organizations', pp. 1–20 in *Research in Social Movements, Conflicts and Change*, vol. 3, Greenwich, CT: JAI Press.

Index

ABC network, ownership 13
accountability
  press 21
  public broadcasting 22
advertising
  by central and local government
    94–5, 128–30, 134
  freedom of 14, 22, 48, 58
  influence of 46, 48
  negative 109
  regulation 48, 59–60
  see also publicity process
agendas
  diverging 121–3
  setting 67, 96–7, 103–5, 107, 112, 129
Agreement for Prevention of Broadcasts Transmitted from Stations outside National Territories 58
Allor, Martin 175
Ang, Ien 175
Arterton, F. 93
Associated Newspapers 5
audience
  anthropology of 186–9
  as citizens 98–100
  as consumers xii
  as embedded 174–8, 184, 187
  fragmentation x, 175
  participation x, 86, 112–13
  in research 173–4, 178–86
  resistance 86
Australia, ownership
  concentration 13–14

Bacon, Francis 171
Bagdikian, B.H. 7
Baker, Kenneth 124–5
Baudrillard, J. 90–2
BBC (British Broadcasting Corporation)
  commercialization 12, 23
  as national public service 22, 84, 108, 132
  regulation 43, 44, 50–1, 53
Bell, Tim 172
Benedetti, Carlo de 4, 8
Berger, P.L. 161
Berlusconi, Silvio 5, 8, 11
Bertelsmann group 2, 5
Birmingham CCS Media Group 116–17
Blackstone, Sir W. 45
Blumler, J.G. xi, 101–13

Blumler, J.G. and Gurevitch, M. 63, 108
Blumler, J.G. et al. 107
Bond, Alan, and ownership concentration 13
Boorstin, D.J. 167, 171
Bourdieu, Pierre 77–9, 91, 181
Braddock, R. 171
Brent Walker leisure group, take-overs 12
Britain
  communication research 142
  privatization 10, 11–12, 13
  and publicity process 108, 109–11
  regulation 41, 42, 43–4, 47, 50–6
  sources 70
British Telecom
  denationalization 10, 25
  and regulation 48, 53–4
broadcasting
  commercial 11, 21–3, 48
  pirate 58
  privatization 11
  public 21–3, 48, 84, 99–100, 111;
    commercialization 11–12, 22, 29;
    Europe 148
  see also interest, public; internationalization; regulation
Broadcasting Standards Council 41, 51
business, as affected with a public interest 30–1

cable television 12, 44, 48, 59, 158
Canada, telecommunications 24
Canadian Broadcasting Corporation (CBC), and public service 22–3
Cantor, M. 165
capital, cultural 81
capitalism, popular 10
Carey, J.W. 154–5, 162
Carlton communications, take-overs 12
CATV 22
CBI, and access to media 66
CBS, ownership 2, 5, 13
censorship 40, 74
change, effects of ix–x, xiii, 19
change, social, and communication research 136–7, 146–7
Channel Four television 12
Child Poverty Action Group 82
China, commercialization 9
Chomsky, N. 168
citizenship, social xii, 4, 85, 98–100, 146

206   *Index*

class, and access to information 18, 28,
    34, 64, 99
Cobb, R.W. and Elder, C.D. 105
Cockerell, M. 70
cognition, influence of media on 102
Collins publisher, ownership 2
commercialization 11–12, 140, 147–8,
    150
communication, public
    access to 32, 34–5, 40, 93, 100, 106,
        117, 139, 147
    definition ix
    historical role ix
    political 84–100, 101–13; evaluation/
        interpretation 97–8; local 111
    and public interest 28–30
    as public utility 30–1, 100
competence, communicative 99
competition 11, 20, 44, 46
conglomerates
    communications 5–6, 8, 11, 13, 20,
        31
    industrial 4–5, 8, 11
    service 5, 8, 11
Connell, I. 117
consumer, culturalist view 114–16
consumption
    patterns 87–90, 92
    and television 180–2, 186–8
control
    cultural 4, 6–7, 15, 127–8
    media xii, 3–4, 5–6, 40–1, 51, 102,
        115, 154
convergence, media 119–21, 127
Cooper and Lybrand report 134
Cooper, T. 163
copyright laws, 28, 46
Corner, J. and Richardson, K. 177
Council of Europe 55–60
    Committee of Ministers 57–8
    Convention on Broadcasting 58–60
    Convention on Transfrontier
        Television 59
Crewe, I. 93, 103
Crouch, C. 83
culturalism
    and European research 141–2
    and news organizations 114–33
Curran, Charles 84
Curran, J. xii, 85, 114–34
Curran, J. et al. 64
Customs, HM 82

D-Notice Committee 51
Dahlgren, Peter 174
Dayan, D. and Katz, E. 171
De Certeau, Michel 178, 181–2, 185
definers
    counter- 66, 68
    primary 64–9, 70–2, 76, 77, 78–9, 82,
        127, 129–30
    secondary 117

democracy, participatory
    and information 18–19, 23–5, 29,
        32–6, 38
    and new technologies 92–3
    and political communication 84–100
    in United States 137, 146
denationalization 10–11
Denton, Charles 12
de-regulation 12–13, 42, 54, 115, 158
determinism
    cultural xi, 85–6; *see also* culturalism
    technological xi, 85
developing countries, access to
    telecommunication technologies
    17
dislocation, European 140
divergence, media
    in agendas 121–3
    explanations 127–31
    in interpretative frameworks 123–7
diversification 5–6
dominance, in media power 63–5, 71,
    78–9, 82
Doubleday, ownership 2
Douglas, Mary and Isherwood, B. 181
Durkheim, E. 157, 160, 166
Durkheim, E. and Mauss, M. 157

elections, and mass media xi, 101–13
English, Sir David 127, 132
equality, in European research 146,
    147
Ericson, R.V. et al. 62, 119
Espionage Act 51
essentialism 92
European Broadcasting Union 56
European Community 56–60
European Convention on Human
    Rights 49, 57–9
European Court of Human Rights 43,
    48, 57–9
European Court of Justice 48, 57, 58–9
exchange theory 73–4

Falklands War, and information
    management 169
family, and television 187–8
Fawcett, Sir James 41
Federal Communication
    Commission 14, 36, 52
Federal Communications Act 1934 24
Ferguson, Marjorie xii, 32, 152–72
Ferruzzi-Montedison conglomerate
    4–5
Fiat group 4, 8
field, intellectual 77–8
Finivest conglomerate 5
Fiske, J. 86, 90, 92, 98, 180
France
    communication research 142–3
    privatization 10, 11
    regulation 45

Frankfurt School 138
Franklin, B. 95
Friedman, A. 5, 8

Gandy, O. 72, 80, 97, 102
Gans, Herbert 61–2, 63, 71, 73–5, 83, 134
Garnham, Nicholas 180
General Electric 2, 13
Gerbner, G. 93
Gerbner, G. et al. 10–12
Germany, Federal Republic
 communication research 142
 regulation 60
Giddens, Anthony 81–2, 156
Giles, Frank 132
Gitlin, T. 81, 172
Glasgow University Media Group 120, 169
Goffman, E. 168
Golding, P. xi–xii, 84–100, 118
Golding, P. and Middleton, S. 71, 118
Gould, Bryan 106
government, *see* state
Greater London Council (GLC), divergent press reports 121–31
Gurevitch, M. et al. 64
Gusfield, J. 77

Habermas, J. 99
Hall, Stuart 116, 119–20, 127, 182
Hall, Stuart et al. 64–9, 71–2, 75, 78, 83, 117
Hamil, S. and O'Neill, G. 86
Harris, R. 169
Harrop, M. 103
Hawke, Bob 13
Healey, Denis 107
hegemony 65, 71
Herald and Weekly Times, Australia, ownership 2, 14
Herman, E.S. and Chomsky, N. 6
Hetherington, A. 118, 131–2
Hillyard, P. and Percy-Smith, J. 95
Himmelweit, H.T. et al. 93, 97
Hirst, P.Q. 83
Hodge, R. and Tripp, D. 177
Hollander, R. 92
Holliday, Richard 127–8
household
 and space–time 159–60
 use of television 187–8

IBA (Independent Broadcasting Authority) 32, 36, 48, 53
identity, cultural 140, 146–8, 175
imagery, iron law of 168
Independent Television Commission 41, 51
information
 access to xi–xii, 4, 6, 18–19, 27–8,

31, 85; inequalities in 17, 34, 85–90, 93, 94, 96–7, 98–100
 commoditization of 17, 28
 gap 96
 interpretation 35
 management x, 64–5, 74, 82–3, 94–8, 145, 153, 164, 167–9
 public 27–8, 34–5, 94–5
 as public utility 30–1
 right to 32, 50, 57
information and communication
 sector 26–8
information society 18, 26–37, 63, 82–3, 91, 145, 147–8
Innis, Harold A. 28, 157, 161–3, 167
innovation, in European research 146–7
integrated services digital network (ISDN) 17, 29, 36
integration, European 140
Intelligence Identities Protection Act 1982 51
Interception of Communications Act 1985 43
interest, public xi
 broadcasting 18–21
 and information society 28–31, 36–8, 145
 and regulation 50–1, 53
 and research 31–8
 telecommunications 24–5
International Chamber of Commerce 58
International Code of Advertising Practice 59–60
International Telecommunication Union (ITU) 25, 27, 31, 54
internationalization ix, xi, xiii, 140, 152, 155
 in broadcasting 17–18, 20–1, 23, 29, 54–5
 of information 27
Interstate Commerce Commission 42
Italy
 communication research 143
 press ownership 4–5
 public broadcasting 11
 regulation 45

Jenkin, Patrick (later Lord) 134
journalism
 and culturalism 114, 116–17
 investigative 67
 sociology of xi, 61–83;
  empirical 69–76
 and space–time 166
journalists
 licensed autonomy 131–3
 relative autonomy xii, 117–21
 role of 107–8, 114
justice, criminal 78, 82

Katz, E. and Lazarsfeld, P.F.   176
Katz, E. and Liebes, T.   177
Kennedy, Edward   14
Kuan-Hsing Chen   91

La Standa department stores   5, 8
Lang, G. and Lang, K.   105, 111
Lash, S. and Urry, J.   91–2
Lasswell, H.D.   157, 161, 163–5, 166,
    186
Lévi-Strauss, Claude   185
libel   20, 50
liberalization   ix, 10, 11, 44
libraries, and access to information
    17, 35
licensing   1, 45, 52
Livingstone, Ken   121–8, 134
lobby system   70, 72, 76
Lockwood, D.   91
London Weekend Television   54
Lowenthal, L.   116
Lull, James   176

McKeon, Richard   182
McLuhan, M.   157, 163, 171
McLuhan, M. and Fiore, Q.   157, 163
Macmillan (New York)   2
McQuail, Denis   xii, 64, 135–51, 174–5
market
    access to   1, 18–19, 21, 23
    ideology of   ix, 9, 18, 145
Marshall, T.H.   98–9
Martinet, André   189
Marxism, on media   63–4
Maxwell Communications Corporation
    press ownership   5
    take-overs   2, 10, 12
Maxwell, Robert   5, 9, 12, 131
Mazzoleni, G.   112
media
    access to   65–9, 74–6, 77–82
    convergence   119–21
    limited effects model   101, 103
    reinforcement thesis   103
media goods, access to   86–90
media-centrism   xi, 61–2, 64, 77, 105,
    141, 169
Melody, W.H.   xi, 16–39
Meyrowitz, J.   171
Michael, J.   xi, 40–60
Miller, Daniel   181–2
Mills, C. Wright   99
Molotch, H. and Lester, M.   73, 75
monopoly
    natural   53–4
    in press ownership   20–1
    state   23, 42, 43–4
    in telecommunications   28, 30–1, 41,
    43
Morison, Samuel   51
Morley, D.   177
movements, social, and media   81
Murdoch, Rupert

press ownership   5, 131, 132–3
take-overs   2, 9, 13, 14
Murdock, Graham   x–xi, 1–15, 88, 118

NACRO (National Association for the
    Care and Resettlement of
    Offenders)   76–7
Naisbitt, J.   171
NBC television   2, 13, 108
Neil, Andrew   132–3
Netherlands, regulation   45
Newcomb, H. and Hirsch, P.   102
news
    as entertainment   156
    management of   169; *see also*
        information, management
    organizations   114–33
    as partial   85, 115
    and political publicity process
        104–13
    television: compared with press   120–
        30; and new technologies   x
    see also definers; sources
News International   5; *see also*
    Murdoch, Rupert
Norway, and foreign programming   11

Official Secrets Act   51
Oftel   25, 36, 46, 48, 53–4
opinion, public
    media influence on   101–9, 129, 164
    media reflection of   114–17
order, in United States   137–8, 146–7
ownership
    concentration   x, 1–2, 7, 13, 131, 147,
        159, 167; factors in   2–3
    conglomerate   4–6, 8
    personal/impersonal   6–7
    powers   7–9, 115, 118, 132–3
    and social theory   3–4
    see also proprietor

Parliament, attitudes to   110–11
party system, decline   105, 146
paternalism, of state   139
PBS (Public Broadcasting Service)   22
Peacock Report 1986   89–90, 115
Pearson Group   9
personalization, political   106
place, in European research   138–9
pluralism   63–4, 68, 71, 75, 78, 117
Police Federation, as source   77
policy, public
    broadcasting   16–19, 21, 23
    information   35–8
    and public relations   169–70
    telecommunications   25–6, 27, 29–34
politics, commodification   167–70
Pope, Alexander   52
populism   110
post-industrialism   92
post-modernism   91
postal services   23–4, 29, 43

power
  institutional, and information
    flow 62–71, 74–6, 78, 83
  in media xiii, 3–4, 6, 7–9, 14–15,
    102, 113, 116–17
  social 91, 113, 117
  and temporality 153–4
powers, separation of 51–2
press
  changes affecting 20–1
  conglomerate ownership 13, 14
  freedom of 1, 20, 45
  private ownership 1–2, 20–1
  tabloid, and media agendas 121–8,
    130–1
pressure groups, as source 71, 76–7,
  79–82, 105–6
Prison Officers Association, as
  source 77, 82
prison reform, and sources 76–7
privatization 2, 29, 43, 53, 67
  advertising 94–5
  and ownership concentration 2–3,
    6–7, 9–15, 42
  and regulation 44
  producers, independent 12, 58
proprietor, editorial influence 1, 7–8;
  see also ownership
public sphere 99–100
publicity process, modern xi, 103–11

radio
  and public interest 21–3
  regulation 54, 55
Radio Authority 41, 51
Ray, Peter 134
RCA records, ownership 2
Reagan, Ronald 9, 14, 106, 169
Reed International 5, 8
Regan, Donald 106
regionalization, of broadcasting 55–6
regulation 21, 24, 28, 30–1, 37, 40–4
  agencies 42, 44, 51–4
  broadcasting 41, 42–4, 45, 54–60
  common carrier/content 43–5, 45–6,
    47–8, 53
  economic 47–8
  European 41, 48, 56–60, 140
  international xi, 31, 41
  and law 40–1, 42, 48–51, 53
  need for 44–6
  press 42, 43, 45
  and privatization 10, 12–15
  telecommunications 43
  see also Britain; United States
Reith, J.C.W. (later Lord) 39
research, communication xii, 31–8, 60,
  98–100, 101–3, 111–13, 135–51
  European 135, 138–51;
    agenda 146–9; and
    integration 144–5; schools 142–4
  United States 135, 136–8, 146, 149
  see also audience; interest, public

rhetoric 182–6
Rice, R.E. 171
Roche, M. 99
Rome, treaty of 57–9
Rosengren, K.E. 141
Ross, E.A. 7
Royal Commission on the Press
  1949 115

Saatchi & Saatchi agency 172
Sahlins, Marshall 181
satellite television 8, 11, 22, 156
  regulation 48, 55, 58, 59
Scandinavia, communication
  research 143–4
Scannell, P. 166, 172
Schlesinger, Philip xi, 61–83, 119, 132,
  134, 166
Scott, John 6
secrecy, and power 74–5
Seymour-Ure, C. 70, 103–4, 106
Sigal, L.V. 70–1, 75, 82
Silverstone, Roger xii, 173–89
Skase, Christopher, and ownership
  concentration 13
Smith, A.C.H. 116
socialism, European 139–40
Sony Corporation 2, 5
sources xi, 61–2, 94–7, 104, 112
  empirical view 69–76
  model 76–82
  non-official 71, 75–82
  structuralist view 64–9, 75–6
Soviet Union, commercialization 9
space
  changes in perception 153–7
  historical approaches 161–5
  influence of electronic media xii,
    152–3, 157–60, 165–71
  social construction 160–1
Spain
  communication research 143
  television 9
speech, commercial, see advertising
Spigal, Lynn 179
sponsorship, of programmes 59
Spycatcher case 18, 50
state
  in European research 139
  and information flow 62–3, 68–71,
    74, 77, 82–3, 94–8
  strategy, source 78–82
structuralism 64–9, 75–6, 127
Sunday Times, editorial change
  132–3
Sweden
  regulation 45
  telecommunications 24–5
Switzerland, regulation 58
symbol, cultural, as barrier 85–94, 96,
  98–100, 105
synergy, effects 6, 8

techno-orthodoxy   xii, 152–3, 157–8, 163
denied   165–70
'techno-Utopia'   92–4
technologies, new
and developing countries   17
effects   x, xi, xii, 2, 19, 20, 22, 55–6;
and European research   141, 145–8, 150
and information society   26–7
and ownership concentration   2–3, 15, 42
Utopian views   92–4
telecommunication networks   23–6, 28–9, 31, 34–5, 53
and space–time   157–8
telegraph services   24, 154–5
telephone services   23–6, 29, 34–5, 43
access to   88, 157
see also integrated services digital network
television
audience   173–89; as active and passive   176, 177–8, 187; analysis of   178–86; anthropology   186–9; plurality of   175; in space and time   175–7
for children   14, 48
commercial, and foreign programming   11, 22
and consumption   180–2, 186–8
effects   165, 177
high-definition   29, 36
news compared with press   120–31
and public interest   21–3
and rhetoric   182–6
and space–time   158–9, 163, 165–6
as technology   178–80, 186
as text   178, 179, 183, 184–5, 186
see also broadcasting; cable television; satellite television
'Television without Frontiers'   58
texts, and political communication   85–94
Thatcher, Margaret   9, 60, 66, 107, 169

Tichenor, P.J. et al.   96
time
changes in perception   153–7
historical approaches   161–5
influence of electronic media   xii, 152–3, 157–60, 165–71
social construction   160–1
Toffler, A.   171
Toshiba, power   8
Tracey, M.   118
trade, financial, and space–time   158
Trades Union Congress (TUC), and access to media   66
Triangle Group, ownership   2
Tunstall, J.   70, 72–4, 118, 131
Turow, J.   102
Twentieth Century Fox, ownership   2

United States
broadcasting regulation   21
ownership concentration   13, 14
public broadcasting   21–2
public policy   36, 168
and publicity process   108–9, 110
regulation   40–1, 42, 45–6, 51, 52
sources   70
telecommunications   24
see also research, communication

VCRs, impact of   22
video, interactive   92–3
voting, change in patterns   103

Weaver, D.   102
Westergaard, John   63
Whale, John   114, 117
White Paper on Broadcasting 1988   41, 51
White, Vivian   125
Wilcox. D.F.   1–2
Williams, F.   171
Williamson, Arthur   127
Wilson, Tony   134
Wober, M. and Gunter, B.   93
work organization, and space–time   159

Index compiled by *Meg Davies (Society of Indexers)*